Perfect Your English

Perfect Your English

The Easy Way

W. H. Ballin

PRENTICE HALL INTERNATIONAL
ENGLISH LANGUAGE TEACHING

First published 1990 by
Prentice Hall International (UK) Ltd
66 Wood Lane End, Hemel Hempstead
Hertfordshire HP2 4RG
A division of
Simon & Schuster International Group

Typeset in 10/12pt Palatino
by Keyset Composition, Colchester

Printed and bound in Great Britain by
Billing and Sons Limited, Worcester

Library of Congress Cataloging-in-Publication Data

Ballin, W. H.
    Perfect your English : the easy way / [W.H. Ballin].
        p.   cm.
    ISBN 0–13–658626–0 : $12.95
        1. English language – Textbooks for foreign
speakers.   2. English language – Grammar – 1950–   I. Title.
    PE1128.B294   1990
    428.2′4 – dc20
                                                                89-49396
                                                                     CIP

British Library Cataloguing in Publication Data

Ballin, W. H. (Warner Harold)
    Perfect your English: the easy way.
    I. Title
    428

    ISBN 0-13-658626-0

---

2 3 4 5   94 93 92 91

To Anna Lise

Contents

Preface   xvii

1 Perfect your grammar   1

  1. The past   1
    We wrote last week   1
    We have written several times   1
    We have been writing   2
    I was writing letters when the roof fell in   3
    We had finished writing when the floor
    collapsed   3
    Habitual action   4
  2. The future   4
    They will play   4
    They will be playing   5
    They are going to play   5
    They are playing   5
    They play   6
    They are about to play   6
    They are to play   6
  3. The subjunctive   8
    Stock phrases   9
    Blessings, exclamations, anthems   9
    If-clauses introducing a hypothesis, a theory, a
    supposition   9
    That-clauses introducing a command, sugges-
    tion, proposal, recommendation   10

4. All about adverbs   11
   Adverbs without -*ly*   11
   Adjective or adverb?   12
   The verbs *to smell, taste, sound* and *feel*   14
   Mixed bag   14
   American department   15
5. Whose genitive?   16
   Double genitive   18
6. Pronouns   19
   Me, myself and I   19
   The rare *one*   22
   His, her or their?   25
   That or *which*?   26
7. A collection of collective nouns   27

8. Comparisons   30

9. – – – (missing words)   32
   Defining relative clauses   32
   The conjunction *that*   33
   The conjunctions *when* and *though*   33
   Participle clauses   34
10. Not what the teacher said   34
   'Don't split the infinitive!'   35
   'The interrogative pronoun "who" is
   subjective; "whom" is objective!'   35
   'Positive comparisons: "as . . . as"; negative
   comparisons: "not so . . . as"!'   36
   'The preposition "in" denotes location; "into"
   refers to movement!'   36
   'Avoid prepositions at the end of a sentence!'   37
   'No sentence fragments!'   37
11. Can this be right?   38

12. Let's hit him in the eye!   41

2 *Perfect your punctuation*   43

1. Full stop [Am.: period]   43
2. Question mark   44
3. Exclamation mark   44

4. Colon 46
5. Semicolon 46
6. Apostrophe 47
   Omissions 47
   Plurals 48
   Genitive 49
7. Hyphen 49
   Compound adjectives 51
   Phrasal compounds 52
   To avoid confusion 52
   Hyphen as word divider 53
8. Dash 54
9. Quotation marks/inverted commas 55

10. Comma 57
    Before conjunctions 58
    Special cases with *and* 59
    Interrupting elements 60
    Participle clauses 60
    Relative clauses 60
    Conjunctive adverbs 62
    To prevent ambiguity 63
    Stylistic aid 63

3 *Perfect your prepositions* 64

1. At 64
   Ability 64
   Big towns/small towns 65
   Exact locations 66
   Time 66
   Directional verbs 66
   Mixed bag 67
2. For 67
3. On 69
4. Out 71
5. Which preposition? 73
   Agree to/agree on/agree with 73
   Angry with/angry at/angry about 73
   Compare with/compare to 73

Concerned about/concerned with   74
In London/to London   74
Mad at/mad about   74
Where do you work?   75
6. Silent parade   76

4 *Perfect your spelling*   78

1. Popular mistakes   78
2. *-able* or *-ible*?   82
3. *-ceed* or *-cede*?   83
4. *-ise* or *-ize*?   83
5. Small letter or capital?   84
    Proper names, historical events, titles   84
    Titles of books, plays, etc.   84
    Specific or general?   84
    Races, religions, ethnic groups, languages 85
    Relatives   85
    Descriptive proper names   86
    God, Jesus   86
    Days of the week, months, holidays   86
    West or west?   87
    The four seasons   87
6. Perfect plurals   87
    Nouns ending in the letters *-s*, *-ss*, *-sh*, *-ch*, and
    -x   87
    Nouns ending in a consonant + *y*   88
    Nouns ending in a vowel + *y*   88
    Nouns ending in a vowel + *o*   88
    Nouns ending in a consonant + *o*   89
    Nouns ending in *-f*   89
    Borrowed (foreign) nouns   90
    Nouns with irregular plural form   91
    Nouns that look like plurals, but are singular
    or plural   91
    Nouns with plural form only   92
    Nouns with no plural form, used in the
    singular only   93
    Nouns with no plural form: singular = plural 93
7. Abbreviations   94

5 *Perfect your correspondence*   98

1. The envelope   98
   Envelope to a private (male) person   99
   Envelope to a private (female) person   99
   Punctuation marks   100
   PO Box   100
2. The letter   101
   Reference   101
   Date   101
   Salutation   102
   Heading   103
   Complimentary ending   104
   Signature (in business letters)   104
   Enclosures   104
3. Style   105
   Cliché collection   105
   Letter endings   109
   Meaningless phrases and words   111
   More scope for improvement   113
   Wrong usage   115
   Keep it simple   121
   The case against *case*   125
   Perfect your diplomacy   126

6 *Perfect your universal English (British English/American English)*   131

1. Spelling
   British English ending *-our* = American   132
   English ending *-or*
   British English noun ending *-re* = American   132
   English ending *-er*
   British English ending *-ence* = American   133
   English ending *-ense*
   British English final *-l* is doubled when a suffix   133
   is added to an unstressed syllable, not in
   American English   133

British English final -*p* is doubled when a suffix
is added to an unstressed syllable, not always
in American English   134
British English *oe* and *ae* (Greek and Latin
words) = American English *e*   134
British English -*ogue* (Greek words) =
American English -*og*   134
Individual differences in spelling; no rules   134

2. Terminology   135
   Things you wear   136
   Around the home   136
   Around the office; to do with work   137
   Things you eat   137
   The automobile   138
   Other technical terms   138
   Mixed bag   138
   Differences that require an explanation   139
3. Pronunciation   140
4. Prepositions   141
   At home/home   141
   For years/in years   141
   Behind/in back of   142
   In Church Street/on Church Street/at No. 16
   Church Street   142
   On behalf of/In behalf of   142
   Out of the window/out the window   142
   Fork out/fork over   142
   To write to/to write   143
   To wash up/to wash   143
   To consult/to consult with   143
   To meet/to meet with   144
   To visit/to visit with   144
   Different than/different from   144
   Half an hour/a half hour   144
   3/4   145
5. Opposite meaning   145
   Should you table it?   145

7 *Perfect your pronunciation and stress*
146

1. Pronunciation 146
   o-u-g-h sequence 146
   Frequently mispronounced words 147
   ch: '*k*' or '*tsh*' 150
   The versatile figure 0 150
   The elusive GHOTI 152
2. Stress 152
   Noun/verb 153
   Noun/adjective 154
   Adjective/verb 155
   Differences between British English and
   American English 155
   Words that can be stressed in two ways 156
   Mixed bag 156

8 *Which of the two?*
158

9 *Perfect your idioms*
185

1. Be 185
2. Call 188
3. Come 188
4. Do 190
   As substitute for another verb 190
   To avoid repeating another verb 191
   To emphasize 192
   In questions 192
   Prepositional idiomatic and other combinations 192
5. Drop 194
6. Fall 194
7. Get 196
8. Give 199
9. Go 199
10. Have 202

11. Knock   204
12. Lay   205
13. Let   206
14. Make   206
15. Play   209
16. Pull   210
17. Push   211
18. Put   213
19. Run   215
    The verb without preposition   215
    Combined with a preposition   216
20. See   218
21. Take   219
22. Tear   222
23. Turn   222

10 Perfect your conversation   225

 1. Greetings, friends!   225
 2. How do you do?   228
 3. Can I help you?   230
 4. Don't mention it   232
 5. Hello, hello!   232
 6. What's the time?   234
 7. How much?   237
 8. Cheers!   239
 9. Perfect your manners   241
    Please   241
    Eh?   243
    Hello!   243
    'Bon appetit'/'Mahlzeit'/'Eet smakelijk'/
    'Velbekom'   244
    'Hup-choo!', 'Atishoo!' and similar noises   244

11 Perfect your vocabulary   245

 1. Single words   245
 2. Colour [Am.: color] scheme   262
 3. Please control *control*   264

4. Please check *check*   267
5. Please decrease *decrease*   268
6. Watch your figures   269
7. More figure work   271
8. Good and bad   273
9. Hot and cold   275
10. Do you like *like*?   278
11. Murder class   280
12. Nocturnal news   282
13. Thing and nothing   283
14. Weather report   285
15. Geography   286
    GB = UK?   286
    NL = Holland?   286
    USA = America?   287
    USSR = Russia?   287
16. Medicine   287
    Sick/ill   287
    Doctor/physician/general practi-
    tioner/specialist/surgeon   288
17. Zoology   289

12 International mistake museum   293

1. Tricky words   293
2. Typical mistakes made by foreigners in
   correspondence   305
   Nouns   305
   Verbs   308
   Adjectives/adverbs   311
   Prepositions   315
   Non-existent abbreviations   317
   Mixed department   318

Word Index   321

Preface

This new version of the two-and-a-half-year course, used for staff training by over 6000 companies in 118 countries, now appears in book form for the first time.

You probably use English at work or for private interest. You probably already know it well or even very well, but now and again you have a few doubts:

Should I have written *have had* or *have been having*?

Why did those English tourists laugh when I mentioned the *backside* of the museum?

Is it *isolated* or *insulated*?

Has *harass* really only one **r** when *embarrass* is written with two?

Why do they so often leave out the comma before *which* and *who*?

Help!

Finding the answers to such questions may not be easy unless you have the time and patience to work your way through a stack of English textbooks. *Perfect Your English* can help you. As it is written for people with your advanced knowledge of the language, we can leave aside elementary matters and concentrate on all areas in which you want to do better.

The subtitle *The Easy Way* tells you that this is not a dry, technical treatment of the often difficult subjects, but a relaxed, easy-to-absorb presentation that is fun to read.

This book is "bilingual" to make it as universally useful as possible. Apart from a complete section on British English/ American English, any differences from the basically British

English text are indicated wherever they occur: for example, *labour* [Am.: *labor*].

My special thanks to Mr A. R. Evans of Armonk, NY, USA for reviewing the manuscript with a scholarly eye. It led not only to useful arguments and improvements, but also to an often hilarious transatlantic correspondence. Come to think of it: serious linguistic matters, but with an element of fun. Exactly what this book is all about.

WHB

1

Perfect your grammar

Anyone who has ever had to learn Latin conjugations or German declensions will admit that English grammar is not difficult. English pronunciation may be unpredictable, verbal idioms a little confusing, and prepositions an occasional headache, but grammar presents few problems.

As logical groundwork for the following chapters, let us make a start with a few items under the general heading of *Grammar*.

1. The past

Here is an up-to-date look at the English past tense, describing something that could have happened just a few minutes ago or even in the distant past on a rainy afternoon in the Stone Age.

● We wrote last week

This is the **simple past**. It describes a **completed event** or **action**, often adding when it happened: *last month, on Tuesday, two years ago,* etc.

● We have written several times

This is the **present perfect tense**. It also describes a **completed event**, but with an important difference: there is a **connection with the present**.

1

The connection is in this case the implication that an answer is still awaited. You use the same tense when you proudly report:

I have seen this film seven times!

Although your sitting through the same picture seven times did indeed represent seven completed events, the link with the present is here the idea that it happened during your **lifetime**. The present perfect tense is used whenever past events add to your list of experiences or achievements:

He has been to Indonesia three times.

She has taken part in the meeting before.

They have never failed to send a greetings card.

Here are two examples that show an interesting difference in the use of the simple past and the present perfect tense:

She did not phone this week.

She has not phoned this week.

The first statement is probably made at the end of 'ie week and implies: no news this week; maybe next week. The second sentence says: we have not heard so far, but there is still a chance.

We sold 320 cranes this year.

We have sold 320 cranes this year.

The first report represents the final total for the year. The second figure is given on the understanding that it happened so far, that there may be more to come.

The present perfect tense is therefore suitable whenever you can add the qualification **so far, up to now** to a sentence.

• We have been writing

This is the **continuous form** of the **present perfect tense**. It describes something that took place **very recently** and is **hardly separated from the present**:

Why are your shoes so muddy?

— We have been digging in the garden.

Where has she been?

– *She has been helping us all morning.*
  Why isn't he home yet?
– *He has been working late.*

You will often hear this tense at the end of radio broadcasts:

You have been listening to the London Symphony Orchestra.

The same tense is used when an activity started in the past and is **continuing into the present**:

They have been manufacturing tractors for 40 years.

This type of sentence is very often wrongly translated from other languages into 'They make tractors since 40 years'. Please make quite sure to use the correct past tense *and* the preposition **for**.

● I was writing letters when the roof fell in

Here we have a mixture of two past tenses. In the main clause the **continuous form** of the **past tense** indicates a past activity of some **duration**. The **simple past** in the subordinate clause shows a short, **completed** event.

● We had finished writing when the floor collapsed

What a dangerous household! Here a **past activity** was **completed** when **another past event** occurred. In the first part of the sentence you use the **past perfect**, or **pluperfect** tense.

● Habitual action

Habitual action can be described in three ways:

When we lived in New Zealand, we visited Taupo twice a year.

When we lived in New Zealand, we used to visit Taupo twice a year.

There is little difference between the two sentences. The phrase **used to** underlines the habit; the plain **visited** could also mean that something just happened, without planned regularity.

When she was in hospital, he would call twice a day.

This grammatically odd use of **would** means the same as **used to** but has a faintly historic ring. It is more likely to be found in an old novel than in everyday conversation.

2. *The future*

There are at least seven ways of expressing the future in English. Here they are, with the verb *play* as example:

They will play.
They will be playing.
They are going to play.
They are playing.
They play.
They are about to play.
They are to play.

There is no shortage of possibilities. Let us examine the various forms and their uses.

● They will play

This is the straight grammatical form. Something will happen at some future time but usually **not very soon**:

The finalists will play at the end of next month.

● They will be playing

This is called the **continuous future**. Something will happen fairly soon and will go on for a certain time. It may be **within a few hours, days** or **months**:

Our team will be playing at 4.30 this afternoon.

They will be playing on Friday.

The second team will be playing later in the year.

This form can also be used to indicate that someone is **taking advantage of an opportunity**. Two examples:

A: *Don't phone him. I'll see him tomorrow.*

B: *Don't phone him. I'll be seeing him tomorrow.*

A: *Leave it to me. We'll talk to them this evening.*

B: *Leave it to me. We'll be talking to them this evening.*

A implies that he will be doing **something special** for the listener. **B** reports that he will be there anyway and will take advantage of the opportunity of putting in a good word for the listener.

● They are going to play

This is the **continuous present** with a future meaning. It applies to something that will happen **within hours, days, weeks** or sometimes even **months**:

Tom and Tim are going to play at the end of the month.

● They are playing

This can, of course, be the present tense, but can also refer to the **near** or even **distant future**.

Jane and Pam are playing at lunchtime.

They are adding a swimming pool next year.

This form is often used with verbs expressing movement: **to come, to go, to arrive, to leave**, etc. It indicates an **intention** of doing something:

I am going to the cinema (this afternoon).

He is coming for lunch (at 12).

She is arriving at 3.

We are leaving in ten minutes.

The time factor in the phrase **to be going** can be very flexible. In February somebody may tell you 'We are going to Greece this year' when the booking has been made for July.

● They play

Slightly less used, this also refers to an event that will take place in the near future:

Liverpool and Tottenham play this afternoon/next month.

Just in case you are beginning to look a little worried now at the sight of all these different versions, please remember two things:

- There is a considerable amount of flexibility in the time factor of the examples given, but don't worry: several versions mean more or less the same when applied to something that will happen within a few hours:

Team A will play this morning.

Team A will be playing this morning.

Team A is going to play this morning.

Team A is playing this morning.

Team A plays this morning.

● They are about to play

We have by now almost reached the present. It is a matter of **minutes** only.

● They are to play

Here the time factor is also flexible. Something may be **hours** or **months** away, but with the implication that the event has been arranged:

Denmark is to play Italy in the quarter-finals.

This sentence may look a little odd to you because in some other languages you would say **against** Italy. You can also add this word in English but usually leave it out when referring to competitive games. A theatre [Am.: theater] critic once used the possibility of a double meaning when commenting:

> *The Finchley Dramatic Society played Shakespeare last night.*
> *Shakespeare lost.*

While on the subject of the future tense, let us clear up the frequent query 'What is the difference between **I shall** and **I will**?' In British English this auxiliary verb is conjugated as follows:

> *I shall*
> *you will*
> *he/she/it will*
> *we shall*
> *you will*
> *they will.*

In American English you use **will** in all cases.

In British English **I will** and **we will** indicate **willingness** to do something:

> *I will be home before midnight* (= promise).
> *I shall be home before midnight* (= time forecast).

In speech and informal writing you can use a simple trick to avoid worrying about **shall** or **will**: contract pronoun and verb to **I'll** or **we'll** and nobody will know the difference:

> *We'll be back for dinner* (= *we shall* or *we will*).

Shall on both sides of the Atlantic shows **compulsion** and can also be applied to the second and third person:

> *He shall do as we say!*

The Ten Commandments are phrased

> *Thou shalt not steal.*

In technical specifications you may find

> *The brass rods shall be free from deformities.*

In American English you can also say I **shall** when expressing a strong resolve. When General MacArthur had to evacuate the Philippines during the Second World War, he vowed 'I shall return'. 'I will return' would have sounded a little half-hearted.

3. The subjunctive

If you ask students of French, Spanish or Italian what they think of the subjunctive, you will probably find that they will give it very low marks for charm or entertainment value.

Good news! The English subjunctive is easy for the following reasons:

- It is used far less than in the Romance languages.
- Conjugation of the **present subjunctive** is the easiest thing in the world: verb forms are the same as the **infinitive** throughout. You don't even have to add the s in the third person singular and can conjugate while thinking of something else: I go, you go, he/she/it go, we go, you go, they go.
- Conjugation of the **past subjunctive** is likewise no problem: verb forms are the same as the **simple past**, except for **to be** which has the form **were**: I were, you were, he were, and so on.
- It is on its way out and may well be obsolete by the end of this century.

Let's see where you do use the subjunctive.

● Stock phrases

The subjunctive is likely to survive in a handful of phrases:

be that as it may
if need be
as it were
come what may
so be it
far be it from me, etc.

Some of these phrases sound a little old-fashioned nowadays. I hardly ever use any of them and feel no ill effects.

● Blessings, exclamations, anthems

(God) bless you.
God be with you.
Heaven help us!
God forbid!

and the titles of the anthems

'God save the Queen'
'Rule Britannia'.

This group is also easy and unlikely to be needed in your daily repertoire.

● *If* -clauses introducing a hypothesis, a theory, a supposition

The most common of these is *If I were you* to introduce a piece of advice based on your vast experience and wisdom:

If I were you, I would accept the offer.

This use of the subjunctive will probably survive for another generation. 'If I was you' still sounds uneducated.

In all other hypothetical statements the subjunctive is no longer being taken very seriously. It used to be strictly applied –

and still is in formal writing – when the **hypothesis** is **impossible** or **doubtful**. Take these sentences:

If this report is true, the company must be nearly bankrupt.

The speaker does not know if the report is true or not. It **may be**. You use the **indicative**.

If this report were true, the company would have been bankrupt long ago.

The report is obviously **untrue**. You use the **subjunctive**.

In less formal writing, however, the **past indicative** is today preferred and may in time completely oust the subjunctive. You may deplore this as an erosion of grammar, or you may welcome it as a useful reform. In the following sentences the grammatically correct form **were** is used in formal writing, but **was** is what you will often hear or read:

We would buy it if it was cheaper.

I wish he was here right now.

They could be in trouble if she was to leave the firm.

The same applies to subordinate clauses that start with **as if** or **as though**:

She felt as if she was walking on air.

He described it as though it was his own idea.

- ● *That* -clauses introducing a command, suggestion, proposal, recommendation, etc.

This is the only group of importance because it shows an unusual trend in grammar: the revival of an old verb form that was becoming extinct.

Although American English often leads the way in simplifying English usage around the world, it here sticks to the more old-fashioned subjunctive while British English prefers the use of **should** and other auxiliaries:

British English:

I propose that he should be appointed General Manager.

*He insisted that they **should replace** it.*

*They asked that she **should be given** a free hand.*

American English:

*I propose that he **be appointed** General Manager.*

*He insisted that it **be replaced**.*

*They asked that she **be given** a free hand.*

American influence is reponsible for an odd development in British English: the return of the subjunctive. In place of the more relaxed constructions with **should** you will often find the more formal-sounding American version with the subjunctive.

4. *All about adverbs*

I listen carefully

You play brilliantly.

He acts badly.

She writes correctly.

It functions erratically.

We read slowly.

You relax completely.

They sleep soundly.

By now you, too, may be half-asleep, thinking drowsily that you merely add -ly to an adjective or participle to convert it into an adverb. I am sorry to interrupt, but this happy rule does not always work. Let us sort out the exceptions.

• Adverbs without -*ly*

*They walk **straight**.*

*He aimed **low**.*

*She works **hard**.*

*We run **fast**.*

*The train ran **late**.*

'Straightly' does not exist. **Lowly** does exist, but it is not an adverb. It is an adjective, used mainly in the old-fashioned phrase *of lowly origin*, meaning *of modest background*. **Hardly** you know, but in its meaning of **scarcely, almost not at all**. As it is always placed before the verb it qualifies and not after it, there can be no mistaking

He hardly works

for

He works hard.

Fast is both adjective and adverb:

A fast car; the car moves fast.

Lately exists, but it means **recently**:

They have lately renovated their offices.

● **Adjective or adverb?**

Why do we say

*She threw the ball **high** into the air*

and not 'highly'? Because **high** does not refer to the act of throwing, but to the position of the ball, i.e. **high** does not qualify the verb; it refers to the object. It is then a predicative adjective, not an adverb.

*She is **highly** qualified*

is different. Her manner of qualifying is high, not she. (She is only 1.30 m.) You need the adverb form **highly**, which in any case never refers to physical height, but means **extremely, very**: *highly emotional, highly effective*, etc.

A few more examples for practice:

*They are **deeply** concerned.*

The extent of their being concerned is deep, not they. **Deeply** is required.

*Still waters run **deep**.*

The waters are deep, not the way they run: you need the adjective **deep**.

We use this grammatical construction loosely.

The manner of using it is loose. A verb needs an adverb: **loosely**.

The bolt securing the door worked loose.

What is loose? The bolt, of course. Therefore **loose**.

He plays bridge badly.

His manner of playing is bad. He is not. (In fact, he is probably quite charming as he trumps his partner's ace.) The verb needs **badly**.

These mussels seem (to be) bad.

The mussels are bad, not the action of the verb 'seem'. The adjective is required.

The radio played much too loud.

Loud is usually preferred when talking about the volume of an instrument or voice, yet you say

They sing loud and clear

but

They complained loudly.

I suppose the difference is that when speaking loud, it's the **volume** that gets on your nerves. When complaining loudly, you are thinking about the agitated **manner of speaking**.

All the above examples with an adjective in place of a suspected adverb yield to the simple analysis:

If you can replace the verb by a form of *to be*, you need an adjective.

We thus find that the ball *is* high, the waters *are* deep, the bolt *is* loose, the mussels *are* bad, and the radio *is* loud.

Do you remember the difference between a transitive and intransitive verb? Vaguely? A quick refresher course: a transitive verb can be used with a direct object.

We write a letter.

An intransitive verb cannot be followed by a direct object: 'the book has disappeared', but you cannot 'disappear' something.

Some verbs can be both transitive and intransitive:

He tasted the milk

and

The milk tasted sour.

This clarification leads us to the next section.

● The verbs *to smell, look, taste, sound,* and *feel*

These verbs take the **adjective**, when used **intransitively**:

*The soup smells **good**.*
*The house looks **attractive**.*
*The pudding tastes **wonderful**.*
*The record sounds **terrible**.*
*We felt **tired**.*

The same verbs take the **adverb** when used **transitively**:

The dog smelt [Am.: *smelled*] *the ground suspiciously.*
She looked at him coldly.
He tasted the hot soup carefully.
They sounded the alarm repeatedly.
We felt the sharp edge gingerly.

Note: **She looks well** refers to her **healthy appearance**. An object **looks good** when it looks **attractive**:

> *This Giant Ice Cream with chopped walnuts and whipped cream on top looks good!*

● Mixed bag

The adjective form is used for no logical reason, but sanctioned by idiomatic usage:

*They always fight **fair**.*
*We play very **rough**.*

*He likes to travel **light*** (without much luggage).

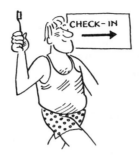

*Go **slow**!*
*Hold **tight**!*
*They arrived **safe** and **sound**,*

but

*They arrived **safely**.*

You may be **fully** aware of certain facts, yet you say

*He knew **full** well (that it was impossible).*

• American department

Real and **sure** are often used as adverbs in informal American English:

*He worked **real** hard.*
*Please write **real** soon.*
*It **sure** was difficult.*
*They **sure** would.*
***Sure**!*

British English would use **really** and **surely** (or **certainly**) instead.

The word **thusly** has been heard on American TV and radio for **in this way**. It does not officially exist, but somehow sounds impressive when uttered in a deep and loud voice.

5. *Whose genitive?*

Are you sure you remember all you were taught about the English genitive case, the possessive? Just in case you are a little doubtful, let's examine some of its peculiarities.

As you know, the apostrophe and letter *'s* play an important part in showing **possession**:

Susan's dress.

Grandmother's cigar, and so on.

Beyond possession in the sense of property, the genitive can also indicate a **descriptive** factor, **originator** or other connection:

Children's footwear.

Tom's new novel.

Women's rights, etc.

The apostrophe + s is not used with ordinary inanimate objects. You do not usually say:

The furniture's value.

The mountain's height.

The forest's trees.

It is better to say *the value of the furniture*, and so on.

The apostrophe + s is not restricted to people only. It can also be used with the following groups of words:

Animals	*The elephant's trunk.* *The lion's roar.*
Countries, some objects	*Norway's export trade.* *The sun's rays.* *The company's pension scheme.*
Indefinite pronouns	*Nobody's business.* *Somebody's umbrella.* *Everybody's concern.*
Some expressions of time and value	*A day's work.* *Last month's salary.* *A dollar's worth.*
A few general expressions	*Duty's call.* *A stone's throw.* *By a hair's breadth.* *For old times' sake.* *For goodness' sake.*
Names ending in *s*	**Historical** names add the apostrophe only: *Jesus' followers.* *Archimedes' legacy.* With other names you add apostrophe + *s*: *Charlie Jones's home.*

You need **no genitive** form with certain combinations of nouns:

Boys school.

Exporters association.

Students federation.

Why no **s**? Because the first word is an **attributive** adjective. A distinction is sometimes made between an **attributive** and a **predicative** adjective. Nothing to be frightened of: an attributive adjective stands next to a noun, usually in front of it:

A blue shirt.

A predicative adjective is linked to its noun by a verb, usually **to be**:

The shirt is blue.

● Double genitive

A typically English oddity is the double genitive, also known as **post-genitive**, the use of a possessive pronoun followed by a noun with apostrophe + *s*:

> *She is a sister of my grandmother's.*
>
> *He is a good friend of my father's.*

This construction can sometimes avoid ambiguity. When I bore you on a rainy afternoon with my album of family photographs, I may explain:

> *And this is a picture of my Uncle Tim.*

This means that the picture shows Tim. *A picture of my Uncle Tim's*, on the other hand, means that the picture **belongs** to him, i.e. it was probably taken by him but need not show him as well.

The possessive *s* can also indicate that something has been left out:

> *She bought it at the butcher's* (shop).
>
> *Let's meet at Macy's* (department store).
>
> *We are staying at my grandparents'* (house).

Another kind of post-genitive is used in these constructions:

> *A friend of mine.*
>
> *That hat of hers.*
>
> *Those plans of theirs.*

What is the difference between *He is my friend* and *He is a friend of mine*? The first is more specific and could mean that he is the **only one** I have. The second is more general and shows that there are many others.

Note: A mistake sometimes heard in countries where a Teutonic language is spoken is 'She is a relative of us'. No, you need the possessive pronoun **ours** here: *She is a relative of **ours***.

Let's quickly run through all of them: **mine   yours   his   hers   its   ours   yours   theirs**. No apostrophe.

Here are a few things worth knowing about the use of the apostrophe + *s*:

Plural	When a noun ends in a plural -*s*, you only need the apostrophe:
	Horses' tails.
	When a noun has an irregular plural without final -*s*, you add apostrophe + *s*:
	Children's toys. *A gentlemen's agreement.*
Compounds	Add apostrophe + *s* to the last noun:
	My brother-in-law's family.

6. Pronouns

• Me, myself and I

This looks like a display of egoism (or egotism; see page 166), but merely introduces a few interesting points about personal, possessive, and reflexive pronouns.

It's me!

You were probably taught at school that if the question is **Who?** (subjective), the answer should contain the nominative, i.e. it must be *It's I*.

How is it then that you are likely to hear *It's **me*** in English-speaking countries? This is one of those cases where colloquial usage, what you say in conversation, overrides theory. As the grammatically correct form *It's I* sounds even a little affected, there is no objection in other than very formal contexts to the more relaxed:

> *It was* **me**.
> *It could have been* **him**.
> *It may be* **her**.
> *It has to be* **us**.
> *It ought to be* **them**.

You will often find this relaxation in comparisons:

> *He looks older than* **her**.
> *They were faster than* **us**.

Some people, trying to be super-correct, say 'between you and **I**'. Although this phrase has a certain elegance to it, the last pronoun should be the objective **me**: *between you and me*.

Wash your hands!

In some languages you do not use a possessive pronoun and simply say *I wash the hands, He nods the head, Please wipe the feet*, and other combinations of verbs and parts of the body. Please be sure to use a **possessive pronoun** in English every time:

> *I wash* **my** *hands*.
> *He nods* **his** *head*.
> *Please wipe* **your** *feet*.

Myself yourself himself herself itself ourselves yourselves themselves

These eight pronouns are used far more often in English than in other languages; for the following reasons:

- They are not only **reflexive** but also **intensive** (emphatic) pronouns.
- In several languages some personal pronouns are the same as reflexive ones.

Reflexive pronouns are used when an action somehow refers back to the subject:

I washed myself.

Did you hurt yourself?

Some verbs can be used with or without a reflexive pronoun:

They worried.   *They worried themselves sick.*

He behaved.   *He behaved himself.*

Less usual in other languages is the **intensive pronoun**, something to give **emphasis**:

I saw it myself.

You said so yourself.

She can easily do it herself.

The pronouns here are in no way reflexive, i.e. they do not refer back to the subject, but mean **personally, on her own**, etc. *He attended* tells you that he was there. *He attended himself* points out that he did not send someone in his place. The intensive pronoun can often sound smoother than the personal one:

This is for advanced students like yourself (or: like **you**).

It was signed by the Minister and myself (or: and **me**).

Definitely not approved are **self** on its own and **goodselves**:

Your parents and self are invited

sounds uneducated. Change 'self' to **you** or **yourself**.

Me, too

Agreement with somebody's statement or suggestion is sometimes translated 'also I' or 'I also'. Both are wrong. *Me, too* is possible but will not get you high marks for educated speech. Your solution is the word **so** plus **do**:

I think it's a good idea. – So do I.

They arrived after lunch. – So did we.

When an auxiliary verb precedes, you repeat the auxiliary:

> *We have decided to stay. – So have we.*
>
> *She can play badminton. – So can I.*

When you are in agreement with a negative sentence, you use **neither** or **nor** in place of **so**:

> *He can't play poker. – Neither can I.*
>
> *We didn't like it. – Nor did we.*

Agreement with somebody's statement can sometimes also be expressed by *same here*. This is suitable only for a casual situation and might be considered slang by some people. Listen to this meeting:

> *I am certainly happy to see you again after all these years! – Same here.*

- **The rare *one***

What's so remarkable about these helpful announcements? The English version is the only one without the impersonal pronoun **si/se/man/on**, etc. This is no accident: the English **one** is used much less than the corresponding word in other languages and can even sound rather stilted in conversation. If you resist the temptation to use it in a translation, you will do a better job.

Here are a few ideas. The literal English version is given for comparison in parentheses after each foreign sentence.

On verra (One will see)

The personal pronoun **we** need not only mean the group to which you belong. It can also be **impersonal**, the world in general. Best translation of the above patient comment from France:

We'll see.

Man nehme einen Liter Wasser (One has to take a litre [Am.: liter] of water)

Instructions of any kind, ranging from how to make a decent bouillabaisse to the right way of landing a jumbo jet with two engines on fire, are given in English in the **imperative**:

Take a litre of water.
Beat it to a thick cream.

Si attende una nuova tassa d'acquisto (One is expecting a new purchase tax)

This depressing piece of news from Italy can become a statement using the **passive voice**:

A new purchase tax is expected.

Zo iets doet men niet (One does not do this (sort of thing))

Again the passive voice, but with an idiomatic twist, this Dutch disapproval is best translated:

This sort of thing is not done.

Done can even be used as an adjective:

It's not the done thing.

Alternatively, you can use the impersonal **you**:

You can't do that!

(Spoken Dutch also has the impersonal **you**: 'je'.)

När kan man träffa honom hemma? (When can one meet him at home?)

This Swedish question is a very indirect way of finding out something that is best phrased in English in a **direct** manner:

When will he be at home?

At what time will he be in?

Man overvejer en skattenedsættelse (One is considering a tax cut)

This unlikely report from Denmark can be translated by bringing in the word **they**, which can also play an **impersonal** part. It is used when referring to people that are in some way assumed to be on the other side of the fence: the government, the employers, the employees, and so on.

They are considering a tax cut.

Se trabaja menos horas hoy día (One works fewer hours nowadays)

As the impersonal **they** in the last example applies to a specific group, you can use the word **people** when you want to be more general:

People work fewer hours nowadays.

Se fala português (One speaks Portuguese)

As you already know, a special bit of shorthand is used for the English version:

English (is) spoken (here).

Slightly nervous, you may ask 'But when can I use the word *one*? Surely, it does exist in English? Yes, it has a place in writing and formal speech whenever the personal/impersonal pronouns

we/you/they may be too direct. A newspaper, for example, could comment on a forecast made by a public company:

Their figures have sometimes been wildly optimistic.
One should not rely on them too much.

Saying **You** *should not rely on them too much* would address itself too directly to the reader, giving him personal advice he may not need. **One** keeps the statement on a more neutral level.

- **His, her or their?**

Arguments sometimes arise when you have this kind of sentence:

Somebody has forgotten his umbrella.

Why the male **his** when the owner could be a woman? It is generally accepted that *his* can serve as a unisex possessive pronoun with such impersonal ones as *anybody, anyone, somebody, someone, nobody, no one, everybody, everyone,* etc. As a compromise in front of a mixed audience, announcements are sometimes amplified to:

Somebody has forgotten his or her umbrella.

In longer sentences with repetitions, however, this can become very clumsy:

If nobody buys more than his or her ration, everyone will get his or her fair share.

Although not, strictly speaking, grammatical, **they** or **their** is becoming accepted in informal contexts. In some way this is even defensible when you consider that *somebody,* for example, can mean *some person* (one) or *some people* (several) when you hear: *Somebody must be responsible for this mess!*

A cynic once commented:

*Nobody would fall in love if **they** hadn't seen it at the cinema,*

treating *nobody* as substitute for *no persons* or *no people,* i.e. more than one.

● **That *or* which?**

Can you see anything wrong with these two headings, taken from London newspapers? Change *which* to *that*, and you will improve the style, because when the antecedent is an inanimate object:

> *Which* introduces a commenting relative clause;
> *that* introduces a defining one.

What does all that mean? Two examples will make it clear:

> *The last letter, which was sent from Madeira, announced their arrival on the first of next month.*

The relative clause is a casual **comment** on the letter. It could be put in parentheses; it could be between dashes. The relative clause is perhaps interesting, but the sentence would also make sense without it. This is a **commenting relative clause**: *which* is better.

> *The letter that was sent from Madeira never reached us.*

Many letters were sent from different places. One got lost. It was the one from Madeira, i.e. we **define** which of the many. We have a **defining relative clause**: *that* is much better than *which*.

> *The train, which is faster on this route than air travel, will be our best solution.*

Here again you make a **comment** about the speed of the train, any train on the route, as opposed to going by plane. On the other hand:

> *The train that leaves at 10.30 will get us there in time*

selects one of several in the timetable; it **defines** the one that will suit you best. You use the relative pronoun *that* for preference.

Going back to our two newspaper headings, we can now reason as follows:

'The firm which shocked Canada – by going away'

The relative clause is not a side comment on the firm. It **defines** which of many was so daring. Therefore: *that* in place of *which*.

'Study centre which helps young immigrants'

There must be many such centres [Am.: centers]. Here again the relative clause **defines** which one. *That* is much better than *which*.

If you are puzzled by the absence of commas in two of the sample sentences mentioned above, see page 60 for rules about punctuation with relative clauses.

7. A collection of collective nouns

All languages have **collective** nouns, words whose singular form means a **group** of people, animals or things. Here are a few of them:

army   audience   board   class   committee   company congregation   crew   family   gang   government   jury majority   minority   number   orchestra   personnel   public staff   team,   and many others.

The choice of the right verb form – singular or plural – should be no problem. In the Scandinavian languages you make no distinction between the two, anyway; in other languages you always use the singular. As you may have guessed already, English prefers to treat these nouns a little differently by admitting the singular or plural verb form. The right choice depends on the following considerations:

If you are thinking of the group as a whole, as a unit, use the singular.

If you are thinking of the individual members of the group, use the plural.

A few examples should make you an expert in one easy lesson:

The **Board** (*of Directors*) *has only limited powers.* (body)
The **Board** *were unanimous in their decision.* (members)

The **committee** *is in session.* (unit)

The **committee** *have approved the plan.* (members)

Our physics **class** *is small.* (unit)
The 1970 **class** *have agreed to hold a reunion.* (all members)

The Cambridge **crew** *is expected to win this year.* (team)
The **crew** *are allowed three hours' rest.* (members)

Their **personnel** *has increased considerably.* (total number) *All* **personnel** *wear uniform.* (members)

*Our **staff has** not changed much.* (establishment)

*Their **staff are** given language training.* (members)

*This **family qualifies** for a tax rebate.* (unit)

*The **family are** very pleased about it.* (members)

You may have been in doubt whether it should be 'The company *is* (or *are?*) introducing a new guarantee'. The **plural** is preferred when the **collective** effort of many people refers to the activities of a company:

*Trans-Globe Airways **serve** caviar in Economy Class.*

You may also find the singular:

*Trans-Globe Airways **is** in financial difficulties.*

Probably because of the caviar.

The collective nouns **government** and **party** take the **singular** verb form in **North America**. In countries using British English you have either the singular or plural, depending on the reasoning mentioned earlier. Although sports teams work (or should work) as one harmonious unit, thus qualifying for the singular, they are always followed by the plural verb form:

*Manchester United **were** defeated at Highbury.*

Three frequent dilemmas:

1. Majority (also **minority**)

An analysis of the function of this word will show you what you need:

*The majority **has** to approve the plan.* (greater part)

*The majority (of tenants) **are** foreigners.* (most tenants)

2. Number

Similar reasoning applies here:

*A number of students **have** not yet enrolled.* (some students)

*The number of students **has** grown.* (quantity)

3. Measurements/units

When you refer to quantities and have **bulk** in mind, you normally use the **singular**:

*About three **pounds** of flour **has** to be added.*

*£550 **is** too much!*

8. Comparisons

Should it be **narrower** or **more narrow**? Is **more pleasant** an improvement on **pleasanter**? Dictionaries will not help you with this kind of problem, but here is a happy thought: there are just a few simple rules which are easy to remember. Exceptions? Of course, as always in English, but even these are nothing much to worry about.

(a) **Adjectives of one syllable (usually of Teutonic origin) take -*er* in the comparative and -*est* in the superlative**

An easy group: **high   low   long   short   old   new slow   fast**, and so on.

These become: **higher   lowest   longer   shortest**, etc.

(b) **Adjectives of two syllables ending in -y, -ly, -le, and -ow take -*er* and -*est***

Another uncomplicated group: **lazy - lazier   lovely - loveliest   noble - nobler   narrow - narrowest**, and so on.

(c) **Adjectives ending in -ant, -ent, -al, -ful, -ive, -less, and -ous as well as adjectives of three or more syllables take *more* in the comparative and *most* in the superlative**

No problem here: **more gallant   most cordial   more useful   most positive   more callous   most resourceful more inquisitive**,   and so on.

(d) **Other adjectives of two syllables take -*er* and -*est* or *more* and *most*, depending on length or harmony of sound**

This is the only rule that can create occasional difficulties, as it is not always easy to decide about euphony, harmony of sound. Let's look at a few words. Valid? 'Valider' does not seem right, so it must be **more valid**. Awkward? 'Awkward-est' sounds awkward, so let's take **most awkward**. Afraid? 'Afraider' can't be right. We stick to **more afraid**.

Some words can take **-er/est** or **more/most**:

> **commonest** or **most common**
> **handsomer** or **more handsome**.

Do you want to know a useful trick? When in doubt, use **more** and **most**. They usually fit. Take a word like **profound**. **Profound-est** is all right, but if you are not sure, try **most profound**. Nothing wrong with it.

In addition, there are a few **irregular comparisons**, but these are for beginners:

> **good – better – best   bad – worse – worst**
> **far – farther – farthest   far – further – furthest**
> **little – smaller – smallest   much/many – more – most**

A few words can have no comparative or superlative, because this elevation would make no sense. These are called **absolutes**. A few typical adjectives in this group:

> **round   square   empty   dead   unique   infinite   perfect**
> **universal   perpetual   true**, and many more.

Take **round**, for example. If the red ball is round, the blue one cannot be 'rounder'. If it looks like it, then the red ball must be slightly oval. Take **empty**: an empty box contains nothing. Another box cannot be 'emptier', i.e. contain less than nothing. Take the word **dead**: Old Joe in the cemetery is dead. He cannot be 'deader' than Lou next to him. They are equally good at it.

Yes, you may hear the exuberant comment 'Her hat was most unique!', but it would be pedantic to raise a finger and object. **Most** is here a colloquially accepted alternative to **very**. When you assure someone that you are 'most grateful', you are presumably not boasting about being the champion in a crowd of thankful people.

A fairly common mistake is using the superlative when comparing only two things. It is **not correct** to say

I learned German and Dutch. Dutch is by far the easiest.

You need the comparative when talking about two things: **by far the easier** (of the two). **Easiest** is one of more than two things.

more beautiful

most beautiful

9. - - - (missing words)

'When in Rome, do as the Romans do.'

This has nothing to do with your planned visit to the capital of Italy. It is an English proverb that tells you that it is always a good idea to adapt yourself to the customs of the country in which you are staying.

Is there anything remarkable about this piece of wisdom? Two words seem to be missing because in other languages you would philosophize 'When **you are** in Rome, do as the Romans do'.

English has several constructions in which you can leave out one or two words without loss of meaning. A few rules will help you to decide when it is safe to adopt this useful economy measure.

● Defining relative clauses

See page 26 for an explanation of the difference between a defining and a commenting relative clause. In some short sentences with a defining relative clause the relative pronoun can be left out:

The film (that) we saw last night was terrible.

This is not the calculator (that) I lent you.

The salesman (whom) you are trying to reach has gone home.

● The conjunction *that*

When **that** introduces a noun clause, you are usually better off without it:

He decided (that) it wasn't worth the risk.

They were sure (that) it would be a success.

That is generally **retained** when the preceding predicate is fairly **long**. Here are the same sentences slightly recast:

He was of the opinion that it wasn't worth the risk.

They seemed to be reasonably certain that it would be a success.

That is also often **retained** after a few verbs that are a little uncommon such as **maintain, assert, allege, emphasize**, etc.:

The pedestrian alleged that the car passed at a speed of 100 m.p.h..

● The conjunctions *when* and *though*

Subject and predicate can be left out after **when** and **though** if the subject is the same as in the main clause and the predicate is a form of **to be**:

She was a champion athlete when (she was) at university.

Though (he was) often absent from lectures, he passed the exam easily.

Mistakes are sometimes made when the subject of the two clauses is not the same. Take this sentence:

When three years old, his parents moved to Canada.

Here you have **two** subjects: **he** and his **parents**. The sentence really means that the parents were three years old when they made the bold decision to emigrate. Not very likely.

Remedy: *When he was three years old. . . .*

● Participle clauses

You need no subject before the present participle if it is repeated in the main clause:

While (he was) waiting, he counted the number of passing cars.

After locking (= she had locked) *the front door, she left quietly.*

Here again, it is important that the subject is indeed the same in both parts of the sentence. Otherwise you may get this result:

Driving across the savannah in a jeep, a rhinoceros suddenly attacked us.

Who was doing the driving? The rhino?

Correction: *Driving across the savannah,* **we were** *suddenly attacked by a rhino.*

10. Not what the teacher said

Language is a living thing: words come and go, meanings change, and even grammatical mistakes – if made often enough by sufficiently many people – may in time become acceptable usage.

When the latest edition of the Oxford Dictionary was criticized for listing certain things that are ungrammatical, the explanation was 'We have to record words and usage as they are, not as they should be'. This may be regrettable, but there is not very much we can do about it.

A few rules and forms of usage may well have changed during

the past decade or two. Here are a few examples where objections to present-day usage would be pedantic.

● 'Don't split the infinitive!'

This old rule means that you should not let a word – usually an adverb – come between **to** and the verb in an infinitive clause i.e. you should **not** say or write:

They decided to drastically reduce their commitments.

The idea is not to separate the words **to** and **reduce**. In this case this is easily prevented by shifting the adverb to the end of the sentence:

They decided to reduce their commitments drastically.

No problem here.

A relaxation of this rule sets in whenever the moving of the adverb or other interrupting element produces a clumsy construction. Take these sentences:

Visitors are requested to kindly refrain from smoking.

If you shift the word **kindly** forward by two words you are really saying that the person making the request is kind, not the one complying with it. In any other position **kindly** sounds silly. Only solution: leave it where it is.

Or:

It is unlikely to really change the result to any extent.

Advancing **really** by two words would attach it to **unlikely**, a word it is not meant to qualify. There is no other suitable home for **really** in the entire sentence. Conclusion: let's leave it where it is.

Modern policy: If it is possible to avoid splitting the infinitive (it very often is), do so. If you produce an awkward sentence as a result, why worry about the rule?

● 'The interrogative pronoun "who" is subjective; "whom" is objective!'

In other words, *Who did it?* asks for the **subject**; *Whom did you see?* tries to find out the **object** of the visit.

Unless they are specially pedantic, your friends in English-speaking countries are likely to ask:

Who did you go out with?

Who is she married to?

Who do you think we ought to invite?

You were taught that it should really be **whom** in these kinds of questions.

Why then the subjective **who** when it should be **whom**? This is perhaps the principal example of how wrong usage can eventually erode the rule. Today, all authorities on good English agree that it is a waste of time to insist on **whom** in other than very formal writing and speech.

> **Modern policy**: Although you may not like the idea, use **who** in everyday speech, and hope that your audience will give you good marks for idiomatic English rather than bad marks for a grammatical error.

Note: **Whom** continues to be used when preceded by a preposition:

To whom did you apply?

● **'Positive comparisons: "as. . . as"; negative comparisons: "not so . . . as"!'**

In other words, it is *as good as*, but *not so good as*. Don't worry. Very few people bother to make the switch to *not so*:

I am not as pedantic as you think.

> **Modern policy**: Standardize on *as . . . . as.*

● **'The preposition "in" denotes location; "into" refers to movement!'**

You sit **in** the bathtub; you step **into** the bath. This is all very logical and easy but you will nevertheless hear:

I saw him put it in his pocket.

You asked me to pour it in the sink.

He told us to get in the car.

She'll get in trouble! (mainly American)

For some reason these are the main examples of combining direction of movement with the preposition *in*. All four sentences are improved by using **into** instead.

Modern policy: Use **into** where needed, but regard *in* -users with tolerance.

● 'Avoid prepositions at the end of a sentence!'

Placing the preposition at the end of a question or relative clause is today the preferred form unless you happen to produce a contract or other formal piece of writing. This idea, pursued by purists only, can produce some very ungainly sentences. Try these, all with prepositions kept tidily away from the end:

Of what were you thinking?

From where does this plane come?

It is the book on which he is working.

Winston Churchill was one of the most brilliant speakers and writers of English of this century. In his younger days he once produced a report that had a preposition at the end of a long sentence. Someone else queried this with the written comment in the margin 'Is this grammatical?'. Churchill wrote back 'This is arrant pedantry up with which I shall not put', neatly demonstrating the clumsiness of the 'correct' position of prepositions.

Modern policy: Follow Churchill.

● 'No sentence fragments!'

You may have learned that a sentence consists of subject and predicate, and expresses a complete thought. In other words, anything lacking subject or predicate is somehow ungrammatical or naughty. Well, it depends. Here is a horrible piece of writing from a full-page advertisement in a London newspaper:

We supply a radio as standard equipment. And through-flow ventilation.

While a heated rear window deals with the cold outside. The rear seats are more comfortable than most front seats. And the trim is high-quality throughout. *And all that for £5495!*

The sentence fragments used here are chopped-up English, mincemeat writing without the slightest merit. On the other hand, sentence fragments are permissible as an aid to vivid writing, for creating an atmosphere:

She awoke. At three. And heard the stairs creak. One at a time. . ..

Alone at last. No people. No telephone. No radio. Paradise!

Making these sentences 'grammatical' by inserting all necessary verbs, articles, prepositions, etc. would remove nearly all suspense or elation.

Modern policy: There is nothing against sentence fragments as an aid to descriptive writing or for creating an atmosphere.

11. Can this be right?

You may sometimes read or hear a sentence which seems to be in some way wrong, not conforming to what you were taught. Perhaps like one of the following:

Aren't I?

Although this may look and sound ungrammatical, it is the acceptable colloquial contraction of **Am I not?**

Can I borrow your car?

Shouldn't it be '**may** I borrow'? Yes, strictly speaking, **can** refers to physical **ability, may** to **permission**:

Can she swim? = Is she able to swim?

May she swim? = Is she allowed to swim?

In colloquial usage, however, **can** is now often preferred when permission is involved. In response to a request it sounds much more friendly than **may**.

You can have the afternoon off

is less condescending, more human than

You may have the afternoon off.

Someone may now ask 'What about **could** and **might**?'. Both are not just the past of **can** and **may**, but can also show some **doubt** regardless of the timing of the event:

They left at 6 a.m. They could be here by lunchtime.

If the weather is good, I might try again.

Could is furthermore the required verb form in **indirect speech** of a statement in the present tense:

They can go. = They were told that they could go.

Might is not used in exactly the same way in indirect speech. If you report *'They were told that they might go'*, you are indicating a doubt, a condition, a qualification. **May** is less vague.

On *either* side

Either normally denotes an alternative: either this or that; either wine or beer.
Colloquially, **either** can also mean **each of two**:

There is a traffic light at either end of this street.

If = although?

Here is an odd way of using the word **if**:

The room was comfortable if a little cramped.

The **if** here means **although** or **but**, i.e. some degree of criticism.

She prefers to type *rather than* write by hand

'Rather than'? Surely you prefer one thing **to** another? Yes, you do in all constructions in which you have a **noun** or **gerund**:

*He prefers tea **to** coffee.*

*She prefers painting **to** drawing.*

When **prefer** is followed by the **infinitive**, you would in theory have this impossible sentence with the word **to** twice:

She prefers to paint to to draw.

Solution: **rather than** in place of **to**. You can also express preference without the verb **prefer** altogether:

I prefer coffee to dessert = I would (I'd) rather have coffee than dessert.

They were very tired on arrival. They seemed cheerful, *though*

What's the **though** doing at the end? Isn't it normally a conjunction, linking two parts of a sentence? True, but in colloquial English you do use **though** at the end of a sentence in place of **however, nevertheless, in spite of, but**, etc., i.e. when you want to indicate something unexpected. A few examples:

The first part was difficult. The second one was much easier, though.

(The second one, **however**, was much easier.)

It may sound incredible. It's true, though.

(It may sound incredible, **but** it's true.)

He is unreliable. You can't help liking him, though.

(You can't help liking him **in spite of** it.)

There is nothing against your using **though** in these constructions in informal writing or conversation. Don't overdo it, though!

Please try *and* finish it by Friday

'And'? Shouldn't it be 'try **to** do something'? Yes, but in colloquial English you often use **and** in **requests**:

Please try and do better next time.

Try and improve on it, if possible.

The *try and* -version in **promises** indicates some optimism about the result:

> *I'll try to get them to sign tomorrow* = I'll try.
>
> *I'll try and get them to sign tomorrow* = I think I'll succeed.

They escaped in a sports car *whose* number we couldn't see in the rain

'Whose number'? Isn't there a rule '**whose** applies to **persons; of which** to **inanimate** objects'?

Whose in connection with inanimate objects often produces a more elegant sentence:

> *Three years ago they bought this piece of land whose value rose sharply when the new motorway scheme was announced.*

Changing this to '. . .piece of land the value of which rose. . .' does sound a bit clumsy.

The multi-purpose **whose** is often a good solution.

12. Let's hit him in the eye!

The position of the word *only* in a sentence can be important. Take the simple sentence *I hit him in the eye*. By placing the word *only* in various positions you can obtain five quite different meanings:

1. *Only I* hit him in the eye. = Nobody else was so cruel. Only I.
2. I *only hit* him in the eye. = All I did was hit him in the eye. Nothing worse.
3. I hit *only him* in the eye. = He was the only victim. Nobody else.
4. I hit him *only in the eye.* = I concentrated on the eye. On no other part of his body.
5. I hit him in the *only eye.* = The poor fellow had only one eye. That's the one I hit.

These examples show clearly:

(a) That the speaker is the kind of person you should avoid.
(b) That you should be careful where you put the word *only* in a sentence.

In English the word *only* has a tendency to place itself before the verb. Very often this does not matter very much. After all, *I paid them only 20 francs* looks the same as *I only paid them 20 francs*.

On the other hand, the position of *only* can sometimes change the meaning of a sentence completely, as the above eye-hitting incident shows. In a legal document the wrong position of *only* can be a very expensive error.

2

Perfect your punctuation

English punctuation has a bad reputation abroad for being difficult, vague, and without clear rules for the unfortunate writer.

That's grossly exaggerated. English punctuation marks are not really difficult. Most of them are used in the same way as in other languages, and the few differences that exist are quickly mastered. Only the comma may sometimes create problems, but I hope to be able to show you that the absence of strict grammatical rules makes it an expressive and quite logical aid in writing.

Let's start with the easy and uncomplicated punctuation marks to get you into the right mood.

1. *Full stop [Am.: period]* (.)

As the term **period** is also sometimes used in English-speaking countries outside North America, let's stick to it from now on to simplify matters. The period ends a sentence. In all languages. As English sentences are (or should be) shorter than those in most other languages, you need more periods in a given piece of writing.

Periods are also used in **abbreviations and contractions**. During the past forty years or so there has been a trend to eliminate the period in abbreviations. I recently read in a 1936 novel that someone 'boarded a **K.L.M.** plane in Batavia'. Nowadays he would 'board a **KLM** plane in Jakarta'.

43

The abbreviations of **well-known organizations, companies, countries**, etc. are therefore best written without periods:

UNICEF   NATO   BBC   TWA   USA   USSR, and so on.

The same applies to internationally recognized abbreviations of units, such as **in** (inches), **m** (metres [Am.: meters]), **g** (grammes/grams), **min** (minutes), etc. These should always be without a period.

2. Question mark (?)

No problems here, but be sure to use the question mark only after **direct questions**.

Can you come on Sunday? is a **direct** question.

I am wondering whether they can come on Sunday is an **indirect** question and no question mark is needed.

Some **requests** are phrased like questions. These are often used in business letters:

Could you please send this by air freight.

This is not a direct question, but another way of saying *Please send it by air freight*. You need no question mark.

3. Exclamation mark (!)

This is used **less** than in other languages, so be careful. As the term implies, an exclamation mark comes after something you **exclaim**, you **shout**:

'Oh!'   'Ah!'   'Ouch!'   'Good heavens!'   'By golly!'

Its use after commands depends on whether it is a strong or a mild order. When you take your dog for a walk and it is time to go home, you may say 'Come along, Fifi'. When independent-minded Fifi fails to take the slightest bit of notice and disappears around the corner, your more forceful order is likely to be 'COME HERE!'. With audible exclamation mark.

Comments introduced by **what** and **how** usually take the exclamation mark:

'*What a swindle!*'   '*How original!*'

I sometimes understate such remarks by using the **ellipsis**, three periods:

After the change of management that dirty old restaurant has become the cleanest and best in town. What a difference.... (Ellipsis followed here by a period.)

Never use more than one exclamation mark. *I had won first prize!!!* may be all right in a schoolgirl's diary, but anywhere else it is considered a bit vulgar. Take this job advertisement in a Swiss newspaper for instance:

Sales/Marketing/Promotion plus the power of positive doing!!!

If you have prooven results that these qualities exist in you and you would like to have the opportunity to make your own future and as much money as you want: With our succesful range of retail products and marketing programme the possibilities are here for you.

The three exclamation marks make the writer sound over-excitable or like a possibly dishonest high-pressure salesman. Besides, his spelling ('prooven') is not too good.

Apply for another job.

4. Colon (:)

The English colon is highly versatile.

As you can see in any English novel, **direct speech** is introduced by a **comma**:

She asked, 'What time will you be ready?'

On the other hand, a **quoted sentence** is introduced by a **colon**, as in most other languages:

As my old instructor used to say: 'When in doubt, shout'.

The colon also signals a **series of items**, an **explanation**:

This sauce is suitable for many kinds of food: meat, fish, salads, and sandwiches.

Their success is due to one thing only: hard work.

The colon is here a substitute for **namely, such as, viz., i.e.,** and others.

You can also put the colon before giving a **reason** or con-sequence:

We came back after only three days: we had run out of money.

There is only one thing to do: we have to sell it.

Not quite so common, but occasionally useful is the colon to mark a **contrasting** thought or statement:

The redesign will take four months: we have barely six weeks left before the exhibition.

The colon is here used in place of **but**.

5. Semicolon (;)

This is an easy stop: stronger than the comma; weaker than the period. It can show a **close connection** between two independent clauses:

The old model had two headlights; the new model has four.

Try this ointment; it may help you.

Before a **conjunction** (*but, although, since, for, as, and*, etc.) you normally use a comma, but occasionally the semicolon is better:

> *The new offices are more spacious, brighter, better planned; and, what's more, they are much nearer our factory.*

The semicolon in this kind of sentence with many commas helps to show where the sentence division begins.

Conjunctive adverbs (*besides, moreover, therefore, however, furthermore*, etc.) usually introduce clauses that call for a slight pause:

> *We get some pocket money of this extra work; besides, it's fun.*

The semicolon can also help to avoid confusion:

> *Most of the work was done by Helen; Jane and Pat taking the line that they were too busy with other things.*

If there is a comma after *Helen*, you will have to read the sentence at least twice before knowing what is meant.

6. Apostrophe (')

Before we start, let's make sure of the correct pronunciation: stress on the second syllable; last syllable pronounced the same way as in 'philosophy'.

The apostrophe is used more in English than in other languages. Here are its main functions.

• Omissions

The apostrophe is used to indicate that one or several letters are missing in a contraction of two words:

> *It's = it is.*
> *You'll = you will.*
> *We've = we have.*
> *Two o'clock*, and so on.

Popular abbreviations tend to lose their apostrophe: *'bus* for omnibus is now *bus*; *'phone* for telephone is now *phone*; and *'flu* for influenza has become *flu*. The absence of figures can also be shown by means of an apostrophe:

In '62 = in 1962.

Letters can also be missing in dialects or other unusual pronunciations of certain words. These can be shown in writing in this way:

Goin' fishin' = going fishing.

'ome, sweet 'ome = home, sweet home.

Very important: please remember that the possessive pronouns **yours, hers, its, ours**, and **theirs** are NOT contractions. **It's** is often confused with **its**. One of the prize exhibits in my collection of Horrible Mistakes is a full-page advertisement run a few years ago by one of the major US oil companies in the most prestigious American business magazine. Here is the headline, with name blocked out in order not to cause red faces somewhere.

WHAT COULD X HAVE BEEN THINKING, PLACING IT'S FUTURE IN THE HANDS OF A VIRGIN QUEEN?

Although the above copy must have been checked and rechecked by many people, that dreadful *'it's'* somehow slipped through.

• Plurals

The apostrophe can help to avoid confusion with certain plurals. When, for example, someone writes 'to chose' instead of *to choose*, you point this out by saying

*'Hey! There are two **o's** in "to choose"'!'*

Without the apostrophe, that 'os' would look strange (unless you can use an italic *o* in printing). If there is no possibility of a confusion, you need no apostrophe: a group of 12 MPs (= Members of Parliament).

In British English an apostrophe is sometimes used with the

plural of **figures**. This practice is less frequent in American English and may be dying out:

All the *5's* = all the *5s*.

In the 1970's = *in the 1970s*.

• Genitive

As you know from your very early English lessons, the apostrophe plays a big part in the possessive form. See page 16 for separate treatment of this subject.

7. Hyphen (-)

Mistakes are often made by foreigners when faced with two nouns. They either use a hyphen where it is not necessary or join the two words into one, when they should be left separate.

A few examples from my collection:

Marketing-Department.
Service-Engineer.
Production-Planning.

These look much better written apart:

Marketing Department.
Service Engineer.
Production Planning.

Speakers of the Teutonic languages often produce the following joined words:

Advertisingbudget.
Salesanalysis.
Drillingmachine.

Please separate these to the tidier-looking:

Advertising budget.
Sales analysis.
Drilling machine.

Although English belongs to the family of Teutonic languages, it does not follow the Teutonic practice of glueing together long words. A lecture on 'atomic absorption spectroscopy' – three manageable words – once came out as 'atomabsorptionsspektrofotometri' in Swedish, a 31-letter monster.

A German letterhead of an 'Energiekostenberatungsgesellschaft' would be far less frightening to potential English clients if translated and dehydrated to 'energy cost consultants', using three easy nouns in place of what could be one of the longest words you can form in German. (There are some longer, artificial creations but they don't count here.) Long, glued-together foreign words look funny to English eyes, so here comes **Rule no. 1** (or Convention no. 1, if you think that rules should be inflexible):

Do not join long nouns. Do not use a hyphen. Write them apart.

When it comes to **short** nouns and other words, you will find that many used to be joined by a hyphen, but are now written as one. In books printed sixty years ago you may come across 'to-day', 'to-morrow', 'type-writer', 'cloak-room', and so forth. These are now *today, tomorrow, typewriter, cloakroom*, and so on. Therefore *snapshot, mailbag, airgun*, and similar **joined** nouns should not be hyphenated.

If you are not quite sure whether a noun can be considered short or not, don't worry. It won't matter much if you join them or write them separately, but please do not use the hyphen:

Tax payer or *taxpayer*

Speed limit or *speedlimit*

Cylinder head or *cylinderhead*.

So here is already **Rule no. 2**:

Join short nouns.

Exceptions? Yes; there are a few, but all of these have logic behind them, the kind of common sense you can apply yourself. **If two joined words look odd, keep them apart to avoid puzzling the reader.**

A few examples:

Stepparent   If your father remarries, you get a stepmother. She could also be called a 'stepparent'. When I first read this joined word I had to look twice: 'stepparent' has the appearance of an adjective. A cousin of 'apparent'? Using the hyphen here can solve the problem and avoid puzzling the reader: *step-parent*.

Grassseed   Three consonants can't be right: *grass seed*, please.

Coworker   Writing *co-worker* avoids the possibility of puzzling the reader who may at first glance take in the word 'cow'.

Seaair   Although certainly short enough to qualify for joining, those two *a*'s do look strange. Solution: *sea air*.

● Compound adjectives

This is a chair of high quality.

In this kind of sentence you talk about **high** (an adjective) and **quality** (a noun).

When you place these two words **before the subject**, you produce the attributive compound adjective **high-quality**. These always need a hyphen:

This is a high-quality chair.

The hyphen helps to make your meaning clear. If you were to write *A high quality chair* (no hyphen), people may interpret this as *A high chair of good quality.*

English has many compound adjectives, words consisting of

combinations of adjectives, nouns, numerals, verbs, adverbs, etc.

low-grade   half-price   first-class   good-looking   all-important, etc.

No hyphen is needed when the first word is an adverb ending in **-ly**: *a badly written report.*

In American English you will find many of these compounds written as one word: *easygoing, oldfashioned, watercooled,* etc. The same applies to such prefixes as **pre-, anti-, co-, ex-, post-, pro-,** etc., which are usually separated by a hyphen in British English, but directly joined in American writing.

It is probable that this reduction in the use of the hyphen will continue, and that joined compounds will eventually be the rule.

Here is an interesting point when you have combinations of **figures** and **measurements**, including indications of **time**. Used attributively, you need a hyphen and the unit of measurement in the **singular**; used predicatively, you have no hyphen, but the unit in the **plural**. If this sounds complicated, here is what I mean:

my *eight-year* old son = my son is *eight years old*

a *twenty-ton* truck = a load capacity of *twenty tons*

a *ten-pound* note = it is worth *ten pounds*.

● Phrasal compounds

Some phrases are normally written as single words, but are joined by a hyphen when used **attributively**, in front of a noun. The phrase *up to date*, for example, is usually written like this:

*Their styles are not quite **up to date**.*

Yet, when placed before the noun, you write

*They presented some **up-to-date** creations.*

Other such phrases are *bread-and-butter, house-to-house, face-to-face*, etc.

● To avoid confusion

Earlier in this chapter we talked about the need to keep some short words apart, because they look odd when joined: **sea air** is better than 'seaair', for example. The hyphen can in some cases clarify meaning or avoid clashing letters with certain prefixes.

The prefix **re-** needs no hyphen when it means *again*: **rewrite, revaluation, restate,** and so on. Sometimes **re-** has nothing to do with *again* and could then easily be confused with the identical word that means something different. A hyphen is then helpful:

> You **resign** (withdraw) from a position, but you **re-sign** when you mean **sign again.**

> You **recover** (get well) from an illness, but when you fix new upholstery material to that shabby armchair, you **re-cover** it.

Clashing double vowels can also be avoided by the hyphen: **re-enter** looks better than *reenter*, **re-employ** is an improvement on *reemploy*, and **re-align** is clearer than *realign*.

● Hyphen as word divider

The division of words at the end of a line (also known by the rather horrible names of syllabication, syllabification, syllabation, and even syllabization) generally conforms to the rules used in other languages. The exceptions in English are fairly logical, so there is nothing to worry about. Here are the main rules:

(a) Avoid word divisions as much as possible

It is always easier to read a complete word than one that has been chopped into two pieces. Avoid separating syllables of one or two letters. You don't gain much, anyway:

> **not**   a-round   re-lapse   de-molish   entertain-ed, etc.

Avoid separating short words:

> **not**   du-ty   la-dy   co-py, etc.

(b) **Retain pronounceable word sections**

Here you can use your own judgement:

> *atmo-sphere   dis-tance   expla-nation*, etc.

This can lead to optional divisions, depending on how you see it. Some people may like **knowl-edge**, because the first syllable is pronounced 'nol'. Others may prefer **know-ledge** as a more logical separation.

So far it's been very easy. English practice differs from what you would normally do in other languages in only one respect, so here it comes:

(c) **Divide prefix or suffix**

This means that it is best to retain an easily recognizable root and divide as follows:

> *divid-ing   differ-ence   depend-able*, etc.

This may occasionally produce an awkward-looking word section on the next line, such as **punct-uation** with those two vowels. In that case use your discretion and write **punc-tuation**.

Modern newspaper production methods or maybe lack of time for proof reading were responsible for some very odd divisions I have seen in recent years:

> thr-ough   pos-tman   forw-ard   sp-eech, and even goa-ls.

Don't let these confuse you.

8. Dash (—)

The dash, a kind of elongated hyphen, is a useful punctuational aid in English writing. Used in **pairs**, it can avoid unsightly commas or heavy-looking parentheses, especially in **interjections** and other side comments:

Her worries, imagined or real, should be investigated.

Her worries (imagined or real) should be investigated.

Her worries – imagined or real – should be investigated.

The last version looks neatest, don't you agree?
Parenthetical remarks can also be longer, as in this example:

Their future prospects – a little difficult to forecast in the present unstable economic climate – nevertheless look bright enough.

The **single** dash is a good stylistic device when adding an **unexpected** conclusion or comment to a sentence:

His latest play is topical, lavishly produced, acted by a cast of major stars – and the biggest flop of this year.

Although their administration is not too reliable, they are a sound company. Don't worry; they'll pay your bill – if they can find it.

9. Quotation marks / inverted commas ('or")

Inverted commas is mainly a British English term. **Quotation marks** is understood in all English-speaking countries and is therefore used throughout this book.

Direct speech is indicated by pairs of quotation marks, either singles or doubles:

They asked, 'How much?'

He answered, "750 yen".

Doubles are more common in American writing; **singles** in British texts.

Both styles can be used together when you want to show **speech within speech**:

"He has that tiresome habit of saying 'eh?' after every question."

or

'He has that tiresome habit of saying "eh?" after every question.'

'He has that tiresome habit of saying "eh?" after every question.'

As in other languages, quotation marks can also be used in handwritten or typed text with titles of **books, plays**, etc. and other inanimate objects that are given a **name**:

'Wuthering Heights'
'King Lear'
the **'Blue Arrow'**, and so on.

(In printed text you may also find capitals: KING LEAR or italics: *King Lear*.)

They are also useful to signal a **quoted** phrase, a **peculiarity** of speech, an **ironical remark**:

'Nitwit' is not exactly a compliment.

She said 'perspire' instead of 'transpire'.

Sir George appeared in a 'comedy' at the Playhouse.

The most devastating use of quotation marks to indicate irony occurred in a TV critic's column in a London newspaper some years ago. A third-rate comedian, who had given a few depressing performances on British TV, announced that he had signed a contract to appear on Australian television. Critic's comment:

Britain's 'loss' will be Australia's 'gain'.

10. Comma (,)

When people complain about difficulties with English punctuation, they usually refer to the comma: 'There are no rules!' 'If I use as many as I think I should, I am wrong!' 'If I use few, I am wrong, too!' 'Help!'

Relax! As you will see, the rules governing the English comma are based on common sense and make it a flexible and useful aid in writing.

In most other languages you still use what is known as **grammatical punctuation** and its corset of strict rules based on syntax. The English comma – and to some extent English punctuation in general – is more concerned with **rhetoric**, with practical considerations, with the need for **helping the reader**. The main functions of the comma are:

- **To mark a natural pause.**
- **To make your meaning clear.**
- **As a stylistic device.**

Let's start with a simple definition:

The comma is a separator. It separates words and sentence elements.

This leads us straight to the main rule:

If a comma does a useful job, use it.

When you have digested this information, you can formulate the following sub-rule yourself:

If a comma does no useful job, leave it out.

Isn't this delightfully simple? Besides, you have two advantages:

1. You need fewer commas than you may be used to. To me, commas look a little like worms and too many of them are not particularly beautiful in a line of writing or printing.
2. Unless you use commas in a wildly eccentric way, nobody can ever accuse you of having made a mistake. **You** thought it was right; it was **your** judgement.

Let us now take a look at the various applications (or omissions) of the comma to see how this common-sense approach works out in practice.

• Before conjunctions

As the comma is a separator, it follows that in **short sentences** there is nothing to separate. Logical conclusion: **no comma**.

I don't know when they will come.

She promised to write if she can find the time.

He knows where he is going.

Let's wait until we hear the signal.

It's expensive but worth every penny.

In **long sentences** you have a **natural pause** before the conjunction. Logical decision: we **use a comma** to separate the sentence elements. Here are conjunctions in three longer sentences. The commas indicate the short pause, the place where you draw breath:

The internal combustion engine was first developed about a hundred years ago, when the need for conserving natural energy resources was of no concern.

The new model has only been on the market during the past six months, but sales already exceed a year's forecast.

She spent five years studying and working in the United States, where she acquired a strong American accent.

The word **that** has less of a pause before it than other conjunctions, even in long sentences. Result: you usually need no comma.

Sometimes you may be tempted to ask, 'This sentence is not really short. On the other hand, I wouldn't call it long. I suppose it's medium. Do I need a comma?' The answer is easy: 'Do what you like. You are the boss. If you think a comma is useful, use it. If you think you can do without it, why not?' What could be easier?

In languages with grammatical punctuation you use a comma before the conjunction *and* whenever it is followed by a clause containing subject and predicate. You do not use it when one of the two is missing. In English you don't have to bother with syntax. All you are concerned with is length of sentence and need for separation. Two examples:

He went by plane and she took the boat.

He went on a three-week fishing trip to Norway, and she took a cruise around the Eastern Mediterranean.

Conjunctions can also be found at the beginning of a sentence, when the subordinate clause comes before the main one. In that case you have a natural pause at the end of the introduction and therefore need a comma:

When we approached the coast, thick fog enveloped the ship.

If their quality does not improve, we have to order elsewhere.

• Special cases with *and*

Don't worry, I am not going to present exceptions to the rules already explained. Here are merely two extensions of entirely logical thinking.

When you enumerate items, you write either **A, B, C and D** or **A, B, C, and D**. Do you need a comma before the word **and**? I don't mind what you do. Writers in American English (and I) prefer the second version with a comma, because it can sometimes help to avoid misunderstanding by stressing that C and D do not belong together:

The mountaineers took along camping equipment, ropes, a box containing food, and two mules.

This is admittedly an extreme case, but the absence of the comma would create the meaning that the poor animals were inside that box.

Sometimes you have **two or more adjectives before a noun.** Take these two sentences:

She is a pretty, talented girl.

She is a pretty little girl.

In the first sentence you have two adjectives of the same weight as subjective opinions. You could also say pretty **and** talented girl. **You need a comma.** In the second sentence you have two adjectives of unequal weight: one expresses an opinion, the other is a fact. You could not join them with the word *and*. **You need no comma.**

A few more examples:

They faced a dangerous, vicious tiger.
They faced a dangerous old tiger.

She wore an attractive, practical dress.
She wore an attractive red dress.

He is a famous, widely copied painter.
He is a famous modern painter.

● Interrupting elements

Inside a sentence you sometimes have a few words that are somehow inserted as comment on the side. As I do not want to confuse you with such grammatical terms as interpolations, interjections, phrases in apposition, parenthetical phrases, etc., let's simply call them interrupting elements. These are always between commas, as in any language:

Our representative, Mr R. D. Brown, will call on you next week.
It's easier, I suppose, than walking all the way.
We can, if you wish, supply it as an extra.

Here again the commas are logical separators.

● Participle clauses

As you usually have a natural pause, you naturally use a comma:

Having nothing else to do, they closed the office and went home.
The dog, sensing danger, became agitated.

Relative clauses

In languages using grammatical punctuation you are obliged to follow the strict rule 'Always put a comma before and after a relative clause!' This can occasionally produce sentences that may confuse the reader. In English you keep out of trouble by using commas only in some cases. Their absence makes your meaning clear. Take this example:

> *The mechanic, who had not slept for 24 hours, was responsible for the defective engine.*

The commas make it clear that the relative clause is a **comment** on the mechanic. You could also use dashes or parentheses in place of the commas. The comment is interesting but not really essential to the meaning of the sentence: the **mechanic** was negligent, i.e. not the manager, the supervisor or the cleaner, but the mechanic. Logically enough, the above sentence contains what is known as a **commenting relative clause**. These always **need a comma**.

Here is the same sentence again:

> *The mechanic who had not slept for 24 hours was responsible for the defective engine.*

What? No commas? Yes, because here the absence of commas changes the meaning of the sentence. The relative clause is not a casual comment on that yawning mechanic, but **defines** which particular mechanic in a group was the guilty one.

This is a **defining relative clause**. The sentence now means: There were several mechanics working on the engine. The one who neglected his work was the fellow who had had no sleep the night before.

Two more examples:

> *Bulgarian peasants, who have long beards, have trouble eating spaghetti.*

Meaning: Bulgarian peasants always have trouble with spaghetti. (All Bulgarian peasants have long beards.)

Bulgarian peasants who have long beards have trouble eating spaghetti.

Meaning: Those Bulgarian peasants who have long beards get their beards mixed up with the spaghetti. (Beardless ones have no problem.)

Airline pilots, who drink a bottle of whisky a day, are dangerous.

Meaning: All airline pilots are dangerous. (Their whisky consumption is one bottle a day. Go by train.)

Airline pilots who drink a bottle of whisky a day are dangerous.

Meaning: Those few (I hope) airline pilots who get through a bottle of whisky a day are dangerous.

Don't you agree that this selective use of commas is far superior to the grammatical system?

• Conjunctive adverbs

The most important ones are **of course, no doubt, therefore, moreover, besides, in fact, accordingly, namely, however, consequently**, and so on.

When they come at the **beginning** of a sentence you usually have a **natural pause** and need a comma:

Besides, it's quicker.

When these words are used **inside** a sentence, you usually have **no pause** and need no comma:

It is therefore cheaper to take full board terms.

An increase is consequently unlikely.

Sometimes you do have a pause, and a comma is useful to show it. I always use commas with the following conjunctive adverbs, but this cannot be called a rule:

They are, of course, much more reliable today.

It will, in fact, be three instead of two weeks.

We could, however, send it later.

She is, no doubt, relieved to be home again.

● To prevent ambiguity

In the introduction I mentioned that the comma can also be used to make your meaning clear, even in constructions where other considerations do not call for it. As here, for example:

Now it all sounds so easy. Before, everything seemed difficult.

The comma after **before** prevents your reading *before everything* together.

● Stylistic aid

Punctuation can sometimes also be a useful stylistic device to give your sentence a desired shade of meaning or atmosphere:

He promised to lead an honest life but he didn't.

He promised to lead an honest life, but he didn't.

He promised to lead an honest life. But he didn't.

The first statement mentions casually that something went wrong somewhere. The second sentence shows disapproval of a broken promise. The third report – introducing a sentence fragment – has an ominous ring about it.

Does any reader still think that English punctuation is without rules, lacking in logic or in any way difficult?

3
Perfect your prepositions

English prepositions can sometimes be a little difficult, because they do not always conform to what you would use in other languages.

*We met **at** university.*

*She is married **to** a doctor.*

*He can sleep **on** the plane.*

are just a few examples.

Let us examine four major prepositions as well as several cases where you may be in doubt about two or three different possibilities.

1. At

You may find the preposition **at** in a few unexpected places. The various applications can be put into a few groups to make matters easier.

• Ability

Probably the most unexpected use of **at** is in constructions in which you refer to **ability, aptitude, proficiency** or their opposites. Let's conjugate to get some practice:

*I am brilliant **at** peeling potatoes.*

*You are not too wonderful **at** skating.*

*He is a genius **at** cooking.*

*She was hopeless **at** poker.*

*We are experts **at** engine tuning.*

*You are no good **at** figures* (= arithmetic).

*They are good **at** Finnish.*

As you can see, you also use **at** when referring to language qualifications. You do, however, use the preposition **in** when combined with the words **fluent, qualified** or **perfect**:

*She is fluent **in** Finnish.*

- **Big towns/small towns**

In is generally used with big towns, **at** with small ones:

*We used to live **in** London.*

*They have a house **at** Esher.*

In can also be used with small towns in three cases:

(a) If the sense of 'inside' is important:

*There is a Roman wall **in** Gloaming-on-Zilch.*

(b) If reference is made to **working**:

*She works **in** Bletchley.*

(c) If the speaker is impressed with the place he is talking about:

*'I live **in** Piddlington!'*

Fact: He lives **at** Piddlington (population: 947).

At is also possible with big towns when referring to a **destination on a route of airports or stations**:

*They got off the plane **at** Rome.*

*They had to get out **at** Milan .*

Or in this kind of sentence:

*The swimming events **at** Barcelona.*

when the complete sentence is likely to be:

The swimming events at (the Olympic Games in) Barcelona.

● Exact locations

At is often used where you would normally expect to find **in** or another preposition:

*You must have met them **at** the hotel.*

*We bought it **at** Smith & Coughie's* (department store).

*It is being shown **at** the Globe Cinema.*

*He learned it **at** school.*

*She probably lost it **at** work.*

By also denotes a location, but often more remote than **at**.

If you are parked **at** the station, you are probably in front of it, where it says NO PARKING. If you are parked **by** the station, you may be somewhere near, maybe even in a side street.

● Time

At is also the principal preposition for indications of time:

At ten past three.

At midday.

At dinner time.

At sunset.

At night.

● Directional verbs

This is perhaps the best way to describe a number of verbs that denote an activity directed towards a person or object. All these need **at**:

*I look **at** you.*

*You point **at** them.*

*He stares **at** her.*

*She aims **at** us.*

*We shoot **at** him.*

*You shout **at** me.*

*They bark **at** everybody.*

Other verbs in this group are **to toss, to hint, to grumble, to throw,** etc.

Be careful with the verb **to laugh**. You laugh **at** a person's jokes or antics, but when you **laugh at a person** (no jokes, no antics), it means that he is not funny but **ridiculous,** i.e. an object of derision:

*When he offered us £200 for the gold bracelet, we just laughed **at** him.*

• Mixed bag

At is widely used in phrases conveying a **degree** or **comparison**:

at best   at worst   at least   at the most   at the latest   at the earliest, etc.

You will also find it in **price** information:

*The house was sold **at** cost price.*

*They sell **at** about $25 each.*

A few other uses worth knowing:

at times = sometimes, occasionally.
at every opportunity = on every occasion.
at random = haphazardly, without aim, without selection:

As all the apples looked perfect, I just took two at random.

2. For

You know all about the use of **for** when referring to **destination**:

*They left **for** Helsinki on Friday.*

*The ship is bound **for** Greece.*

*The plane is taking off **for** Montreal.*

You do not need **for**, however, when thinking more about movement from one place to another than destination:

> *They flew to Houston on Tuesday.*
>
> *The ship sails to Naples every week.*
>
> *The plane goes all the way to Nairobi.*

When you refer to **distance**, you have two constructions; one with preposition, the other without:

> *He ran for a mile before he found shelter.*

The **for** shows that the poor fellow had to run 1.6 km **without knowing beforehand** that it was going to be that far.

Here our boastful athlete knows his daily ration and needs no **for**. The sentence *I spent four years in New Zealand* can be translated into various languages word for word. But when you use another verb (i.e. not *spend*) and can add **for a period of**, you need the additional preposition **for**:

> *He stayed there for (a period of) three months.*
>
> *She was away for two hours.*
>
> *They lived in Africa for six years.*

No language uses the equivalent **pour/für/para/per/voor** or **for/för** (Scandinavian) in this kind of construction.

For can indicate that the period of time was **known beforehand**:

His company sent him to Japan for a year

means that he was exiled for a fixed period of twelve months. On the other hand:

He stayed for two years

can also indicate that nothing was arranged beforehand. He simply stayed that long.

There are a few more unusual uses of for, which are best demonstrated by short sentences and comments, where necessary.

*Please **ask for** him at the reception desk.*

*Let's **ask for** more iced water.*

*We are **longing for** some decent weather.*

*He **waited for** her at the corner.*

The above four sentences may look elementary, but in *He waited for her at the corner*, for example, Teutonic languages would use 'on' after the verb, and Romance languages no preposition at all.

*She is usually **taken for** an American* (assumed to be; rightly or wrongly).

*He is often **mistaken for** a native.*

***For all I know**, he is no longer alive.* = **As far as I know.**

*They can sue us, **for all I care**.* = I **don't care** at all.

***For all that**, we are still fond of him.* = **In spite of** all that.

*I believe they left **for good**.* = **For ever**, permanently.

3. On

A rough classification may be useful here. **On** can indicate some form of **contact**. It can be on top of:

*The flowers are **on** the table.*

It can be an upside-down arrangement:

*A fly can walk **on** the ceiling.*

It can be at any angle:

> *The clock is **on** the wall.*
>
> *She wore a cameo **on** her blouse.*

I suppose rivers have some contact with towns in such names as Stoke **on** Trent. You have heard of Newcastle **upon** Tyne? Why **upon** and not **on**? There is no rule. **Upon** is on its way out in this kind of combination and as good as dead in general speech and writing. It used to give a more emphatic or formal ring to such phrases as

> *It depends entirely upon you*

but today **on** is perfectly all right. Retain **upon** only in 'Once upon a time,' when you introduce a fairy tale, and you need never give another thought to 'Is it **on** or **upon**?'.

Connected with newspapers only, you also have **on** as short for **on the staff of**:

> *She is working **on** the 'Evening Bleat'.*

On applies to a **specific day**:

On Christmas Eve.
On the 28th of the month.
On Wednesday.

When mentioning a period of time, not just one day, you use **at**:

At Christmas.
At the end of the month.
At mid-week.

The **subject** of some brain work is introduced by **on**:

> *He wrote a book **on** China.*
>
> *She gave a talk **on** first aid.*
>
> *I'd like some information **on** Mexico.*

In all these sentences you could also use **about**:

> *I'd like some information **about** Mexico.*

On is also used in connection with **sustaining life**, either the food or the money needed for it. (Most European languages use 'of' here.)

*They thrive **on** worms and beetles.*

*She is living **on** her pension.*

On + gerund or noun can indicate that something took place **immediately**:

*He sent a cable **on** reaching his office.*

***On** arrival at the airport she found the missing key.*

A temporary condition is often indicated by **on**:

*The garage was **on** fire.*

*She should be **on** duty.*

*They are (again) **on** strike.*

A few general expressions with **on**:

*It is **on the cards** that they will cancel.* = **Possible**, likely.

*They did the repair **on the cheap**.* = **Cheaply**, but with an implication of poor quality.

*Have you (got) a match **on you**?* = On your **person**.

*They visit us **off and on**.* = At **irregular** intervals.

*We have too much work **on hand**.* = Pending, **to be done**.

*Are they **on the level**?* (slang) = **Honest, serious**.

4. Out

This is a preposition with few problems. It is of special interest to us because of its versatile use as a prefix to a verb. It then indicates superiority, inferiority or at least some kind of comparison. The resultant **out**-verb often needs a fairly long sentence in a translation. As here:

*She **outclassed** them all.* = She was very much **better** than all the others.

*He **outwitted** them all.* = He was much **cleverer** than all the others.

*They were **outgunned**.* = The others had **more/heavier/**longer-range guns than they.

She outlived him by ten years.

*She **outlived** him by ten years.* = She lived ten years **longer** than he did.

*This model is **outdated**.* = This model is **out of date**.

*He has **outgrown** his school uniform.* = He is now much **too big** for it.

*We were **outpointed**.* = We **lost** on points.

*They **outbid** us.* = Their bid was **higher** than ours.

*We were **outnumbered**.* = The others were **more numerous**.

Out in front of a noun can be found in:

*She is an **outpatient**.* = She goes to the hospital for medical attention; she is **not** a patient **in** the hospital.

*We store it in an **outhouse**.* = **Separate** building or hut.

*He was an **outlaw**.* = **Fugitive** from the law.

*It's a small **outlay**.* = **Expense**.

*He wore an **outsize** hat.* = **Extra large**.

*They are **outdoor** fiends.* = They love the **open air**.

Other uses of **out** worth knowing are:

*It was an **out-and-out** swindle.* = **Complete** swindle (expressing indignation).

*The hotel is **out of the way**.* = **Not centrally** located; hard to reach.

*Before the week is **out**.* = Before the **end** of this week.

5. Which preposition?

You may sometimes be a little doubtful which preposition to use with certain verbs or nouns. Here are a few:

● Agree to/agree on/agree with

When you say 'yes' to a suggestion, request or proposition, you **agree to** it. You give your **consent**:

*He finally agreed **to** the plan.*

When all people in a group say 'yes', giving their **joint agreement**, they **agree on** something:

*They (all) agreed **on** the location of the new factory.*

You **agree with** a **person**, i.e. you think that what he or she says or writes is correct:

*I agree **with** his reasoning.*

● Angry with/angry at/angry about

You are angry **with** or **at** a **person**:

*She was terribly angry **with/at** him.*

Angry **about** refers to the **reasons** for your strong emotions:

*They are angry **about** the poor service.*

● Compare with/compare to

When you look at the **difference** between people or things, you compare one **with** the other:

*They compared the cost of a new car **with** that of a second-hand one.*

Compare to is much less frequently used. It means referring to a **similarity** between two things, **liken** one to the other:

> *They compared the new conductor to von Karajan.*

This is a compliment. It means that *the new conductor is in the same league as von Karajan.* On the other hand, if some ballerina's dancing is compared **with** that of Pavlova, the result can easily be rather less flattering.

Note   In British English somebody started a trend a few years ago by using *compare to* when it should really be *compare with*. As the difference between the two is useful and still largely respected in American English, please try to preserve it.

• Concerned about/concerned with

Concerned about is **worried**:

> *They do not seem greatly concerned **about** the cost.*

Concerned with refers to your **work** or some other responsibility:

> *He used to be in sales. Now he is concerned **with** advertising.*

• In London/to London

When using the verb **to be** and referring to a **specific visit** to a town or country, you say **in**:

> *I was **in** Helsinki last summer.*
>
> *We were **in** Holland three months ago.*

To is used when talking about **visits in general**, usually phrased in the present perfect tense:

> *Have you ever been **to** Helsinki?*
>
> *We have never been **to** Holland.*

• Mad at/mad about

Mad at has no connection with insanity, but is the colloquial equivalent of **angry with/at**:

> *She has been mad **at** him for months.*

Mad about has a connection with craziness, but only as far as it is used in several other languages when referring to **extreme enthusiasm**:

Gerry is mad about motor bikes...

Carrying enthusiasm further and applying it to a **person, mad about** means **in love**:

John is mad about Mary.

● Where do you work?

This simple question can produce replies with four different prepositions:

*I work **in** a bank.*

*You work **at** the National Bank.*

*He works **for** the Gas Company.*

*She is **with** World Travel.*

What's the difference? **In** refers to a place of work in **general** without mentioning name or location. **At** is more **specific**. A few examples:

*I work **in** a library.*	*I work **at** the Hampstead Library.*
*He works **in** a bank.*	*He works **at** the Central Bank.*
*She works **in** a boutique.*	*She works **at** Madame Bouvier's (boutique).*

For is mainly used by people not working in an office, i.e. representatives, service engineers, and others who could not truthfully say that they are to be found in a certain location. A geologist, digging in some remote desert 3000 miles from home, may explain to a curious camel:

*I work **for** the Globe Oil Company.*

With is the right preposition when using the verb **to be**:

*I am now **with** Brown, Brown, McTavish & Jones.*

6. *Silent parade*

Teaching means explaining. Here is something different: no explanation at all, just a parade of English prepositions that are not the same as those you would use in translations into most other languages:

*She is married **to** a Norwegian.*

*He lives **with** his parents.*

*I don't know what happened **to** him.*

*We talked **to** them this morning.*

*She is suffering **from** some tropical disease.*

*He is in bed **with** the measles.*

*They showed their distaste **for** the performance.*

*I am allergic **to** beetroot.*

*They are indifferent **to** it.*

*She objected **to** it.*

***For** the following reasons. . . .*

*The bridge slopes **at** an angle of 20 degrees.*

*They were oblivious **of** the rain.*

*We depend **on** it.*

*Are you averse **to** prepositions?*

*We heard it **at** school.*

*It was delivered **against** Order No. 456.*

*It is closed **for** repairs.*

*Fulham lost **to** Arsenal in the final.*

*When he saw that we were all against it, he gave **in**.*

*They met **on** the plane to Stockholm.*

*It will be closed Monday **through** Thursday.*

The last **through** is a useful American way of saying Monday, Tuesday, Wednesday **and** Thursday. The British English 'Monday to Thursday' can leave the listener or reader in doubt whether Thursday is included or not.

4

Perfect your spelling

English spelling can sometimes be a little tricky or inconsistent. Mainly for two reasons. One is that English has many homophones, words that sound alike but don't look alike. When you hear 'rain', someone may mean *rain, reign* or *rein*. The other reason is that English words are often spelled differently from quite closely related words in other languages. Here are a few common spelling mistakes with explanations or comments.

1. Popular mistakes

Correct	Comment
accidentally	'Accidently' is often seen.
acquaintance	*Acquiesce, acquire, acquit* and their noun forms are the other words with that important **c**.
accommodate	Leaving out one **m** is the most common mistake you find in English-speaking countries.
address	Several languages have only one **d** here. English has two.
aggressive	Double **g**, please, even if *agree* only has one.
bachelor	The first syllable may sound like 'batch', but the written word has no **t** in it.
bankruptcy	Don't forget the **t**, although it is hardly audible when the word is spoken.

basically	'Basicly' is a common mistake. *Publicly* is the only word ending in -*ic* which can be formed into an adverb by adding only the -*ly*.
Belgian	In English-speaking countries people often write *Belgium*, the name of the country, when they mean *Belgian*, the adjective or noun.
benefited	Only one **t**, although it may sound as if it had two.
catastrophe	The last syllable is pronounced as in 'philosophy', but note the spelling **phe**.
cemetery	Three **e**'s here.
commitment	Leaving out one **m** is another mistake often found in English-speaking countries.
committee	Some languages have a single **m** and a single **t** here. English has two of each.
dessert	Double **s**, if it is the dish after your main course at lunch or dinner (stress on last syllable).
	Desert, with one **s** and the stress on the first syllable, if it is that sandy area with maybe an oasis here and there.

developed	Just single consonants.
discreet	There is also the rather rare adjective *discrete*, meaning *having a separate existence*.

eccentric	Some languages have 'exc' or 'exz' instead.
ecstasy	Some languages write it 'ext'.
embarrass	If you leave out one **r** you have reason to be embarrassed.
enthusiastic	'Enthousiaste' is French, but not English.
exaggerate	Double **g** but only one **r**.
fiery	The noun is *fire*, but for no logical reason the adjective has that unexpected extra **e** in it.
flexible	'Flexable' is a common mistake in Continental Europe. Please also see *able/ible* on page 82.
forty	Again a lack of spelling logic, when you consider that it is *four, fourteen*, but *forty*.
fulfil	Although consisting of *full + fill*, one **l** is dropped twice in British English. American English has *fulfill*.
handkerchief	Although the **d** is not pronounced, don't forget it. Confusing factor: the popular abbreviation is *hankie*.
harass	Not like embarrass, because here you have only one **r**.
height	Probably just a typing error, but 'heigth' has been seen in letters.
incidentally	Nouns ending in *-ent* always form the adverb by adding *-ally*, not just '-ly'.
independent	This is the adjective and noun. Writing '-ant' is a mistake probably due to the existence of the noun *dependant*.
independently	'Independentally' was seen in a full-page advertisement in a major American magazine.
indispensable	Why the occasional 'indispensible' when even in French it is spelled as in English?
lightning	This is the electric discharge in nature. Not to be confused with *lightening*, the gerund or present participle of the verb *to lighten*, i.e. to make lighter.

literature	Scandinavian languages may have 'litt', but note the English way.
to lose	One **o** only. Possible confusing factor: the adjective *loose* has two.
lying	The gerund or present participle of the verb *to lie* has this vowel change.
marmalade	English has an **a** in the middle, some other languages an 'e'.
mattress	Some languages have only one **t** or even a **d** instead.
Mediterranean	The only doubled letter is the **r**.
occurrence	Double **c**, double **r** + **-ence**.
paraffin	English has a double **f**, not double **r**.
parliament	No other language has that extra **i** in it.
pastime	A pastime helps you pass the time but minus one **s**.
permissible	**-ible**, please.
personnel	The stress on the last syllable is probably the reason why some people write 'personell'.
proceed	See also *eed/ede* on page 83.
promissory	A written promise to pay is called a promissory note with double **s**.
pronunciation	The pronunciation is the way you *pronounce* something. Not very logical.
questionnaire	Double **n** for no special reason.
responsible	The French suffix '-able' is responsible for a common mistake.
satellite	One **t** but double **l**.
separate	Surprisingly many people write 'seperate'.
solicitor	Single consonants throughout.
to soothe	Careful with that final **e**, not found in the similar verb *to smooth*.
stationary	If it doesn't move, it's *stationary* (adjective). If it is the writing material, it's *stationery* (noun).

subscription	When you subscribe to a publication, you take out a subscription. Similar transitions are in *describe/description* and *prescribe/prescription*.
superintendent	Not much logic here, because the *attendant* at the car park may be promoted to *superintendent*.
tendency	With *-ency*.
truly	Adjective: *true*; adverb: *truly*.
turpentine	Other languages have 'ter' as first syllable.
tyranny	Think of the spelling *tyrant* and you will never double the **r**.
voluntary	Careful with the second vowel, which is **u** in English, but **o** in a few other languages.

2. -ABLE or -IBLE?

There is no reliable rule whether any given adjective should end in -**able** or -**ible**, but as the -**ible** group is smaller than the -**able** opposition, this list of the most important words should help you make the right decisions.

accessible	discernible	permissible
admissible	divisible	plausible
audible	edible	possible
collapsible	eligible	reprehensible
combustible	exhaustible	resistible
compatible	fallible	responsible
comprehensible	feasible	reversible
contemptible	flexible	sensible
corrigible	gullible	susceptible
corruptible	intelligible	tangible
credible	legible	visible
defensible	negligible	
digestible	perceptible	

As you may sometimes be in doubt about the negative versions of these words, please remember that most have the prefix **in-**. All words beginning with the letter **p**, have the prefix **im-**: *impossible, implausible*, etc. All words beginning with the letter **r** take the prefix **ir-**: *irresponsible, irreversible*, and so on. The few exceptions are: *unfeasible, unintelligible, illegible, unsusceptible*.

3. -CEED or -CEDE?

This is a much easier group, because once you remember that there is exceed, proceed, and succeed, other verbs must always end with **-cede**:

accede	concede	recede
antecede	intercede	retrocede
cede	precede	secede

Small exception: there is also supersede, with an **s** in the middle.

4. -ISE or -IZE?

British and American English are on common ground when using the ending **-ise** for a group of verbs. Here are the most important ones:

advertise	compromise	improvise
advise	despise	revise
arise	devise	supervise
comprise	disguise	televise (etc.)

Other verbs, based on the Greek ending *-izo* (to make, to become, to use) always have the ending **-ize**. It is a very large group, but a few examples will give you an idea of its members:

authorize	economize	realize
baptize	legalize	recognize (etc.)
capsize	organize	

Also, their noun forms such as authorization, realization, etc.

Note: It is analy**se** in British English, but analy**ze** in American English.

5. Small letter or CAPITAL?

English shares with all major European languages (German is the exception) the pleasant custom of using a small initial letter for all nouns: **m**ouse elephant **b**liss **t**oothache.

As you may already suspect, this happy rule does not apply every time, so let us look at the finer points, the possible surprises, the exceptions on the road to perfection.

● Proper names, historical events, titles

As in your language, you need capitals here:

> Laurel & Hardy.
> the Treaty of Rome.
> the Queen of Sheba.

This is the easiest group of all.

● Titles of books, plays, etc.

You generally use capitals for all words except short prepositions and articles:

'A Tale of Two Cities'
'Hungarian Without Tears'.

In most other languages you would use small initial letters except for the first word.

● Specific or general?

> *The old Admiral wrote more memoirs than the other admirals.*
>
> *When he served in the Army, he came into contact with the armies of other countries.*
>
> *The Minister attended the weekly meeting of ministers.*
>
> *The Church maintains several churches in the mountain regions.*

Here you have the difference between the **specific** word with capital and the **general** noun, written in the usual way with a small initial letter. The Admiral we know, the Army of the country, the Minister we talk about, the Church as an institution and not as a building.

Titles, events, institutions, bodies, etc. are treated in this way:

Our Government and allied governments.

World War II was a six-year war.

The State deals with other states.

The late King George was one of seven kings at the wedding.

● Races, religions, ethnic groups, languages

Nouns and adjectives have capitals:

Caucasian
Buddhist
Slav
Cantonese

The word **Negro** is now taboo in North America and **coloured** [Am.: **colored**] is going out of fashion. The right word is now **black**, usually with a small initial letter:

The population is now mainly black and Puerto Rican.

An ideological concept would have capitals: Black Equality. Capitals for **black** and **white** can also be found when racial division is stressed:

The Blacks objected to the plan.

● Relatives

Your **parents** are Father and Mother when addressed:

Could you please help me, Mother?

In other constructions, usually with a possessive pronoun in front of it, you need no capitals:

My father should be able to help us.

Uncles and **aunts** are usually written with a capital when combined with a name:

It is possible that Uncle Fred will be here.

Otherwise it is:

My uncle was here yesterday.

Brothers and **sisters** have no capital when they are relatives:

Your brother Tim called me.

Our sister Julie will come later.

When written with a capital, brothers and sisters can mean something different: **Sister Julie** is likely to be a nurse or nun, **Brother Tim** a member of a religious order.

● Descriptive proper names

Capitals are not needed for proper names or adjectives that have become general descriptive terms:

american cloth
brussels sprouts
french fried potatoes
french window
india rubber
panama hat
spartan education
venetian blind
wellington boots.

If you like french fried potatoes, you are an easy-to-please visitor. If you prefer French fried potatoes (imported from France), you are a very expensive guest.

Similarly, a hard task may be *herculean*, and your milk *pasteurized*.

● God, Jesus

Personal and possessive pronouns are written **He** and **His** in theological texts.

● Days of the week, months, holidays

These are always written with a capital letter:

Wednesday
February
Easter

Slightly different from some languages where you find 'onsdag', 'février', and 'påsk'.

● West or west?

You use a capital when you refer to a **region**:

He is going to live in the North.
They sought their fortunes in the West.

You need no capital when referring to **direction of movement**:

Danish weather forecasts usually mention westerly winds.
They changed direction and headed east.

● The four seasons

No capitals are needed unless they are **personified** as in poetry, for example:

'When Winter comes on wings of snow,
It can get pretty cold, you know.'

If you don't think much of my poetry and want to write something better yourself, I don't mind. But please remember that in conventional poetry every line should start with a capital. Like the *It* above.

6. Perfect plurals

If you think that adding an **s** to a noun is all you have to do in English to produce the plural form, you are an optimist.

Let's make sure we know about the most important peculiarities of the English plural.

● Nouns ending in the letters -s, -ss, -sh, -ch, and -x

Add **-es**:

As the plural of **gas, wish,** and **tax** would look a little strange if written 'gass', 'wishs', and 'taxs', we almost automatically add -es and produce:

gases   losses   wishes   beaches   taxes.

● Nouns ending in a consonant + *y*

Add -s, but change the y to **ie**:

babies   cherries   parties.

Proper nouns (names) and distinctive suffixes retain the -y in the plural:

*There are two **Henrys** in our class.*

*Reunification of the two **Germanys**.*
*They can be considered **standbys**.*

● Nouns ending in a vowel + *y*

Just add **-s**:

boys   monkeys   plays.

The plural of **money** is sometimes also spelled **monies**.

● Nouns ending in a vowel + *o*

No trouble here; you simply add the **-s**:

cameos   folios   ratios   studios, etc.

• Nouns ending in a consonant + *o*

A small number of what could be called **familiar**, fairly frequently used nouns take the ending **-es**:

echoes   heroes   mosquitoes   potatoes   tomatoes.

Eliminating your spelling dilemma, a few nouns can be written with an **-s** or **-es** in the plural:

banjo(e)s   cargo(e)s   domino(e)s   flamingo(e)s   ghetto(e)s
motto(e)s   tornado(e)s   torpedo(e)s   zero(e)s.

There is some small difference in the preference between the two endings between British English and American English. It can perhaps be said that as soon as a noun becomes more common in everyday usage, the tendency towards a plural **-es** increases. The word **ghetto**, for example, is now frequently used in journalism in connection with any ethnic minority in any part of the world. The plural **ghettos** is now increasingly written **ghettoes**.

All other nouns ending in the letter **-o** take the simple **-s**. These are mainly abbreviations of certain technical words:

photos (photographs)   radios   dynamos   stereos   magnetos, etc.

or words that somehow look more foreign than our old friend **potato**, for example:

albinos   halos   infernos   manifestos   provisos   solos
sopranos   tobaccos, etc.

• Nouns ending in -*f*

Belief, chief, relief, and **roof** take the **-s**; most others change the **-f** to **-v** and add **-es**:

calves   halves   leaves   loaves   selves   shelves   thieves
wolves.

Nouns ending in **-fe** behave in the same way: **knives, lives,** and **wives.**

Five words in this group can be regular or irregular:

dwarfs/dwarves   elfs/elves   hoofs/hooves   scarfs/scarves
wharfs/wharves.

• Borrowed (foreign) nouns

Generally speaking, there is a tendency to add the plural -s without worrying too much about the language of origin.

Although the Italian plural is 'maestri' and 'crescendi', for example, the English version would be:

maestros   crescendos   stilettos   falsettos, etc.

A little extra care is required with a few words. Luckily there are not many.

The ending **-um** usually has a regular plural:

**asylums   forums   lyceums   museums   pendulums
premiums   quorums,**   etc.

Some words retain the Latin plural form:

**addendum/addenda   datum/data   erratum/errata
maximum/maxima   medium/media   minimum/minima
stratum/strata**.

The plural **mediums** exists, but is then confined to mean those persons found at occultist meetings who tell you that Uncle George (dead since 1967) wants to talk to you.

The foreign **-on** becomes **-a**:

automaton/automata   criterion/criteria   phenomenon/phenomena.

The ending **-is** becomes **-es**:

**analysis/analyses   axis/axes
basis/bases   crisis/crises   oasis/oases   parenthesis/parentheses
thesis/theses**, etc.

The endings **-ex** and **-ix** become **-ices**:

index/indices   vortex/vortices   appendix/appendices.

The plural of **index** and **appendix** can also be regular, depending on meaning. In mathematics you have **indices**, but tables of contents in books are **indexes**. Additions (in books, for example) are **appendices**, but an experienced surgeon may boast that last month he removed 27 **appendixes**, i.e. cured people who had appendicitis.

Nouns ending in **-us** generally add **-es**, but a few special plurals exist:

alumnus/alumni   bacillus/bacilli   fungus/fungi   nucleus/nuclei radius/radii.

Pronunciation of the final **i**: 'eye', i.e. **radii** = 'ray-dee-eye'.

French nouns used in an English context can be a little inconsistent. You have **bureau/bureaux, tableau/tableaux** but usually **plateau/plateaus** (less frequently **plateaux**).

This is all you have to know about plural **-s** anomalies, but here are a few additional points about unusual plural forms.

• Nouns with irregular plural form

You probably know all of these. Let's have a sixty-second refresher course:

child/children   foot/feet   goose/geese   louse/lice   man/men mouse/mice   ox/oxen   penny/pence   tooth/teeth woman/women.

Brother has the irregular plural **brethren**, if you don't mean your parents' sons but **fellow members** of a religious or other order, society, association, etc.

• Nouns that look like plurals, but are singular or plural

This group is fortunately very small:

corps (from the French)   **headquarters   series   species.**

A few examples:

*The first series **was** excellent.*

*The last three series **were** sold out.*

*This species **was** discovered two years ago.*

*These species **are** now extinct.*

*Their headquarters **is** at Aldershot.*

*All headquarters **were** moved last year.*

Note: the word 'serie', often seen in letters, does not exist.

One noun that also looks like a plural, but is always used with the **singular** verb form is the word **news**. The news **is** good or bad.

● Nouns with plural form only

These words are always written with the plural -s:

> **alms barracks dregs eaves goods means measles mumps odds riches tidings**.

The verb form must also be in the plural:

> *The dregs **were** still visible.*

Behaving in the same way are a few objects that are more or less symmetrical in construction:

> **bellows breeches forceps pants pincers pliers scissors shears spectacles tongs trousers**.

As you can usually put the words *a pair of* in front of them (*I bought a pair of pants*), you always use the verb form in the plural as well, even though you are referring to one single object only:

> *The scissors* (one article) **are getting blunt**.

To make things more difficult, however, I have to mention that you do use the singular when *a pair of* is added:

> *This pair of scissors **is** blunt!*

A few words of Latin or Greek origin also have the plural version only, but can have the singular or plural verb form:

> **athletics ceramics economics ethics hydraulics mathematics phonetics physics politics statistics tactics,** etc.

The **singular** verb form is used when you refer to these words as **subject for study**:

> *Statistics **is** easy!*

Otherwise you use the plural:

> *Statistics **are** in this case unreliable.*

• Nouns with no plural form, used in the singular only

advice baggage furniture information luggage produce transport.

You say

Most of their furniture is of teak wood.

The produce is sold through a government agency.

• Nouns with no plural form: singular = plural

Most of these are animals:

cod deer fish fowl grouse salmon sheep swine trout.

sheep   sheep

It is therefore one deer or twenty-seven deer; one salmon or two thousand salmon; one trout or fourteen trout. You once saw the word 'fishes'? Yes, it does exist, when you refer to **varieties** of fish, not just fish in general:

I wonder if there are any fish in this lake.

The bay is famous for its exotic fishes.

Aircraft is the only non-animal in this group:

*It looks like **an** amphibious aircraft.*

*They own **two** executive aircraft.*

I recently saw a brochure on package tours to East Africa. It promises the reader that he will see 'lion, zebra, rhino, and other wild animals in their natural surroundings'. Only one of each?

No; the singular here is hunters' jargon, a little misplaced in this context. As you and I are likely to bounce along in a jeep, merely trying to do our shooting with a camera, we are interested in lions, zebras, and rhinos in the plural. The more the better.

7. Abbreviations

If you are a football fan, you may be surprised to hear that **fan** is short for *fanatic*. (We like football, but we are not really fanatics, are we?)

Riding on a bus, you are probably in no way concerned about the fact that your vehicle used to have the Latin prefix 'omni': omnibus. When shouting 'Taxi!', you have better things to do than give a thought to the origin of this abbreviation: *taximeter*, that box near the driver which shows the rapidly increasing amount you will have to pay at the end of the trip.

Abbreviations often seem to slide into a language, becoming the accepted word in **conversation**, more frequently used than the original. Few people have **influenza** nowadays. Not because it has died out, but because millions simply have **the flu**, first spelled **'flu** to indicate that it was an abbreviation, now just **flu**.

Here is the first selection of the most important English abbreviations you are likely to meet. The elementary ones (zoo, photo, phone, etc.) have been left out.

ad	**Advertisement**. You may hear 'let's place an ad next week', 'that was a good ad'. The UK abbreviation **advert** is unknown in North America.
amps	**Ampères**: nobody ever says ampères.
bra	**Brassière**: if you do wear it, it's always a **bra**.
budgie	**Budgerigar** (not American): that mini-parrot known in North America as **parakeet**.
exam	**Examination**: students never take examinations; they take exams. At least in conversation.
gym	**Gymnasium** or **gymnastics**: when you go to the gym, you wear gym shoes. (Pronounced 'jim'.)

hippo   **Hippopotamus**, that endearing animal usually seen only with its head sticking out of the water.

lab   **Laboratory**: you may be told 'this was tested in the lab'.

memo   **Memorandum**: this need not be the stiff, official document you may suspect. An Office Memo (pronounced 'memmo' or, jocularly, 'meemo') may merely tell you that the toilets on the sixth floor will be closed for repairs until the end of the month.

mike   **Microphone**: Mike (Michael) is talking into a mike.

op   **Operation**: the surgical job. Also **ops**: military exercises.

perm   **Permanent wave**: your hairdresser will give you a perm.

pram   **Perambulator**: the rather clumsy (British English only) word for **baby carriage**. When you want to give Baby some fresh air in the park, you have to push the pram.

pro   **Professional**: this can refer to a sportsman or woman; to someone who thoroughly knows his job.

recap   **Recapitulate**: in TV panel games you may hear the chairman recap (= repeat) some information: 'Let me recap.'

revs   **Revolutions per minute**: the **rev counter** in your car indicates the **r.p.m.** of the crankshaft. **Revving** (yes, two 'v's!) means putting your foot on the accelerator of your stationary car and producing the 'vroom-vroom-vroom' sound to impress nearby citizens.

rhino   **Rhinoceros**: pronunciation 'rye-no', not 'ree-no'.

specs   **Spectacles**, now more generally called **glasses**. Also **specifications**. Maybe you need your specs to read the specs.

sub   Three possibilities: **submarine**, the submersible boat. **Substitute**, used in North America only. **Subscription** (British English only), the membership fee for a club or association. The American equivalent of this kind of subscription is **dues**: union dues, club dues, etc.

Sub is not short for subscription to a publication.

telly   'On the telly' is the more working-class term for the more general 'on TV', i.e. on **television**.

vet   **Veterinary surgeon: animal doctor** or **veteran** (American only): a former member of the Army, Navy or Air Force. The British equivalent is **ex-serviceman**, with no abbreviation.

You may also come across the verb **to vet**, which is not an abbreviation of anything, but a useful word to know. It means **check, examine**: you can vet that stack of applications on your desk. You can also be *vetted for security*. Someone will dig into your past to see whether you can be trusted with the drawings for the new nuclear submarine.

Some abbreviations are just letters. Here are a few interesting ones:

C/F B/F   When you write a column of figures and reach the bottom of the page, your **C/F (carried forward)** shows that the depressing summary is being continued. The **B/F (brought forward)** before the first figure at the top of the next page shows that it is not the start of something new but a continuation.

IOU	The receipt for a personal loan could be written 'I acknowledge herewith that I borrowed the sum of £2.60 from Jack Pratt'. Much shorter and perfectly legal is putting **IOU** (**I owe you**) on a piece of paper, adding the amount, and signing it.
PTO/p.t.o.	When you are writing a letter and have reached the bottom of the page, **PTO** tells the reader **Please turn over**, i.e. 'I am continuing on the reverse of this sheet'.
RSVP	These four letters can be seen on the bottom of printed invitation cards. Oddly enough, they stand for the French 'Répondez, s'il vous plaît', i.e. **Please reply** (whether you can come or not).

5

Perfect your correspondence

Let's write a letter! We are not concerned with what you want to tell him, her or them. That's your problem. But we are going to look at:

- General points regarding letter and envelope.
- Matters of style.

1. The envelope

Whenever I have to write a letter, I usually start with the envelope. If you have equally eccentric habits, please join me right away.

Although you may think that an envelope to someone in an English-speaking country need not look much different from something you send locally, there are nevertheless a few conventions and ideas worth knowing.

• Envelope to a private (male) person

Mr Michael R. Jackson

is nowadays quite safe in most cases.

In the UK it used to be *Michael R. Jackson, Esq.* (no **Mr** in front, but **Esq.** after the name), but this is now as good as dead. I might still use it:

- When I think that the person is very important or an elderly gentleman.
- When I know that the person thinks that he is very important.

Academic qualifications are generally shown by letters after the name, such as:

Mr John Mitchell, MD
Mr Peter J. Langdon, LL.D
Mr Ian S. Shaw, PhD, and so on.

Although these are, in fact, *Doctors* (of Medicine, Law, and Philosophy, respectively), you are still all right with the simple **Mr** in front of the name.

• Envelope to a private (female) person

There are now four possibilities:

Miss Irene Hughes = single; adult or child.

Mrs George L. Grant = married; very formal; used when her first name is not known.

Mrs Mary Dale = married; normal/less formal widowed or divorced.

Ms Betsy Pond = may be single, may be married, may be widowed, may be divorced.

The last, more neutral version is quite useful when you do not know whether a woman is married or not. **Ms**, pronounced 'mizz', has a buzzing sound, like a bee circling a jam jar. In Hong Kong, for example, *Ms* is used in all documents relating to women.

Good news: I have noticed that in some countries, the USA, Sweden, and Finland, for example, only the name of the person is often mentioned, with no title in front. This trend seems to be spreading. If it becomes general in a decade or so, your troubles will be over.

• Punctuation marks

The English comma serves to separate words and to avoid confusion, as you heard earlier in the book. There is consequently not much logic in still using commas in any part of the address. The use of a period after initials seems to be dying out as well. Therefore:

Mr. J. G. Edwards,
11, Surrey Street,
London W.C.2.

is now often:

Mr J G Edwards
11 Surrey Street
London WC2R 2PS

• PO Box

If the letterhead of a company mentions both the street as well as the post office box number, there is obviously no need to put both on an envelope. The postal staff sorting your letter at destination need only one of the two.

Whenever I write to foreign countries, I also think of those postal workers and put Postfach, BP, CP, Apartado, Postboks, Box, Postbus or PL as their local version of PO Box.

2. The letter

Starting at the top in a business letter, we have the following items:

● Reference

Some letterheads include the printed **Your ref.:** and **Our ref.:**, which make things easy for you. Where these are not given, the tidiest solution may be making the other people's reference part of your opening sentence. If you underline it, staff sorting the mail at destination is unlikely to miss it.

Something like this:

We thank you for your letter of September 15th,
reference BLR/VS, and are glad to tell you that. . .

Your own reference could then be put at the *bottom of your letter* on the left-hand side. This may be better than squeezing it somewhere between the letterhead and the date.

● Date

The last time I counted there were about a dozen different possibilities:

10th March 1999–   10th March, 1999–   10 March 1999–
March 10, 1999   March 10th, 1999   March 10 1999
1999-03-10   10-3-1999   10:3:1999   10/3/1999   3-10-1999
10.3.1999

As this is very confusing, here are a few comments:

In the **USA** and **Canada** the sequence **month-day-year** is preferred. The most common way of writing the date is:

March 10, 1999–

When this is written entirely in figures, it therefore becomes

3-10-1999

To people anywhere else this means 3rd October, not 10th March. So be careful when interpreting all-figure dates in letters from America. As yours could cause misunderstanding over there, it is better to write the month in letters.

In 1967 the International Organization for Standardization advocated the version **1999-03-10**. My own correspondence files show little support for this idea so far. **10.3.1999** is not recommended. It is all right in several European countries, but not normal in English-speaking ones. My own preference is for the version **10th March 1999** for the following reasons:

- It has the most logical sequence day-month-year.
- It is free from punctuation marks.
- It avoids the possibility of the Anglo-American misunderstanding mentioned above.

• Salutation

The way you address the other people or person is called the salutation. There are several possibilities, depending on whom you are writing to and in which country.

To individuals

Dear Sir,

Dear Mr White,

Dear Madam,

Dear Auntie Flo,

It all depends on your relationship. There is no 'Dear Miss'. **Dear Madam** is suitable for a **Miss, Mrs** or **Ms**. Punctuation: the **comma** in countries following the British system:

Dear Mr Jackson,

the **colon** in North America:

Dear Mrs Black:

In some countries people may have titles, such as

Direktor Gerhard Schmidt
Civilingeniör Lennart Persson
Rektor Povl Nielsen, etc.

but in a letter to persons with equivalent titles in an English-speaking country, they are all addressed as just plain **Mr**. You cannot write 'Dear Director Kendall'.

To companies

> *Dear Sirs*, (British system)
>
> *Gentlemen*: (American style)

In the less likely event of your writing to a firm consisting of two or more women, you would use **Dear Mesdames**. In letters addressed to an individual in a company your salutation would depend on your relationship. If you know him, it could be **Dear Mr White**; if you want to be more formal, **Dear Sir**.

Letters sent **for the attention** of a person in a firm are not personal letters. They should still be opened **Dear Sirs** or **Gentlemen**. The added **For the attention of Mr J. G. Morgan** (in North America usually just **Attn.: Mr J. G. Morgan**) merely serves to direct the letter to JGM quickly. Do not start it 'Dear Mr Morgan'.

• Heading

A heading, also called **subject line**, is a useful device. It gives the reader some clear information right away and can make sorting of the incoming mail at destination easier. Besides, it avoids a long opening sentence, which often goes like this:

> *We thank you for your letter of April 8th regarding insurance cover on goods returned for replacement.*

A heading gives you greater clarity and the opportunity of using a more adventurous opening gambit than the weary 'we thank you for your letter. . .':

> *Dear Sirs,*
>
> <u>*Insurance cover on goods returned for replacement*</u>
>
> *Your letter of the April 8th raises an interesting point. . .*

• Complimentary ending

Your choice of valediction again depends on whom you are dealing with. A table may help:

	British style	American style
Letter to an individual, (formal)	*Yours faithfully,*	*Cordially yours,* *Very truly yours,* *Yours very truly,* *Yours truly,*
Letter to an individual, (personal)	*Yours sincerely,* *Yours truly,*	*Sincerely,*
Letter to a company	*Yours faithfully,*	*Very truly yours,* *Yours very truly,* *Cordially yours,*

If the American choice seems confusing, simply stick to **Yours sincerely** for personal letters and **Very truly yours** for formal ones.

In a letter to a friend the word **love** is usually a good ending in place of any of the above phrases.

• Signature (in business letters)

Even though you may be writing an impersonal letter, likely to produce an answer not addressed to you, it is always a good idea to type your name under the signature. It gives the other people useful information on what that weird-looking scrawl means. In addition, they may wish to talk to you on the telephone and need then not ask the operator to find out who might be hiding behind the reference 'DFH'. If your job function is reasonably impressive, you may wish to add it under the name for additional identification.

Bare initials and names are usually assumed to denote a male person. If this description does not fit you, add **Miss, Mrs** or **Ms** in parentheses before or after the typed name.

• Enclosures

If you have to send something with your letter in the same envelope, put **Encl.** at the bottom left of the page and mention what it is. This is mildly interesting for the recipient, but can be very helpful to you. As enclosures are often assembled after a letter has been completed,

Encl.   Invoice
Guarantee Certificate
Wiring Diagram
Maintenance Instructions

can be a useful check list.

3. Style

When writing to your relatives or friends, you probably sound like you speak. In business letters, however, where people often write to others they have never met, there is often a tendency to sound more solemn, more important, sometimes a bit pompous.

To make a start, here are a few typical clichés found in letters from English-speaking countries.

• Cliché collection

By return of post

This is a very strong demand, which other people often find quite impossible to meet, no matter how efficient they are. Besides, if they are competent, they will probably deal with your request quickly, anyway. If they are hopeless, you will have to wait; despite your 'by return'.

A more effective way of making your problem more compelling, more convincing is giving the reason for your urgency. A few ideas:

Your immediate confirmation will be essential, as we receive requests for accommodation every day.

Please send the invoices before the weekend. The ship sails on Friday of next week.

We need the floor plan straight away. The machine will be here this week.

These requests are likely to produce better results than a flabby 'by return of post', which is often considered just another stereotyped phrase.

At your earliest convenience

This i⸱ obviously not as strong as *by return of post*, but is too meek. It seems to whimper 'whenever you can manage; we know you are busy with more important things'.

Spell out when you do need what you are asking for. Use more definite sentences on the model of those under the above heading.

At an early date

This phrase is much too vague, both as promise and as request. Try to be more precise. A promise could mention:

A four-door model is expected to be ready before the end of the year.

A request could ask:

Please send the Affidavit within ten days, as we still have to register the Deed.

In due course

These three words can mean very little. The writer of the letter may be thinking of two weeks when he promises to send you something 'in due course'. You, on the other hand, may consider two weeks ridiculously slow.

If you mention the expected period of time, you will appear to be more personally interested. If you cannot be too exact, try the following:

In about a week or so.

In about ten days' time.

In roughly three weeks.

In a week or two.

All these are sufficiently vague to give you some extra time, if necessary.

The only defensible use of *in due course* could be in the request *Please send us a bank transfer in due course,* where the exact time limit could sound a little dictatorial.

Herein, therein, hereof, thereof, hereto, thereto, hereafter, henceforth, etc.

These compounds should be confined to legal documents. Anywhere else you will produce a better style by either leaving them out altogether or by using something more simple. A few ideas:

the conditions herein specified = *the conditions specified* (in the contract)

the certificate attached hereto = *the attached certificate*

as stipulated hereafter = *as stipulated below*

will henceforth be discontinued = *will be discontinued from now on*.

A letter recently seen confirms the receipt of a brochure and 'thanks for the information contained therein'. Nothing impolite or incomplete in the shortened:

We received your brochure and thank you for the information,

or simply

(We) thank you for the brochure.

Fewer words = a better style.

Our cheque [Am.: check] in the amount of £85

In the amount of means **for**. Let's be lazy, use one word in place of four, **and** sound more modern:

Our cheque for £85.

Please do not hesitate to let us know

Many sales letters still end with something like this:

If you require more detailed information, please do not hesitate to let us know.

There can only be one of two reactions to what you told them:

(a) They are interested in your offer. If something was not clear enough, they will ask you. Very soon. No hesitation.
(b) They are not impressed. You will never hear from them again.

The above sentence can always be left out. It is unlikely that a potential customer will be sitting there, hesitant or scared to open his mouth.

We have written to them re your insurance claim

Don't use **re** as a shorter version of **about**, which is more natural, relaxed, and human. **Re** should be confined to legal documents, where the summary of a court case may have the heading

Re Joseph R. Soap vs. United Umbrella Co.

The bill of lading is now to hand

Nobody would say 'to hand' in a conversation, yet this old-fashioned phrase can still be found in business letters. Improvements:

The bill of lading has now arrived.

We have received the documents.

Rest assured

To me, this moth-eaten recommendation always sounds a bit like 'sleep well'. If you leave it out, you will sound more trustworthy. Compare these two statements:

Rest assured that all insurance claims will be settled promptly.

All insurance claims will be settled promptly.

Don't you agree that the second version is more convincing?

The motor is now in stock. Same will be sent together with the machine

Never use **same** as a pronoun. It is not merely out of date, but even sounds a little uneducated. Use **it, they, this** or other more direct words:

It will be sent with the machine.

They will leave on Tuesday.

The ten-word sentence

We have received your translation and thank you for same.

can become the modernized six-word statement

We thank you for the translation.

• Letter endings

76.3 per cent of all English letters mailed by companies in eleven European countries at 6 p.m. yesterday had a participle ending*.

What is a participle ending? It is the last paragraph in a letter that starts with the **ing** -form of a verb: **thanking** you, **looking** forward, **hoping**, and all the rest. There are three things against it:

1. You will not find this ending in any good modern book on English correspondence.
2. The writer has to use three lines for his final paragraph instead of one:

   Looking forward to hearing from you,
   we remain, (we are)
   yours faithfully,

   The middle line is often left out, but this is grammatically wrong. The participle must be followed by the subject (**we**).
3. The information given in this paragraph is usually quite unnecessary.

Let us take a closer look at some of the most widely used endings to find out why we can do without them.

---

*I haven't the slightest idea whether this is right or wrong, but I thought some readers might be impressed by statistics.

Looking forward to hearing from you

If you write to someone for information, you naturally expect an answer, look forward to some reaction.

Awaiting your reply

Once the writer has sent off a letter asking for something, he or she will indeed wait for an answer. Naturally.

Hoping to receive your early reply

Nobody likes to wait six weeks for an answer, so there is no need to mention everybody's preference for a quick response.

Looking forward to your news with much interest

An extended version of the above phrase, adding the reassurance that a reply will be of interest to the writer. But of course.

Thanking you in anticipation/Thanking you in advance

I know you do use these expressions of premature gratitude in several languages, but they have no place in a modern English letter. You would not use them on the telephone, not even to a total stranger, so why sound different in writing?

Make your request in a friendly way, and you can forget about this old cliché, often added to a letter without much thought.

Trusting to have been of service to you

This phrase is all right in some languages, but in English it sounds a little servile.

Trusting that this action will meet with your approval

This phrase shows some form of inferiority complex on the part of the writer who seems to say 'I hope I managed to do the right thing'. Be bold: leave out this expression and show that you have no feeling of insecurity.

Assuring you of our best attention at all times

Don't assure people of something expected of you, anyway. Efficiency has to be shown, not promised. When you offer goods or services in a well-written letter that deals with all questions a customer may have asked, you will automatically give the impression that 'best attention' can be expected from you. At all times.

Seeing these popular endings unmasked in this cruel way, you may ask 'what on earth **can** I say instead?'

It's easy: NOTHING. Just the usual **Yours faithfully, Very truly yours** and any of the other ways of closing a letter, discussed on page 104.

Make sure that your letters are written in a friendly style and they will not sound at all abrupt when closed by these two or three words instead of by a self-evident or meaningless three-line paragraph.

• Meaningless phrases and words

The following don't mean very much when looked at closely.

According to our records

You can usually do without this statement. Take the following situation: someone asks about the date something was sent. The reply often states:

According to our records, the goods left here on the 17th.

If the writer can confirm the exact date, he has looked it up somewhere. Naturally.

Attached herewith

Reduce these two words by 50 per cent and improve your style as a result. 'The sales conditions attached herewith', becomes simply:

The attached sales conditions.

For your information

When you send out printed details, you are doing so for the purpose of giving information to the other people.

> Our latest brochure is enclosed for your information

tells the recipient something self-evident. Why not leave out the last three words? They may be all right when you send a copy of your stinking letter (= strong complaint) to the gas company for the information of your lawyer. Just to keep him informed.

Involved

There is nothing wrong with **involved** in these two sentences:

> *It's a good idea, but it sounds rather involved.*

Involved here means **complicated**.

> *When they moved to the new district, she became involved in charitable affairs.*

She became **occupied by, entangled with, mixed up with** activities connected with charity.

> As an *adjective after a noun*, the word *involved* is always unnecessary:

> *We can also send it by airfreight. The extra charge* (involved) *will be about £35.*

An acknowledgement of receipt will oblige

The verb at the end seems to hang in the air. Oblige whom? Roger in the Filing Department? Mary in Accounts? The direct **please** -message solves the problem:

> *Please send a receipt.*

> *Please let us have a receipt.*

Actually

This word is often found in British correspondence. It can usually be left out:

> We confirm that the replacement tank was actually shipped on the 15th of last month.

Actually is correct when you do mean **really, in reality**:

> *It sounds incredible but it actually happened.*

Relevant

Relevant is usually irrelevant:

> The packing list is inside crate No. 4. The relevant invoices were sent by airmail three days ago.

Test: leave out **relevant** and ask yourself whether anything important has been lost.

The word **relevant** is useful when you want to make clear that something is not irrelevant, i.e. that something does indeed apply to the matter discussed or referred to:

> *The first witness had not seen the accident properly and his statement was of little value. The second witness saw at least part of the scene. His report was more relevant.*

Writing 'revelant' (with switched consonants) is a frequent spelling mistake.

• More scope for improvement

Approximately

Thirteen letters make this one of the longest adverbs in the business. Shorter and equally suitable versions are **about** and **roughly**. Slightly more colloquial are **some** and **around**:

> *This repair will cost about 800 Kroner.*
>
> *It should take roughly two months.*
>
> *That bone is some six thousand years old.*
>
> *The average temperature in July is around 24 degrees.*

As per your instructions

As per admittedly has the advantage of shortness, but if we want to improve our style, we have to make the sacrifice and write:

In accordance with your instructions.

Please return the order form duly signed

I have always considered **duly** slightly insulting. How would you translate it in the above sentence? Perhaps **correctly, as it ought to be, in the right place,** and other very elementary pieces of advice.

Less potentially insulting and more friendly solution:

Please sign the order and return it to us.

It will be forwarded next week

There is nothing against the simple verb **to send**. It is suitable for anything between a letter weighing 16 grammes and 356 tons of mild steel reinforcing rods:

The missing tools will be sent tomorrow.

A better use of **to forward** is 'to send something on to a **second destination.'** That letter arriving at your hotel after you left will (if you are lucky) be forwarded to your home.

Per airmail

By is better than the Latin **per**:

It was sent by airmail.

While on the subject of **per**, you are probably used to

£30,000 per year (usually **p.a.** = per annum)
100 kilometres per hour
$400 per square foot.

This is suitable for formal writing. In conversation and informal writing you would normally say:

£30,000 a year.
100 kilometres an hour.
$400 a square foot.

Prior to

Before is always better. Write as you would say it:

The car will be undersealed before shipment.

Said

Do not use **said** as an adjective, unless you are drawing up a legal document in old-fashioned English. Use the definite article, demonstrative or possessive pronoun, whichever fits:

It was included in said consignment = *in the consignment*.
It was credited to said account = *to your account*.
Said clause can be deleted = *this clause*.

Under separate cover

This does not tell the other people very much apart from the fact that it is useless to go on searching in the same envelope. By all means say *separately*, but be helpful by adding how the other article was sent:

The operating instructions are leaving separately by printed matter mail.

The test sheets are being sent separately by the driver of the delivery truck.

● **Wrong usage**

There is something not quite right with all of these frequently used phrases and words.

We kindly inform you

A very frequent mistake, made in letters from any country, including English-speaking ones. **Kindly** in front of a verb in the imperative or applied to other people does indeed mean **please**:

Kindly send the operating manual as soon as you can.

Could you kindly return the surplus battery.

Nothing wrong with these sentences, although **please** would sound more natural, more the way you would say it over the telephone.

The mistake is made when **kindly** is attached to **we** or **I**. It then really means that the **we** or **I** is the kind person, surely a misguided boast. 'We kindly inform you,' can only mean 'We are being kind by informing you,' which is hardly what the writer had in mind. Remedy:

We are glad to tell you.

We are pleased to inform you.

and other, more modest statements.

Enclosed please find our invoice

A very popular request, but not very good style. Let's look at it closely. When I tell you *'please come, please write* or *please show me,* I am asking you to do something, because the verb is in the **imperative**.

In that case 'please find' must logically mean 'please look for it', asking the recipient of the letter to poke his nose into the envelope to see what he can find. Silly? Yes, so you need a simple statement, not a request:

We are enclosing our invoice.

We enclose our delivery note.

Our Certificate of Origin is attached.

Please advise us when the pump will be ready

The verb **advise** should be confined to its basic meaning of **give advice**, i.e. telling an undecided person what you would do in a given situation. Avoid a certain bureaucratic chill by making the following change:

Please let us know when the pump will be ready.

If you are the one giving the happy news, simply say *we are pleased to tell you*, not advise.

We anticipate no further delays

If you are a little surprised about the treatment just given to your old friend **advise**, let me add that **anticipate** should also be left to its real meaning. Real meaning? Yes; this is not **expect**, but **forestall, act before something happens, do something beforehand**:

We do not want to anticipate the opening of the show by unveiling our new model this week.

This means that we do not want to do anything beforehand. Although **expect** looks less impressive than **anticipate**, it has one major merit: it is the correct word. 'We anticipate no further delays', should become:

We expect no further delays.

We would appreciate to receive it very soon

You expect to receive, hope to receive, are glad to receive, want to receive. When you use **appreciate** and **look forward to**, however, you need the gerund, the **ing** -form:

*We would appreciate **receiving** it.*
*We look forward to **receiving** it.*

They obviously have no intention to replace the faulty valve

In other languages the noun **intention** is followed by a verb in the infinitive. Not in English:

*They have no intention **of replacing** it.*

The mistake was probably due to the fact that the verb **to intend** is indeed followed by the infinitive:

They intend to come later.

Deem

Refuse to be impressed when you read:

We do not deem it necessary to change our accounting system for the time being.

The writer does not deem anything. He **thinks** or **considers**. **Deem** has a place in legal English:

Unless four weeks' notice of termination is given in writing, the lessee will be deemed to have agreed to one year's extension of the lease.

This means that unless the tenant says 'no', he will be **assumed** to have said 'yes'.

Feasible

Someone may report:

It is quite feasible that they will come later.

What is meant here is simply **possible**, nothing else. **Feasible** is in order when used to mean **capable of being done, practicable,** i.e. adjectives usually applied in connection with a project, idea, plan:

This suggestion sounds a bit crazy, but our technical people tell us that it is quite feasible.

Perhaps

This word is sometimes used as synonym of *please*:

Could you perhaps make sure that the optical attachment is packed in a separate box.

Perhaps introduces an element of vagueness into a sentence, so use it only when you really want to be vague. The above sentence should read: *Could you please make sure. . .* . If you want to make your request a little stronger, shorten it to *Please make sure. . . .*

Point of interest: perhaps is used less in American English than in British English. At the beginning of a sentence it is always replaced by **maybe**:

British English: *Perhaps they'll come tomorrow.*

American English: *Maybe they'll come tomorrow.*

Transpire

It may somehow look impressive when you read:

We are not sure what transpired at the meeting.

The writer meant nothing more exciting than **happened**, and should have used this unassuming word. The correct meaning of **transpire** is **become known, leak out,** i.e. often some unexpected or embarrassing development:

They denied all knowledge of the faulty pipes, but it transpired three weeks later that the foreman had warned management about it twice.

It will be replaced, irregardless of the nature of the damage

There are two words that mean the same: **regardless** and **irrespective**. 'Irregardless' is an interesting cocktail you will be unable to find in a dictionary. Best policy: use one of the two existing words.

We now have to proceed with alternate plans

The president of a major American corporation recently made this important announcement. The importance to us is the wrong use of the word **alternate**.

The adjective and noun **alternate** refers to **two things** that **vary** in accordance with a **regular pattern**: your wallpaper may have alternating red and white stripes; if you work every second Saturday, you work on alternate Saturdays; if you and a friend take turns driving a car for three hours at a time, you are alternating the driving duties. The electrical current shown by that up-and-down symbol ∿ is **alternating current**, abbreviated **A.C.**

Those plans mentioned in the heading, however, are **alternative** plans, a similar-looking adjective with which **alternate** is often confused. **Alternative** means **one or more other possibilities**:

> *We have to make alternative plans.*

Alternative, derived from the Latin 'alter' (one of two; the second of two) used to be applied to only **one** other possibility. This restriction is no longer valid, and you can correctly refer to several alternatives.

There is no possibility of us agreeing to this proposal

The word **agreeing** is here a **gerund**, a verbal **noun**. This verb form has the function of a noun. In place of **agreeing** you could also use the noun **agreement** and change the sentence to:

> *There is no possibility of our agreement to this proposal.*

The noun agreement is preceded by what is here the **possessive adjective** *our*. Since a gerund does the work of a noun it needs this possessive form (our) *not* a personal pronoun (us). Corrected version:

> *There is no possibility* of **our** agreeing. . .

As you will come across the wrong pronoun frequently in **informal** language, here are the better forms in parentheses, if you are interested in perfection:

> Do you mind me smoking? (***my*** *smoking*)
> The odds against him winning are high. (***his*** *winning*)
> She remembered us telling her. (***our*** *telling*)
> There is no point in you waiting any longer. (***your*** *waiting*)
> I can't imagine them being that generous. (***their*** *being*)

The BBC made this mistake last week when reporting:

> The rules do not prevent them joining the federation.

Here you have two corrected possibilities:

> *The rules do not prevent* **them from joining** *the federation.*
> *The rules do not prevent* **their joining** *the federation.*

On the other hand, you may have heard this kind of sentence:

I heard him talking about me.

There is nothing wrong with the personal pronoun **him** here, because **talking** does not have the function of a noun but is the **present participle**: he was in the act of talking when I heard him. You could also have said:

I heard him talk about me.

The borderline is sometimes not completely clear, but you can generally rely on the following rule:

> You need the **possessive adjective** when you can use a **noun** in place of the **ing** -form:
>
> our agreeing = our agreement.
>
> You need the **personal pronoun** when you can say *in the act of* in place of the **ing** -form:
>
> saw him swimming = saw him in the act of swimming.

Some flexibility now exists when you have this type of genitive form:

They objected to my sister being late.

Although 'my sister's being late' is grammatically correct, the added *s* can make the sentence sound a little pedantic. Solution: leave it out.

• Keep it simple

In some languages the word *simple* is not far removed from *primitive*. In English, too, when you refer to a *simple fellow*, a *simple soul*, but in business communications simplicity is a **virtue**.

Your letters will then be **shorter**, a great advantage to the busy reader at the other end who may have to look through that stack of mail on his desk. Your letters are likely to be **clearer**, as they will be free from unnecessary ballast that so often leads to misunderstanding. Your letters will also probably sound more **friendly**, more the way you would say it in person, without long and possibly even pompous phrases.

How to do it? Here are a few ideas:

Convert the long phrase into one word

Take the phrase **in view of the fact that**. It has six words, yet whichever way you look at it, it really means no more than **because, as** or **since**. One word in place of six: an excellent economy measure.

Here are a few sentences containing phrases of several words (written in bold face), which can be replaced by one preposition or conjunction (given in parentheses).

Pension payments vary **in relation to** *length of service.*	**(with)**
You may be right **with regard to** *next year's economic trends.*	**(about)**
It will have no effect **in terms of** *our ability to compete.*	**(on)**
The opening will be delayed **due to the fact that** *some actors are still held up by fog at London Airport.*	**(because)**
We heard a lecture **on the subject of** *nuclear energy.*	**(on)**
A medal will be given **in respect of** *safe driving.*	**(for)**
Similar problems may apply **with regard to** *export orders.*	**(to)**
This illness is more widespread **in the case of** *people over 70.*	**(with** or **in)**
It has been changed **in order to** *simplify dismantling.*	**(to)**
The site was surveyed **in connection with** *the next Olympic Games.*	**(for)**
The chart will be useful **with a view to** *assessing our sales trend.*	**(for)**

We ought to increase stocks **in view of the fact
that** prices are likely to go up next quarter.   **(because)**

The rear entrance will be closed **until such time as**
the road extension has been completed.   **(until)**

There may be changes **with regard to** company policy.   **(in)**

Leave out words that mean very little or nothing at all

The loss of the words in parentheses means a gain in style:

(It will be noted that) *prices have been reduced by 3½%.*

(We wish to point out that) *the brushes were definitely sent together
with the paint.*

(For the sake of good order) *we confirm that the missing tools were
sent this morning.*

She was unaware (of the fact) *that the others had already left.*

The new park is much bigger (in size).

The table is oval (in shape).

Other cumbersome constructions can be streamlined by re-
arranging the sentence. You have ten words in the sentence

There are no problems as far as *finance* is concerned.

Say the same with six words:

*There are no problems **with** finance.*

Try this one:

*Production is running ahead of schedule, but **the situation** is less
satisfactory **from the point of view of sales**.*

The sub-clause consists of 13 words and manages to sound
pretentious. Collect the double bonus of an unpretentious as well
as clear statement by rephrasing to five words:

*Production is running ahead of schedule, but **sales are less
satisfactory**.*

Be careful with the words *situation, nature,* and *character*

As we have just seen, the word **situation** can make a sentence longer than necessary. So can **nature** and **character**.

The delivery situation is now easier.	(six words)
Delivery is now easier.	(four words)
She has had an illness of a minor nature.	(nine words)
She has had a minor illness.	(six words)
This claim is of a doubtful character.	(seven words)
This claim is doubtful.	(four words)

Saving a few words may by itself not seem so very important, but as you are at the same time improving your style, the changes are worth making. An improvement usually requires more effort. Here you need fewer words, less effort.

Avoid the impersonal *it*-sentence

Writing is a substitute for speech. When you write to other people, you talk to them in a letter. Do so in a **direct** way and avoid all those vague phrases beginning with **it**:

It is regretted = *we regret.*
It has come to our notice = *we have heard.*
It will be appreciated = *you will understand.*
It would be appreciated = *we would be grateful.*
It will be our endeavour = *we will try.*
It will have to be decided = *you will have to decide.*

'It will be noted' can either be left out or transformed into something more forceful. Take this sentence:

It will be noted that prices have been reduced by $7\frac{1}{2}$ per cent.

If this $7\frac{1}{2}$ per cent does not amount to very much, at least shorten your modest boast to:

Prices have been reduced by $7\frac{1}{2}$ per cent.

If the $7\frac{1}{2}$ per cent is something that will give your competitors sleepless nights, why not make a noise about it?

We have reduced prices by $7\frac{1}{2}$ per cent.
You will be glad to hear that we have cut prices by $7\frac{1}{2}$ per cent.

Avoid the old-fashioned *would* -construction

Would is doing an acceptable job when used to indicate a **condition**:

> *We would come if we could.*

Would sounds very old-fashioned when used in the following way, which has nothing to do with the conditional mood:

> (In reply to your letter) *we would inform you. . . .*

You often find this phrase in letters from UK government departments or from writers over a certain age. It sounds chilly and impersonal. Remove the chill by removing *would*:

> *We are glad to tell you*
> *We can tell you*
> *We are pleased to confirm*

and similar ways of saying exactly the same thing in a less starchy, more friendly way.

Avoid abstract nouns

An abstract noun needs a verb to go with it; often also an article, a preposition, a personal pronoun. Use the verb form only and you can save all that ballast. Here's how it can be done:

We **are in receipt of** = we **have received/we thank you for**.
We **have given consideration** = we **have considered**.
We **are of the opinion** = we **believe**.
We **wish to convey our appreciation** = we **appreciate**.
We **have arrived at a decision** = we **have decided**.
We **wish to express our regret** = we **regret**.
We **are in a position to deliver** = we **can deliver**.
They **expressed their willingness** = they **agreed**.

Which column sounds more human, more friendly?

• The case against *case*

The noun **case** has its uses: *in any case, in case of fire,* a *case of typhoid fever,* and so on. There are, however, many instances in which

case has no useful function. Here are a few case-less improvements:

The case with case	Case-less
This is specially prevalent in the case of old people.	*This is specially prevalent **with** old people.*
Their complaints are in many cases unjustified.	***Many** of their complaints are unjustified.*
This illness is nowadays much less common than was the case fifty years ago.	*This illness is nowadays much less common than fifty years ago.*
Breakages are in every case due to bad packing.	*Breakages are **always** due to bad packing.*
Management is in many cases out of touch with foreign markets.	*Management is **often** out of touch with foreign markets.*
Most tours include full board, but in a few cases only breakfast is provided.	*Most tours include full board, but **a few** only provide breakfast.*
It is definitely not the case that we have approved this expenditure.	*We have definitely not approved this expenditure.*

● Perfect your diplomacy

No one is perfect. Unless people always give you fantastic service or you happen to be exceptionally tolerant, you will sooner or

later have to complain to somebody about something. There are usually two ways of doing so in a letter: the straight and potentially rude way or the path of diplomacy. Let us join the Diplomatic Corps for one easy lesson and see how we can make noise in a tactful manner. The secret is often the use of the verbs **seem** and **appear**.

You forgot to send

This is a direct accusation. As you may possibly not have looked in the right place, leave the door slightly open by saying instead:

You appear to have overlooked sending.

We do not seem to be able to find.

We cannot find.

This is wrong

This dogmatic statement is unlikely to widen your circle of friends. Say exactly the same in a more pleasant way with:

There seems to be a mistake.

This appears to be incorrect.

We cannot quite reconcile.

You misinterpreted our instructions

In other words: you are pretty stupid. Diplomatic version:

It appears that our instructions were not quite clear.

You sent the wrong invoice

The 'you' at the other end may not have been the guilty person. Perhaps there was some mistake in their mailing department. If you write:

We received the wrong invoice.

you are saying exactly the same in a milder manner.

The use of **seem** and **appear** in these more tactful versions of letters of complaint has two advantages:

(a) You are not directly accusing anyone.
(b) If you are proved wrong, you made no major accusation. Things only 'appeared' to be as you said.

Another device for treading carefully is the **understatement**, a form of verbal camouflage for which the English are famous. It cloaks a statement in a variety of negatives and adjectives to cushion the impact of what is being said. It doesn't really deceive anyone of a certain intelligence, but at least it sounds more elegant. Here is how it can be done.

Bare fact
They set fire to their warehouse, collected the insurance, and solved their financial problems overnight.

Understatement
The fire in their warehouse was possibly not entirely unconnected with one or two financial problems they seem to have been having this year.

Bare fact
His proposal is nonsense.

Understatement
We are not fully convinced that his somewhat unorthodox proposal is necessarily the right solution.

Bare fact
He didn't study and failed the examination.

Understatement
It is not altogether unlikely that his reluctance to study had some bearing on his marked lack of success in the examination.

Understatement is not so common in America, where the inhabitants are often the descendants of people from countries where emotions are not so restrained. As part of your Anglo-

American education let us listen to comments on identical situations and events from natives of the British Isles and from the USA.

English understatement	American realism
I suppose this meat could perhaps be a little more tender.	This meat is as tough as old boots!
Our hotel room at the coast was not exactly the Ritz.	The room was awful!
His speech at the convention could really have been a little more interesting.	It was the dullest speech I've ever heard.
Their ideas are perhaps a little unconventional.	They're crazy!
She's not exactly the world's greatest cook.	She'll ruin corn flakes!

Note The use of understatement needs a little extra care and a light touch. Otherwise it can sometimes sound like clumsy sarcasm.

A few readers may now be a little worried after seeing some phrases they have been using almost daily in letters described as poor style. 'Where do I find a list of better expressions?' Fortunately there is nothing new to learn. All you have to remember is a simple rule. Here it is, beautifully framed:

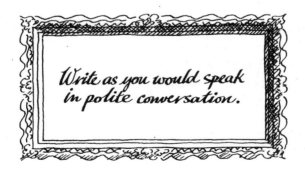

Write as you would speak in polite conversation.

In other words, if you would say it, you can write it. If you would not say it, why write it?

Whenever you are in doubt about something, take a hard look at it in the light of the above rule and you will know immediately whether it is acceptable or not. Three test cases:

- Would you say 'enclosed please find the money' when handing somebody an envelope? No; you would say that it *is enclosed*.
- Are you likely to tell a new customer 'I assure you of my best attention at all times' when he visits your office? Of course not. If your assistance is prompt and efficient, he will know that your attention is pretty good. If you are not too helpful, he knows that your assurance is an empty promise.
- When your car is blocking the entrance of the local fire brigade, do you explain to the policeman 'I'll move in due course'? Unless you enjoy being towed away, you avoid vague forecasts and try to be *more exact* about the timing.

Do you get the general idea? If something sounds pompous, old-fashioned, unnecessary or even silly when you say it, why should you write it?

6

Perfect your universal English

British English/American English

Suppose you make a phone call through an operator. Elsie in London may ask you 'Are you through?', meaning 'Are you connected?'. When you answer 'Yes', she will sigh happily and leave you alone to talk.

Janey in Minneapolis may also ask you 'Are you through?' If you answer 'Yes', she will cut you off straight away, because to her the same question means 'Have you finished?'

If you were taught British English at school, you have to know something about American usage to understand spoken and written English wherever it may come from. If you were brought up on American English, it is useful to have a reasonable knowledge of the spelling and terminology used in countries following the British system.

The borderline is often not very clear. Canadians – constitutionally in the British orbit – speak and write American English.

Australians and New Zealanders use British English, but with many local or American terms. On the other hand, some Americans will be familiar with many British terms; others may know hardly any.

This chapter deals with the essential differences between the two systems. Having lived in the UK, Canada, and New Zealand, with long stays in the USA and Australia, I should be a fairly reliable eye and ear witness for you.

1. Spelling

Differences in spelling can be put into two groups: the first group is subject to clear rules, and you can safely 'translate' a word from one type of English into the other. The second group has no rules, but as it consists of no more than two dozen words, you should have no trouble in learning them.

Here comes the first group. British English is always given in the left-hand column in this chapter.

● British English ending *-our* = American English ending *-or*

colour	*color*
labour	*labor*
honour	*honor*
flavour	*flavor*, etc.

American English is far more logical by sticking to *-or* throughout. British English has such inconsistencies as **colour/discoloration, honour/honorary, humour/humorist, vapour/vaporize**. Also **candour** but **pallor, rancour** but **squalor**, and other oddities. If there should ever be a popularity contest for International English, I shall vote for the American system.

• British English noun ending -*re* = American English ending -*er*

theatre	*theater*
centre	*center*
fibre	*fiber*
metre	*meter*, etc.

The above 'metre' is 1000 mm. In British English you also have the spelling 'meter,' but it then means either **verse rhythm** or **measuring device**, as in gas meter, volt meter, and others.

Exceptions to this rule are **acre** and **massacre**, which are spelled in this way on both sides of the Atlantic. Reason: if written with the 'cer' at the end, they would have to be pronounced like the first syllable in 'certain'.

• British English ending -*ence* = American English ending -*ense*

licence	*license*
defence	*defense*
offence	*offense*
pretence	*pretense*, etc.

British English has *license*, but this is the verb, not the noun. You would then correctly write that:

They were licensed to use the licence.

• British English final -*l* is doubled when a suffix is added to an unstressed syllable; not in American English

dialled	*dialed*
labelling	*labeling*
marvellous	*marvelous*
panelled	*paneled*
totalling	*totaling*
travelled	*traveled*
woollen	*woolen*, etc.

● British English final -*p* is doubled when a suffix is added to an unstressed syllable; not always in American English

If you were taught British English at school, you may find it odd to see *kidnaping* and *worshiper* in American publications, but these spellings are quite correct.

Exception: It is *developed/developing* everywhere.

● British English *oe* and *ae* (Greek and Latin words) = American English *e*

haemorrhage	*hemorrhage*
gynaecology	*gynecology*
anaemia	*anemia*
mediaeval	*medieval*
foetus	*fetus*, etc.

Most British medical journals now use the spelling *fetus*. It is *manoeuvre* in British English, but *maneuver* in American English. Both are pronounced 'manoover'.

● British English -*ogue* (Greek words) = American English -*og*

catalogue	*catalog*
dialogue	*dialog*
epilogue	*epilog*
monologue	*monolog*, etc.

● Individual differences in spelling; no rules

First column British English, second column American English.

aluminium	*aluminum*
(stress on third syllable)	(stress on second syllable)
axe	*ax*
cheque	*check**

---

*Cheque is also used in North America. The spelling *Travelers Cheques* (looking like an Anglo-American mixture) used by some US banks is therefore correct.

cosy	*cozy* (also *cosy*)
draught	*draft*
gaol	*jail*
goodbye	*goodby* (also *goodbye*)
grey	*gray*
kerb	*curb*
mould	*mold*
moustache	*mustache*
plough	*plow*
programme†	*program*
pyjamas	*pajamas*
sceptical	*skeptical*
tyre	*tire*
vice (the clamping tool)	*vise*.

Don't be confused by the 'home-made' spelling **thru** and **tonite**. They are unlikely to be approved by any future dictionaries. Some more respectable-looking words can also be misleading. An American politician once made a speech and used the word *normalcy* in place of *normality*. It was his invention, but the word has remained in the American language ever since.

2. Terminology

When it comes to differences in terminology – Jack in Birmingham (West Midlands) wears *trousers*, Jack in Birmingham (Alabama) wears *pants*; that sort of thing – we have to limit ourselves strictly to essentials.

Trifling differences (*cookery book/cookbook; driving licence/driver's license*, etc.) have therefore been omitted. The selection of words is grouped under eight headings.

---

†*Program* in connection with computers.

● Things you wear

dinner jacket	*tuxedo*
ladder (in stocking)	*run*
made-to-measure (suit)	*custom-made*
nappy (babies only)	*diaper*
trousers	*pants*

● Around the home

bat (table tennis)	*paddle*
chest of drawers	*bureau, dresser*
cupboard	*closet, wardrobe**
curtains	*drapes* (if opaque)
	curtains (if net or lace)
cutlery	*flatware*
dustbin	*trash can, garbage can*
flat	*apartment†*
greaseproof paper	*wax paper*
jug	*pitcher*
lift	*elevator*
luggage	*baggage‡*
pack of cards	*deck of cards*
rubbish	*garbage, trash*
tap	*faucet*

---

*A *closet* is usually built-in, a *wardrobe* movable. You also have *kitchen cupboard* in American English.

† Also used in British English.

‡ Light baggage is also known as *luggage*.

tin (for food)	*can*
torch	*flashlight*
verandah	*porch*

Note: The difference between the American *garbage* and *trash* may be worth knowing. Garbage is generally the domestic and often smelly waste you throw out. Trash can be anything you want to get rid of: when you move house, you are always surprised how much trash you have to get rid of.

● Around the office; to do with work

bank note	*bill* (e.g. pound note, but dollar bill)
bill of lading	*waybill*
carriage paid	*freight prepaid*
current account	*checking account*
to engage staff	*to hire staff*
personal (phone) *call*	*person-to-person call*
to *post a letter*	*to mail a letter*
postman	*mailman*
return ticket	*round-trip ticket*
rise (in salary)	*raise*
scribbling pad	*scratchpad*
shareholder	*stockholder*
single ticket	*one-way ticket*
the (telephone) line is engaged	*the line is busy*
timetable	*schedule*
trunk call	*long-distance call*
unit trust	*mutual fund*

● Things you eat

biscuit	*cookie*
lump sugar	*cube sugar*
minced meat	*ground meat*
sweets	*candy*
underdone (meat)	*rare*

● The automobile

bonnet	*hood*
boot	*trunk*
caravan	*trailer*
gear lever	*gear shift*
lorry	*truck*
paraffin	*kerosene*
petrol	*gasoline, 'gas'*
puncture	*flat*
saloon car	*sedan*
silencer	*muffler*
windscreen	*windshield*

● Other technical terms

aeroplane	*airplane*
(railway) carriage, coach	*car*
goods train	*freight train*
(radio) *valve*	*tube*
railway	*railroad*
spanner	*wrench*
subway (passage under street)	*underpass*
tram	*streetcar, trolley car*
underground (train; Métro)	*subway*

● Mixed bag

autumn	*fall; autumn* (literary)
cheek (impudence)	*gall, nerve*
high street	*main street*
holiday(s)	*vacation**
interval	*intermission*
ironmonger's	*hardware store*
pavement	*sidewalk*
(stand in a) *queue*	*line*
shop	*store; shop* (if small)
timber (cut wood)	*lumber*

---

*Vacation also exists in British English, where it is mostly applied to the universities and the law courts.

• Differences that require an explanation

Public school/private school

Full marks to American English for logic: in America a **public school** is for the general public. It is free, financed by the State. A **private school** is not for everyone, because you have to pay. No complications here.

In British English a **public school** is by no means for the broad public. Not everyone can get in, not everyone can afford the fees. (An American may therefore explain that this kind of public school is a private school. . . .)

Slightly dizzy, you may ask 'If in the UK a public school is a private school, what do they call a really public, i.e. non-paying school?'. This is called a **state school** or, more often, **comprehensive school**, i.e. the non-paying school usually financed by the local city or borough council.

Ground floor/first floor

If you have to climb no stairs, you probably live on the **ground floor**. At least in Europe. In America you start counting at ground level and call it **first floor**. So the second floor in Manchester (England) would be the third floor in Manchester (New Hampshire), and so on.

Chemist/druggist

In Britain medical prescriptions are sold by a **chemist**, also called 'the chemist's', if you have the shop in mind. His American colleague is a **druggist**. He works in a **pharmacy**, a word used in British English mainly for the science or business connected with medical prescriptions.

The American **drugstore** originally did sell pills for your headache and other troubles, but has branched out in all directions. The well-organized drugstore of today also sells soft drinks, light meals, magazines, books, records, ice cream, etc.

The British English term **chemist** is therefore not very clear. It can be a person who has something to do with your cough drops or someone who has studied **chemistry**.

To let accommodation/to rent accommodation

If you do not own the place you live in, you **rent** it from the owner. On both sides of the Atlantic. If you own a house or apartment and let someone else live in it, you **let** it in British English, but **rent** it in American English.

If this sounds confusing, let me clarify the situation in this way:

	British English	**American English**
The owner	lets to the tenant	rents to the tenant,
The tenant	rents from the owner	rents from the owner.

3. Pronunciation

As advanced student of English you know the main differences between a typically British and American accent. Here are a few points you may find interesting.

These are some of the principal differences in pronouncing words, left column British English, right column American English.

	Pronounced as if written	**Pronounced as if written**
anti-	an tea	ant eye
clerk	clark	clurk (rhymes with 'work')
lever	leever	levver ('e' as in 'ten')
lieutenant	leff tenant	loo tenant

patent	pay tent	pattent
route	root	rowt ('ow' as in 'cow')
schedule	shed you'll	sked you'll
semi-	sem-ee	sem eye
vase	vahz ('a' as in 'calm')	vayze (rhymes with 'blaze')

The American **tomato** rhymes with **potato**, which seems logical, yet the British **tomato** sounds like 'tomahto'. The American double _t_ sounds like a 'd': **butter** = 'budder', **pretty** = 'priddy'. The single American _t_ within a word also sounds like a 'd': **forty** = 'fordy', **mighty** = 'mighdy'.

When someone tells you that he 'wayded', he may mean _waited_, maybe for a train, or _waded_, i.e. walked in shallow water. The American _t_ is often ignored when preceded by the letter _n_: _twenty_ sounds like 'twenny', _plenty_ like 'plenny', and so on.

4. Prepositions

There are a number of interesting Anglo-American differences in the use of certain prepositions.

• At home/home

If you do not go out, you stay **at home**. At least in British English. In American English you will report that you stayed **home**; without preposition.

• For years/in years

If you have not seen Jack since 1978, you report in British English that you have not seen him **for years**. In American English you deplore that you have not seen him **in years**.

The same difference applies to the expression **for ages/in ages**, meaning colloquially 'during a very long period of time':

They haven't invited us **for** ages.

We haven't seen them **in** ages.

• Behind/in back of

The American English **in back of** sounds odd in the UK, but is quite acceptable American for **behind**:

> *He stood in back of us during the game.*
> *It's in back of the house.*

• In Church Street/on Church Street/at No. 16 Church Street

In British English you live **in** a street, road, avenue. In American English **on**:

> *They live in Thurlow Road, London.*
> *He lives on Dean Street, Las Vegas.*

As soon as you mention the number, however, both sides of the Atlantic agree on **at**:

> *She used to live at 48 Prescott Road.*

• On behalf of/in behalf of

> *She attended on behalf of her brother.* (British)
> *She attended in behalf of her brother.* (American)

• Out of the window/out the window

In British English you look out **of** the window, throw something out **of** the window (disgusting!), and even (I hope not) fall out **of** the window. In American English you omit the preposition and simply look out the window, throw something out the window, and fall out the window.

• Fork out/fork over

A little slangy, but worth knowing. This verbal idiom means **pay**, with the implication that somebody is **reluctant** to part with money:

> *In the end he forked out forty pence!* (British)
> *In the end he forked over seventy cents!* (American)

● To write to/to write

Citizens of the UK and Commonwealth countries sit down to **write to** their friends. Holders of US passports simply write their friends. No *to*.

If they don't write, they may get **into** trouble. Not Americans who will get **in** trouble. In extreme cases wrongdoers may be put **into** prison. In America people are put **in** jail.

● To wash up/to wash

Do you know the definition of a bohemian? Someone who washes the dishes **before** a meal. You and I like to get them cleaned after we have eaten. In British English I drag you into this by suggesting that we should **wash up**, meaning the **dishes**. In American English I would propose **doing the dishes**, because in North America **to wash up** means a minor **personal** wash, usually of the hands.

While we are on the subject of washing, please remember that the British English **sink** is found only in the kitchen, laundry room, garage, etc. The same object in the bathroom or toilet is a (wash)**basin**. In American English a **sink** is a sink; anywhere in the house.

● To consult/to consult with

In British and American English you consult an expert. When saying **to consult with** in American English you indicate a more detailed or formal discussion of your troubles:

He will have to consult a lawyer,

but

*He consulted **with** his lawyer for three hours.*

• To meet/to meet with

The American version **to meet with** indicates an **arranged meeting,** not a casual encounter:

We met them at the airport (purely by chance).

*We met **with** them to discuss the reorganization* (arrangement).

British English has simply **to meet** for both cases; without preposition.

• To visit/to visit with

The American English **to visit with** means staying with people, not merely spending a few hours:

We visited her in hospital (short bedside stay).

*I visited **with** them during the summer* (longer stay).

In British English you never use **with**. The sentence 'we visited them last year' can therefore either mean a very brief appearance or a long stay.

• Different than/different from

In American English it is quite acceptable to say:

Our hotel room is different than yours.

British English is different. It much prefers:

Our hotel room is different from yours.

• Half an hour/a half hour

This is admittedly not a prepositional difference, but I think I can squeeze this item into this section without your noticing it.

British English has:

This will take half an hour.

We'll see you in half an hour.

American English usually prefers:

This will take a half hour.

We'll see you in a half hour.

● **3/4**

Another fraction, called **three-quarters** in British English, but usually **three-fourths** in American English.

5. Opposite meaning

The difference between some British English and American English words and phrases can be small or it can be considerable.

Here is an interesting case: the British expression means more or less the opposite of the American one.

● **Should you table it?**

When someone in the UK has a brilliant idea and wants it to be discussed or decided at an official meeting, he **tables** it. This is a very formal expression. It requests that a proposal, motion, suggestion, etc. should be **put on the table** and be made a part of the agenda or official business.

When someone in North America has a not so brilliant idea and wants it discussed at a meeting, some of his colleagues may think that this would be a waste of time. They may then suggest that this proposal should be **tabled**, but they mean that it should be **dropped under the table**, i.e. not be made a part of the business. In other words, in British English you table (propose) useful subjects; in American English you table (let die) useless ideas.

Beyond the information on British and American English given in this chapter, any differences between the two are pointed out whenever they apply to words or phrases in other parts of the book.

7

Perfect your pronunciation and stress

English pronunciation can sometimes be difficult. Rules exist but are not reliable because of the many possible exceptions.

Two 'technical' points: phonetic symbols are not used in this chapter, as I never considered the system of near-hieroglyphics specially helpful. So if we discuss the two ways of pronouncing the word *row*, for example, we say that it can either rhyme with 'cow' or 'low'.

The stress is shown in **bold face**. Like this: **ne**cessary shows that the stress is on the **first** syllable.

1. Pronunciation

• o-u-g-h sequence

Did you know that these letters can be pronounced in seven different ways? Here they come:

Pronounced Most important words in group
as in

buff	*enough* *rough* *slough* (to shed snake skin) *tough*
off	*cough* *trough*
true	*through*
low	*(al)though* *dough* *furlough*

cow	*bough* *Slough* (the British town)
	slough (swamp)
caught	*bought* *fought* *ought* *thought*
cup	*hiccough* (mainly written *hiccup*)

This group, with so many possibilities, is the most difficult. Pleasant thought: the rest will be much easier.

• Frequently mispronounced words

A few brief comments alongside each word should help:

aborigine	A native of a country before the arrival of the settlers (now mainly applied to the original inhabitants of Australia) is pronounced 'abbo-**ri**-dji-nee'.
admirable	Take no notice of the verb *admire*, stress the first syllable, and pronounce the second one as in 'mirror'.
anemone	A flower (or primitive animal) with an unexpected sound: 'an-**ne**-mo-nee'.
antipodes	Regions at the other end of the world from us are *antipodes*, stressed '**anti**podes', with the last syllable to rhyme with 'freeze'.
bow	This rhymes with 'low' if it means: (a) A knot with two loops, e.g. a bow tie. (b) What you need to play a violin, cello or double bass; what is essential in archery. It rhymes with 'cow' if it means: (a) What you do when you incline the top part of your body or your head. (b) The front end of a ship.
Cambridge	The first syllable is pronounced as in 'came', not to rhyme with 'tram'.
clerk	In British English it rhymes with 'dark'; in American English with 'Turk'.
comparable	The parent may be the verb *compare* but the adjective has the stress on the first syllable, with the second more or less neglected: '**com**-prabble'.

forehead	Not like 'fore' + 'head', but as '**forred**'.
fuchsia	A pretty flower with a crazy pronunciation: like '**few**-sha'.
gauge	To rhyme with 'page'. No problem in American English, where it is written *gage* (or sometimes *gauge*).
gross	Although it may look as if it ought to rhyme with 'loss', it has the long vowel sound as in 'road'.
indict	This may look like 'predict', but is pronounced to rhyme with 'invite'.
infamous	As this is not the opposite of *famous*, but means *of bad reputation*, its pronunciation is also less reliable: '**inf**emmus', with stress on first syllable.

infamous

famous

irreparable	The parent is the verb *repair* but the adjective contains no *i* and has the stress on the second syllable, with the rest of the word neglected: 'ir-**re**-prabble'.
margarine	Mostly pronounced 'mar-dje-reen', ignoring the usual rule that the letter **g** before **a, o** or **u** has the hard sound as in 'gas'.
mortgage	No **t**, just '**mor**-gidge'.
muscle	Ignore the **c** and pronounce it as if written 'mussel'. On the other hand, *muscular* retains the **sk** -sound.

personnel	Stress on the last syllable: '**person**nel**', i.e. not like the adjective pronounced as '**per**sonal'.
preface	Looks like 'pre' + 'face', but the first syllable sounds like in 'preposition' and has the stress. The second syllable sounds like 'fiss'.
preferable	The relationship to the verb *prefer* does not extend to pronunciation. Stress the first syllable and neglect the second one: '**pref**frable'.
ratio	As 'nation': 'ray-shee-oh'.
recipe	Not very logically, you say '**re**-sippy'.
row	This rhymes with 'slow' if it means:
	(a) What you have to do to get anywhere in a rowing boat.
	(b) Objects arranged side by side: a row of houses, a row of seats.
	It rhymes with 'cow' if it is the colloquial expression for noise or a quarrel.
salmon	The l is not pronounced in these words:

> *almond* *alms* *balk* *balm* *calm* *caulk* *folk*
> *palm* *psalm* *qualm* *salmon* *talk* *walk* *yolk*.

	Some people say 'goff' for golf, but this seems to be going out of fashion.
subtle	Another silent letter, the b. The word sounds like 'suttle'. In the same group are:

> *bomb* *climb* *comb* *debt* *doubt* *dumb* *lamb*
> *limb* *plumb* *plumber* *thumb* *tomb*.

superfluous	Following no rules whatever, this word has the stress on the second syllable, which is pronounced to rhyme with 'fur'.
victuals	Two oddities: the c is silent, and the last syllable is pronounced in an unexpected way. Say as if written 'vittles'.
z	The last letter of the alphabet is pronounced 'zed' in British English; 'zee' in American English.
. . . .	What are these? Points? No, these are *dots*. Morse code consists of *dots* and *dashes*.

45–50	If these are house numbers, it is 'forty-five **to** fifty', of course.
	If they are something else; a model number, for instance, it is 'forty-five **dash** fifty'.
348/829	The slanted line between the two figures is pronounced '**stroke**': 'three four eight **stroke** eight two nine'. (Sometimes also '**oblique**'.)
8‰ (= 0.8%)	Say 'oh point eight per cent'. What's happened here? The symbol for 'per mille' does not exist in English. You then have to use **per cent** and give the figure a decimal point.

- ## ch: '*k*' or '*tsh*'?

The **ch** in words derived from Greek is almost always pronounced '*k*'. The best-known examples are *archaic   archangel architect   archives   character   chasm   chemistry   choir   chorus chronicle   chronometer   chrysanthemum   psychology*, etc.

When the prefix *arch-* means *chief*, the **ch** sounds like in '*march*': *archbishop   archdeacon   archduke*, etc. The exception is *archangel*, as mentioned in the paragraph above, and a few rare words such as *archiepiscopal   archidiaconate   archimandrite*, etc.

- ## The versatile figure 0

Did you know that you can pronounce it in six different ways, depending on the context?

My telephone number is 200 50 36

When spelling a number out aloud, perhaps to a telephone operator, you say 'two double oh five oh three six. 0 = **oh**.

228 should read 2280

You point out the missing 0 by saying that there is a **nought** missing in the first figure. American English prefers the word **zero** . 0 = **nought** or **zero**.

Temperature: − 30°

When referring to a scale with plus and minus divisions, you use the word **zero**. Thirty degrees below zero. 0 = **zero**.

The conversion factor is 0.46

This decimal fraction can also be written **.46**, i.e. without the 0. You have two ways of saying this figure aloud: **oh point** four six or simply **point** four six. In a multiplication you would say 'you have to multiply all prices by point four six'. 0 = **oh point** or not mentioned.

Wimbledon score: 6–2   6–0

In lawn and table tennis you call 6–0 '*six-love*'. What has love got to do with a poor score? It's a little intricate, but let's try: the figure 0 looks a bit like an egg. The word *egg* is *l'oeuf* in French. As *l'oeuf* looks a little like *love*, we have the equation

0 = egg, egg = l'oeuf, l'oeuf = love, love = 0

Voilà!   **0 = love**.

Using similar reasoning, British English has the expression **duck** (from duck's egg) for a zero cricket score. If you are *out for a duck*, you are *out for nought*. In American English you have **goose egg** for the lowest result in school.

Arsenal-Tottenham: 3-0

In all other sports with a point count the figure 0 is called **nil**: the score was three nil. 0 = **nil**.

In some languages the figure 0 is similar to the English word *null*. This has nothing to do with numbers. You can find it in the phrase **null and void**, meaning **not valid**:

> *The lottery was declared null and void when certain irregularities were discovered.*

● The elusive GHOTI

A more relaxed concluding paragraph in this chapter is a contribution attributed to George Bernard Shaw, who shared your opinion that English pronunciation was not exactly the most logical thing in the world. He invented the word GHOTI to show that:

> GH should be pronounced like the **gh** in the word 'tough', i.e. **f**.
> O could sound like the **o** in 'women', i.e. **i**.
> TI ought to be pronounced like the **ti** in 'nation', i.e. **sh**.

Following these 'rules', GHOTI should be pronounced 'fish'!

Not necessarily. Another, newer theory is that when asked to read GHOTI aloud, you should keep your mouth tightly closed, as it has no sound value at all.

Proof:

> GH as in 'though', i.e. not pronounced.
> O as in 'people', i.e. not pronounced.
> T as in 'listen', i.e. not pronounced.
> I as in 'parliament', i.e. not pronounced.

Therefore GHOTI = ————————!

2. Stress

What book are you reading right now? *Perfect Your English*? On which syllable did you put the stress in the word *perfect*? If on the **first** syllable, you made a mistake. That's how the **adjective** is stressed. In *Perfect Your English* you have the **verb** *to perfect*, with stress on the **second** syllable. Surprised?

Many of my foreign friends have a very good English accent. They have no problem with the *th*, the *r* or the *w*, and generally pronounce words beautifully. Yet here and there they lose valuable points by putting the stress on the wrong syllable. English stresses are fortunately not as unpredictable as pronunciation in general.

The examples are best read aloud. When nobody is listening, of course.

● Noun (stress on first syllable)

Verb (stress on second syllable)

Some of the nouns and verbs are not related – an **ob**ject and something to which you ob**ject**, for example – but they are nevertheless given in one line to resolve any doubts. Short sentences or phrases will be useful in your reading exercise.

Noun	Verb
a strong **ac**cent	an ac**cen**ted (or ac**cen**tuated) syllable
a drug **ad**dict	ad**dic**ted to work
our faithful **al**ly	al**lied** nations
a positive **at**tribute	at**trib**uted to negligence
an international **com**bine	let's com**bine** them
her powder **com**pact	the sand is com**pac**ted
outrageous **con**duct	it con**ducts** heat
a minor **con**flict	con**flic**ting reports
a **con**test of strength	the verdict is con**tes**ted
our new **con**tract	she con**trac**ted yellow fever
an old **con**vict	con**vic**ted for embezzlement
a religious **con**vert	con**ver**ted to 220 volts
lost in the **de**sert	de**ser**ted by their friends

a magazine **di**gest	di**gest** your food
her **dis**card was the ace	let's dis**card** the surplus
a 20 per cent **dis**count	you can dis**count** the story
the rear **en**trance	an en**tran**cing dress
our official **es**cort	we were es**cort**ed out
very daring **ex**ploits	he is being ex**ploit**ed
I need only an **ex**tract	the tooth was ex**tract**ed
burning **in**cense	they looked in**censed**
a steep **in**cline	we are in**clined** to agree
an enormous **in**crease	prices were in**creased**
sounds like an **in**sult	don't in**sult** him
an unidentified **ob**ject	I ob**ject** strongly
our building **per**mit	they won't per**mit** it
a useful **pres**ent	pres**ent** arms!
farm **pro**duce	pro**duced** on the farm
very fast **prog**ress	they pro**gressed** slowly
an interesting **pro**ject	our pro**ject**ed expenditure
limited **pros**pects	pros**pect**ing for gold [Am.: **pros**pecting]
a world **re**cord	re**cord**ed for posterity
uncollected **ref**use*	we can't re**fuse**
an export **re**ject	it was re**ject**ed
a tricky **sub**ject	sub**ject**ed to a test
a building **sur**vey	they sur**veyed** the site
the principal **sus**pect	I'd never sus**pect** him
a sudden **trans**fer	she was trans**ferred** to Paris

● **Noun (stress on first syllable)**	**Adjective (stress on second syllable)**
a pop **con**cert	con**cert**ed action
alcohol **con**tent	they seemed con**tent**
blue **over**alls	our over**all** impression
the London **Under**ground	they live under**ground**

---

*Refuse is what you throw away. It is also called **rubbish, garbage** or **trash**.

- **Adjective (stress on first syllable)**

  She is **ab**sent
  abstract paintings
  a **fre**quent visitor
  she speaks **per**fect Dutch

Verb (stress on second syllable)

  he ab**sen**ted himself
  the figures were ab**strac**ted
  they fre**quent** this bar
  per**fect** your Urdu!

- **Differences between British English and American English**

Nouns

British English	American English
ad**dress**	**ad**dress
alu**mi**nium	alu**mi**num (no 'i'!)
detail	de**tail**
frontier	fron**tier**
in**qui**ry	**in**quiry
in**tri**gue	**in**trigue
la**bo**ratory	**la**boratory
maga**zine**	**ma**gazine
millio**naire**	**mil**lionaire
Portu**guese**	**Por**tuguese
Pyre**nees**	**Py**renees
re**cess**	**re**cess
re**search**	**re**search
tele**vision***	**te**levision
vermouth	ver**mouth**

Verbs

frus**trate**	**frus**trate
harass	ha**rass**
lo**cate**	**lo**cate

Secondary stresses in American English

In British English the endings **-ary, -ory**, and **-ery** are often telescoped and more or less swallowed up. In American English

---

*Now increasingly also **te**levision.

they are enunciated separately. The word **cemetery**, for example, sounds like 'semmatree' in British English, but more like 'sem-me-ta-ry' in American English, i.e. four syllables, with nearly even stress on all. Words like **voluntary, necessary, category**, etc. are treated in a similar way.

• Words that can be stressed in two ways

ab**do**men	**ab**domen
comparable	com**pa**rable
controversy	con**tro**versy
	(British English)
de**co**rous	**de**corous
formidable	for**mi**dable
	(British English)
hospitable	hos**pi**table

• Mixed bag

The adjective *alternate* is stressed on the second syllable; the verb *to alternate* on the first.

Berlin in Germany is stressed Ber**lin**. Berlin (USA) is stressed **Ber**lin. When the German Berlin is used as an adjective, the stress changes to the first syllable: *A **Ber**lin Diary*. It is **Prin**cess Margaret when a name follows. Otherwise the stress is on the second syllable:

*I believe she is a prin**cess** or something.*

When you have **New, Old, North, West, Little, Lower**, etc. as adjective or prefix with geographical names, you do not normally stress these, i.e. you do not say '**New** England' to point out the difference from the England on the other side of the Atlantic. Names like **New Zealand, Northampton, Westchester, Great Yarmouth**, and so on, have even stress on all syllables.

The most common mistakes heard in my travels? Here they are:

Heard	Should be
component	com**po**nent
display	dis**play**

distribute	dis**tri**bute
insurance	in**sur**ance
percentage	per**cen**tage
to **per**fect	to per**fect**
New York	New **York** (or even stress)
necessary	**ne**cessary (but ne**ce**ssity)

8

Which of the two?

Mistakes are frequently made in English when you have the choice between two similar words. Is it *continuous* or *continual*? Other pairs may not look alike, but you may ask yourself when you can't fall asleep at three o'clock in the morning: 'What *is* the difference between *client* and *customer*?'

Here is a collection of some tricky pairs that may have bothered you in the past.

Adhesion/adherence

Both have a common verb **to adhere** which means **to stick**. **Adhesion** is the **physical** condition:

This paint has excellent adhesion.

Adherence has the **figurative** sense:

They are to be admired for their adherence to moral principles.

Admission/admittance

Admission means **permission of entry**. It can be physical:

The admission of immigrants had to be restricted.

It can be the price of a **ticket**:

Admission: £1.50.

Admittance is a formal term for **right of entry**. A notice that says NO ADMITTANCE on a door means KEEP OUT.

Using the two words together, you could say that a drunk was refused admittance to the show even though he had paid his admission.

To affect/to effect

These two verbs are often mis-spelled, also in English-speaking countries. The reason may be that they have a common noun: **effect**.

To affect means **have an influence** on something:

The strong wind affected the tennis game.

To effect means **cause, bring about**:

The new manager effected an improvement in the EDP Department.

The adjective **affected** can also mean the same as in many other languages: displaying mannerisms that are not natural.

Amiable/amicable

Although your Latin may be rusty these days, you probably still recognize that these two words must have something to do with 'friend'.

Amiable is always applied to **people** who are **pleasant, easy-going, likeable**. **Amicable** cannot be applied to people, only to **relationships** that are **friendly**. Using both words in one sentence, you could comment:

The two amiable proprietors had an amicable business relationship for many years.

Beside/besides

Beside refers to the **physical** situation. It means **side by side, close to**:

He sat beside her.

Still in a sense physical, but used figuratively are:

Beside the point, meaning **irrelevant**,

and the slightly old-fashioned expression:

*He was **beside himself** with rage,*

which indicates a really boiling temper.

Besides is used in two ways: as an adverb in the sense of **moreover, in addition**:

He has not improved; and besides, he does not seem to care.

Less frequently, it can also be a preposition, meaning **apart from**:

Besides curtains, they also sell sun blinds.

Blink/wink

Both have something to do with the movement of the eyelids. **Blink** is what you do involuntarily every few seconds with both eyelids. A wink is the lowering of one eyelid to give a **signal**. Here is the difference, shown in artistic form in its three stages:

Not quite logically, **wink** (not **blink**) is used in phrases connected with sleep:

I didn't sleep a wink last night = got **no sleep** at all.

They had forty winks after lunch = a **brief sleep**, a **nap**.

Blush/flush

When you are temporarily red in the face, it can be the result of either *blush* or *flush*. **Emotion** (embarrassment or shyness) makes you **blush**:

When he complimented her on her first-class work, she blushed.

Physical exertion causes you to be **flushed**:

She was flushed after running for the last bus.

An in-between situation can exist when you are red in the face because of a mixture of emotion and physical causes. You can, for example, be flushed with excitement.

Childish/childlike

Childish is no compliment. It means **immature**:

His reaction to their mild letter of complaint was very childish. (He sulked for months!)

Childlike can be a compliment, as its meaning of *like a child* refers to **positive attributes** such as innocence, grace, honesty, etc.:

The movements of the dancers had a childlike grace.

Contents/content

Contents is what you find in some form of **container**: the contents of a bottle, bag, box, book, and so on. Make sure you use the plural. In other languages you use the singular. **Content** is the **presence of one element in another**, often expressed as a percentage or proportion: the water content in my glass of wine, the copper content in an aluminium [Am.: aluminum] alloy, etc.

The **content** (singular) of a book or a speech can also mean the **essential element**:

It's a bestseller, but devoid of serious content.

Continuous/continual

Continuous means **without interruption, all the time, non-stop**:

There is a continuous performance from four to eleven.

Continual means **very frequent**:

They are notorious for their continual complaints.

Nobody can complain 'continuously'. People have to sleep some of the time.

Note: **Constant** is near in meaning to **continuous**, but not quite non-stop: her constant companion, constant headache, constant worries.

Customer/client

A **customer** buys **goods** and pays a **price**. A **client** buys **professional services** and pays a **fee**.

Professional services are provided by lawyers, architects, accountants, and various consultants, who do not sell goods but give information or advice in some form or other. Doctors and dentists are also part of the professional group. They have **patients** and charge a **fee**.

The English word **profession** means the same as in your language:

He is a carpenter by profession.
She is a professional tennis player.

The English expression **the professions**, however, refers to a group of activities that require **academic** training, a university education:

He is not sure yet, but will probably go in for one of the professions.

Definite/definitive

Definite means **certain, clearly defined**:

Their arrival time is now definite.

Definitive means **final**, often implying not merely the last, but also the best:

It is probably the definitive book on the Vietnam war.

This sentence means that the author has treated the subject so much better than anyone before him, that it will be *the* book on the war in Vietnam.

Using the English **definitive** may be specially tempting to speakers of languages that have 'definitivo', 'definitiv', and similar words. Please remember that the correct equivalent is **definite**.

Department/division

In one of your idle moments – perhaps when sitting at your desk in the office this morning – you may have been wondering whether there is any difference between these two words.

If you are thinking about the organization in a company, American usage prefers **division** for all but the tiniest sections in a firm:

Chemical Division
Marketing Division
Export Division.

British usage has always preferred **department**, reserving **division** for major integrated parts of a company:

Export Department
Marketing Department
Consumer Products Division.

Division, with its military connotation, somehow sounds more impressive than **department**. That must be the reason why companies outside North America tend to use it increasingly for modest departments that would previously not have qualified for this distinction.

This idea that the division is bigger than department is reversed when it comes to the government. Then **department** is really the big thing. The **State Department**, for example, is that vast United States ministry known in other countries as Ministry for Foreign Affairs, Foreign Ministry, Ministry for External Affairs, and similar more descriptive terms. (It is called **Foreign Office** in the UK).

Distinct/distinctive

Distinct is **clear**: a distinct difference, distinct outline, distinct advantage. **Distinctive** means being **different** from something else. You may need a distinctive trademark, distinctive design, distinctive slogan, i.e. something that stands out, something that people will recognize because it is striking.

Combining the two, you could say that a signpost can be made more distinctive by using more distinct lettering.

Eatable/edible

Eatable means that something is of a **quality** suitable for eating. As comment on somebody's standard of cooking it expresses a very low degree of enthusiasm:

How did you like her dinner?

Well, it was eatable. . . .

Edible means suitable for human consumption, because the food contains nothing that will poison you. Illustrated books will enlighten you on edible and **in**edible mushrooms, for example.

Negative form of **eatable: uneatable.**

Economic/economical

Economic refers to the science of **economics**. You can have economic factors, an economic return on investment, an economic business. People can never be called economic.

Economical is the opposite of wasteful and can be applied to people and objects. If money is involved, **economical** is simply **money-saving**.

He is very economical in his buying habits = **spends little**.

The new engine is highly economical = **uses little** fuel.

In a court case someone once admitted that he had been *economical with the truth,* a very elegant way of saying that he was not telling the whole truth.

Efficient/proficient

Efficient is **competent, well organized**. It can be applied to people or things:

She is incredibly efficient.

Proficient means **qualified, skilled**, an **expert** at something. It can be applied to people only:

They are proficient in (at) braille.

It is quite possible that someone proficient (who knows his special field) can at the same time be inefficient, if he forgets to answer letters or has a messy workshop.

E.g./i.e.

These two abbreviations are often confused. An **example**, a **limited selection** is introduced by **e.g.** This is short for 'exempli gratia'. When reading it aloud, say *for example, for instance* or, if you insist, 'ee-gee':

They manufacture medical appliances, e.g.
syringes, catheters, surgical instruments, etc.

An **explanation**, a **definition** is introduced by **i.e.** ('id est'). Say 'eye-ee', 'namely', 'that is' or 'that is to say' when reading it aloud:

They have three major product lines, i.e. chemicals, pharmaceuticals, and cosmetics.

Egoist/egotist

The extra **t** makes a considerable difference, although both people are not wildly attractive characters. An **egoist** is the same kind of person you have in other languages; someone who thinks only of himself; someone who is **selfish**. An **egotist** (remember that **t** to denote *talking*) is a person who **talks a lot** about **himself**.

An egotist is probably also an egoist, but an egoist is often no egotist. (He keeps very quiet while he is gobbling that pound of chocolates when nobody is looking.)

Electric/electrical

Electric describes **individual products** that are in some way **actuated by electricity**:

electric light   electric train   electric motor, and so on.

It includes electric eel and electric shock. **Electrical** describes anything else **connected with electricity**, also the **collective nouns** of electricity-powered products:

electrical engineer   electrical science   electrical appliances
electrical phenomenon, and so forth.

Using the two adjectives in one sentence you would be quite correct in saying:

Our electric toaster is an electrical appliance.

Note: In some languages you have the abbreviation 'el-motor'. This does not exist in English. It is always **electric motor**.

Error/mistake

The difference between the two is not enormous, but **error** is usually less serious than **mistake**.

If I ask you to multiply 312 by 758, and you tell me that the result is 236,498, you probably made a slip when typing the last digit. I would call this an **error**. If you tell me that you bought a company two years ago, which has so far lost two million dollars, you made a mistake. (How could you do such a thing?)

Every/each

Here is something for the connoisseur. **Every** applies to an **unspecified** number of objects. **Each** is usually better when the number of objects is **known** or **small**.

Examples: *In Glasgow you find a pub in every block.*

You do not know the number of blocks in merry Glasgow. You are making a general statement, therefore **every**.

There is an entrance at each corner of the park.

You know that the park has four corners. Therefore **each**.

Here are two nearly identical sentences with a difference in interpretation:

Every airliner has a Certificate of Airworthiness.

All airliners have it. A general statement.

Each airliner has a Certificate of Airworthiness.

Each single aircraft I am talking about; presumably of one specific company, production run, type.

Exceptional/exceptionable

Exceptional is, of course, something that is an exception, **unusual, abnormal**:

We had an exceptionally wet summer three years ago.

Exceptionable is mainly used in the negative form **unexceptionable**. It means **acceptable**, not open to objection:

I have read the conditions. They seem unexceptionable.

To take exception to something means to **disapprove**, raise an objection.

You will probably find exceptionally good weather unexceptionable.

Fast/quick

These two are not completely interchangeable. **Fast** refers to **speed** of movement or action:

A fast train.

A fast run.

Quick relates to the **length of time** an event or action takes:

A quick meal.

A quick reply.

Using both adjectives in one sentence, you could say:

They had a quick crossing because the boat was fast.

He had a quick meal because he is a fast eater.

Exception department: **quick** can mean speed if the movement or action is not sustained, abrupt:

Try to get that window seat! Quick!

or

He is an odd kind of man, with very quick, nervous movements.

Farther/further

Good news! **Further** can now safely be used in place of **farther** although there is a difference according to the dictionary. **Farther** is the comparative of **far** and thus relates to **physical distance**:

London-Eastbourne is farther than London-Brighton.

Nobody will be worried if you use **further** here. **Further** means **additional, other, subsequent**:

We have to await further developments.

Floor/storey [Am.: story]

Floor indicates the **position** in a building: second floor, top floor, etc. **Storey** refers to the **height** of a building: a ten-storey apartment block.

In future/in the future

In future means **from now on**, starting now:

All goods will in future be sent by our own transport.

In the future is more vague and means at some unspecified **later** date:

We hope to be able to send all goods by our own transport in the future. (As soon as we can afford three trucks.)

While talking about 'the future', here is one small point you may find interesting. If today is the 5th of the month and you want to say that something will happen on the 26th, you have three ways of putting it:

In three weeks.
In three weeks from now.
In three weeks' time.

When using the last version, please don't forget the apostrophe in writing:

In five hours'/days'/months'/years' time.

Historic/historical

Historic refers to something important that is or will be **remembered in history, recorded by history**: a historic meeting, historic decision, historic voyage, historic landmark, etc. **Historical** is the adjective for all other purposes when you mean **to do with history**: a historical play, historical novel, historical costumes, etc.

Human/humane

Human is the more frequent adjective when referring to matters concerning **homo sapiens**: human habitation, human failings, human ancestry, etc. **Humane** means **benevolent, compassionate**: humane treatment is decent treatment.

If/whether

In many constructions these two words are indeed interchangeable:

I am not sure if this is possible,

or

I am not sure whether this is possible.

The main difference is that **whether** is always assumed to be followed by **or not**. This means that in questions or requests an answer is usually expected. Take these two almost identical sentences:

Let me know if you can come.

The stress is here normally on the word *know*. The speaker or writer tells you here: *If you can come, please let me know.* (If you can't, don't bother to notify me.)

On the other hand, someone may tell you:

Let me know whether you can come.

This says: *Please let me know whether you can come or not.* An answer is required.

Imply/infer

Many people think that these two mean the same thing. There is a difference worth remembering.

Imply is what the speaker or writer does: says, suggests, **insinuates**, hints at something that can be interpreted in a certain way. **Infer** is what the listener or reader does: **concludes**, guesses, deduces, thinks.

Taking the two together, you could say:

When she implied that she was very busy, he inferred that he was not welcome.

The two nouns are **implication** and **inference**. (**Inference** has the stress on the first syllable. The remainder is pronounced like the same syllables in 'reference'.)

Incredible/incredulous

Both have something to do with **believe**, as anyone will tell you who has ever battled with Latin.

Facts, events, reports, and other **impersonal** things are **incredible** (or **credible**): they are hard to believe. **People** can be **incredulous**, i.e. they don't believe what they read or hear.

The two together:

He was incredulous when he heard their incredible story.

Insulated/isolated

English has two words, where other languages only have one. **Insulated** is the technical word: protected against **electricity, heat** or **cold**. **Isolated** is the general adjective. It is used for anything that is **separated, kept apart**:

When the tide rose, he found himself isolated on a tiny rock.

You have heard of an **isolating switch**? This has nothing to do with insulation but **isolation**, because it **separates** circuits.

Last/latest

Last denotes **final** or **most recent**. This can be confusing: *her last book* can mean that she never wrote any others or that it is her most recent literary effort. **Latest** makes the position quite clear; it means the **most recent** of several, leaving open the possibility of more to come: our latest model, their latest publication, her latest hairstyle.

There is obvious scope for ambiguity in the many languages that have only one word for **last**.

Less/fewer

An interesting pair. **Less** is followed by a noun in the singular and is used when referring to extent, degree, and **quantity in bulk**. **Fewer** is followed by a noun in the plural and refers to quantity in terms of **units**.

A few examples:

less milk	*fewer bottles*
less help	*fewer assistants*
less money	*fewer pesetas*
less expense	*fewer bills*
less weight	*fewer kilos*

Libel/slander

Both mean the same: making false, damaging statements; **telling lies** about a person or company.

Libel, however, is something **written**, usually a newspaper article. **Slander** is spreading all that nasty information **verbally**. As it is much easier to prove written defamation than word-of-mouth comment, you will sometimes hear about a libel suit; hardly ever about legal action involving slander.

Lie/lay

These two are often mixed up in English-speaking countries, mainly in the past tense.

There are two separate verbs: **to lie** means **to recline**, to be in a **horizontal position**. It is **irregular: to lie – lay – lain**.

He likes to lie in bed until lunchtime.

The book lay on the shelf.

The ring must have lain on the counter.

It is an **intransitive** verb, i.e. you cannot add a direct object. You may lie on the floor, if you like that sort of thing; but you cannot 'lie something on the floor'. You then need the other verb: it is **to lay**, which means **to place, to put**. It is irregular: **to lay – laid – laid**. It is **transitive**, i.e. it can be followed by a direct object:

Let me lay the table.

She must have laid it there by mistake.

The ostrich laid an enormous egg.

A frequent mistake is saying 'he lay it on the table'. As you now know, it should be:

*He **laid** it on the table.*

Note Just to complete the picture, there is also a third verb **to lie**, which means telling something that is **not true**. It is regular: **to lie – lied – lied**.

Long/lengthy

These two often mean the same, except when referring to something you have to read or listen to, when **lengthy** can imply that you were **bored**:

He produced a lengthy report after his trip to Korea.

Many pages, but not terribly entertaining.

Much/many

In the same way as *less* and *fewer*, *much* applies to **bulk**, mass, an unspecified quantity. **Many** are objects you can **count**:

much money	*many guilders*
much demand	*many orders*
much traffic	*many cars*
much food	*many dishes*

The same definition applies to **much worry/many worries** and **much trouble/many troubles**. **Much worry** is the total extent of your problems. **Many worries** are the individual headaches that bother you.

Murder/assassinate

The difference is simple: you and I are murdered. Statesmen and other **important** people are **assassinated**.

Offer/quotation

An **offer** is more general. It can be verbal or in writing. It is often applied to bulk goods with a variable price:

We are interested in an offer for 250 tonnes of prime bleached sulphite pulp.

The American unit of weight is still called **ton**.

A **quotation** is more formal. It is always in writing and is the best term for a **detailed proposal**:

Please let us have your quotation for Model KLB 2000 with power feed, rotary table, and grinding attachment.

An **offer** is often based on a price calculation, a **quotation** on a fixed price list.

Outside the office you also have a verbal **offer** when you tell someone how much you are prepared to pay. For a used car, for example. An offer at an **auction** is called a **bid**.

Official/officious

No problem with the adjective **official**, which means the same as in other languages: properly **authorized**. **Officious** describes a person who is over-keen to give service, who rushes around and upsets people. The best noun would be **busybody**. An officious waiter can ruin your carefully planned business lunch, if your guest becomes irritated and is in no mood to discuss the proposed contract.

Older/elder

Older is the general-purpose comparative form of old: *old – older – oldest*. **Elder** and eldest refer to family members and are always attributive adjectives: *my elder brother, my eldest sister*. You cannot say 'my brother is elder than I'.

On time/in time

On time means **punctual**:

The train is on time.

In time means **not late**, before the last minute. **In good time** gives you a little extra:

We should get a window seat if we get there in (good) time.

Passed/past

Identical pronunciation can cause mistakes; **passed** is a **verb** form, the simple past or past participle of **to pass**:

She passed the test.

They passed over the bridge.

Past is here a **preposition**, applied to **time** or **space**:

It is now half past ten.

The ball whistled past the goal post.

Practical/practicable

Practical has to do with **reality**, with **practice**, with a **good idea**:

It seems the only practical solution.

You are a practical person if you can knock a nail into the wall without hitting your thumb. **Practicable** means **possible,** something that can be **put into practice**:

This idea is unfortunately not practicable.

This means *it can't be done*. A practical suggestion may not be practicable.

Negative versions: **unpractical** and **impracticable**. ('Impractical' can be found in American English.)

Practically is colloquial for **almost**:

The book is practically finished.

Price/prize

Price is, of course, the **value** of something in terms of money or effort. **Prize** is what you receive as reward in a **competition**. If you come first in a race, you will receive First Prize, complete with that **z**.

The other Teutonic languages and French have only one word for the two.

Principle/principal

As these two sound completely alike, spelling mistakes are not uncommon. **Principle** is a noun and means the **motive** guiding an **action** or **attitude**.

It looks narrow-minded, but we have to respect his principles.

It can also be the **basic element**:

I am not worried about the extra 50 cents. It's the principle that bothers me.

Principal as adjective means **main, chief, first, foremost**:

Their principal export is bananas.

As a noun it means the **head** of an **institution**, usually of a school or college:

Let's see the Principal about Willie's bad exam results.

In business an agent may refer to the firm or person he **represents** as his principals:

We are authorized to sign on behalf of our principals.

Question/query

A **question** is a straight request for information. The person asking it may know something about the subject; he may know nothing. A **query** is the result of some doubt in the mind of the speaker or writer who usually knows something about the subject.

Clever you and I, listening to the lecture on 'The Advantages and Risks inherent in Pressurized Water System Nuclear Reactors', may afterwards raise a query. Jack over there, who slept solidly throughout the talk, will wake up and ask a question.

Readable/legible

Readable is easy to read because of **style**:

The highly complicated subject was treated in a readable manner.

If you want to make sure that your books are read by a wide

audience, you must make them readable, i.e. easy to understand, a pleasure to read. **Legible** is also easy to read, but because the printing or writing is **clear**:

Some pages in this old bible are hardly legible.

Small/little

Small is the **neutral**, general-purpose word, but **little** has an **emotional** element and conveys a personal attitude to the object.

They have a small fox terrier

describes size in a detached, matter-of-fact way.

You should see their little cocker spaniel!

indicates that the speaker is rather fond of the little fellow.

Another use of **little**, often unconnected with physical size, is as reinforcement of a negative opinion. When you say 'He is a nasty man!', you are obviously not over-impressed by his charm. When you hiss 'He is a nasty little man!', he must be very nasty indeed.

Large/big

The difference is the same as that between *small* and *little*. **Large** is for **sober** comment; **big** for a more **personal** or emotional opinion.

An advertisement for a house, for example, may mention '*large dining room*'. When you have seen it, you are likely to tell your friends: '*It's got a big dining room*'.

Stimulus/stimulant

As you can guess, these two words have something to do with getting things to move a bit faster, raising the interest level and other developments in the right direction. **Stimulus** is the **abstract** term:

His enthusiasm was a tremendous stimulus to all of them.

Stimulant is the **concrete** article, usually something you swallow to prevent you from going to sleep.

Tall/high

Both mean a certain distance from the ground. **Tall** implies a **narrow base**, something **slender**: a tall chimney, a tall mast, a tall person. **High** has a base of a certain **width**: a high wall, a high mountain, a high fence.

When you are in doubt about someone who is tall but by no means slender (Fatty weighs 150 kilos), call him **big**. If a person is described as 'high', it means that he or she has had too much alcohol or drugs.

Uninterested/disinterested

These two are very often mixed up in newspaper articles and even in books written by people who should know better. The difference is quite clear and should definitely be preserved.

Uninterested means **lacking in interest**, by far the more frequently used of the two. **Disinterested** means **unbiased**, impartial, without self-interest or personal motive that could influence your attitude.

The judge and jury in a court room must be interested in the case being tried, but must at the same time be disinterested. If a company is on trial and one of the jurors owns shares in it, he could not claim to be disinterested, i.e. to be free from the thought that an adverse verdict might hurt his pocket.

    uninterested = **lack of interest**
    disinterested = **disinterest**

Very/much

Very usually qualifies an **adjective** to indicate **degree**: very funny, very deep, very loud, and so on. **Much** qualifies **participles** to indicate **degree**: much admired, much discussed, much appreciated, and so forth.

Very can also be used to qualify a few **participles** that have assumed the meaning of adjectives. All of these have something to do with **emotions** or **state of mind**:

very pleased
very alarmed

very worried
very frustrated
very impressed
very elated

Whenever you are in doubt about **very** or **much**, use a simple trick: say **rather** (weaker than very/much) or **greatly** (stronger than very/much). They usually fit: *greatly perturbed, rather bothered, greatly underrated,* etc.

Waste/wastage

Waste is usually **avoidable**: a waste of food, money, time, etc. **Wastage** is generally **unavoidable**. It is the natural loss of a substance through evaporation, normal leakage, and similar causes: wastage of fuel in a tank, water in a cistern, and so on.

Whisky/whiskey

Whisky is from **Scotland; whiskey** from **Ireland** or **North America**.
   Plurals? *Whiskies* and *whiskeys*, respectively.

Sometimes you have the choice between three or even four vaguely similar words. Which do you choose?

Beautiful/handsome/pretty

Generalizing a little, I recommend **beautiful** for male babies and female persons of all ages.
   Handsome is suitable for males beyond the baby stage and women of slightly advanced age when beauty may be combined

with a certain dignity. The description 'a handsome girl' usually indicates a cautious assessment by the speaker, i.e. the girl has perhaps a bit of a horse face, but is otherwise not too repulsive. . . .

Pretty is applied to small girls and young women. If you are a woman of forty, you will prefer to be called pretty rather than handsome.

Multi-purpose, uni-sex adjective, suitable for babies as well as grandmothers or grandfathers of 80? **Good-looking**.

Boat/ship/vessel

A **boat** can be of any size, from a rowing boat to an ocean liner. Be careful with professionals, however, because you will not be asked to the captain's table again after telling the master that his forty-thousand ton liner is a beautiful 'boat'. The correct word is **ship**, an ocean-going vessel. **Vessel** is the formal or generic term.

Former/ex/late

Former means still alive but **no longer in the same job** or position: our former manager, a former employee, one of my former pupils, etc.

Ex- means the same as former, but often with the implication that the departure was **not quite voluntary: ex-husband, ex-President, ex-mayor**, etc.

The **late** Jock MacTavish does not mean that Jock arrived at 4.30 when he should have been there at four o'clock. It means that he is **dead**. You do not need **late** when it is generally known that a person is no longer alive:

It is attributed to President Truman

but

It belonged to her late grandfather.

Journey/voyage/trip

Journey is **any** kind of **travel** of a certain distance. **Voyage** looks like the French 'voyage' but means **travel by sea** only. Both terms have lost the race against **trip**, that very short and ordinary-looking word. **Trip** used to mean a short journey by **land, sea** or **air**. Now it can be travel of any distance:

We are going on a trip to the mountains. (23 miles)

Have a good trip! (They are flying around the world.)

Trip is not suitable when referring to distance or time. You then need the other two words:

She has a journey of eight miles to get to the office.

Europe–Australia can mean a voyage of five weeks.

Likely/apt/liable

Likely indicates that something is **expected** to happen, that it is probable:

The application is likely to be approved tomorrow.

Apt is applied to people or animals and denotes a **tendency**, a characteristic action or reaction:

She is apt to be offended by your lack of interest.

Liable is similar in meaning to **likely** and **apt**, but has a **negative** connotation, i.e. that something unpleasant will happen:

If you use this shampoo, your hair is liable to fall out.

Packet/parcel/package/pack

Packet is usually **small**, often machine-wrapped:

A packet of envelopes.

Parcel is of **medium size**, usually what you can carry or send through the post. The wrapping is normally done by an amateur like you and me. **Package** is bigger than a parcel. If you send me three towels, you make a parcel. If you send two dozen, you make a package.

Pack can be the American equivalent of **packet**:

A packet of cigarettes (British) = a pack of cigarettes (American).

It is also a container for easy carrying. A *six-pack of beer*, for example. **Back pack**? That's the modern type of **rucksack**.

Sufficient/enough/adequate/ample

Sufficient is the same as **enough** but more formal. **Adequate** is just enough and no more. 'Our hotel room was adequate' indicates no special enthusiasm. **Ample** is **more than enough**:

Stop! Seven potatoes is ample!

Under/below/underneath

Under is the most common preposition of the three. It describes **situation** or means **less than**:

I found it under the house.
It cost under ten dollars.

Below applies to **situation**:

They live below us. (This can be more than one storey lower)
A fracture below the knee.

It is also used in a few expressions:

below expectations
below freezing point
below his rank
below the belt, etc.

Underneath describes **situation**, usually the immediate under-side:

It was underneath the table top.
They live underneath us. (On the floor directly under ours)

Beneath is little used. It survives in such phrases as 'it was beneath his dignity'.

Wages/salary/fee

Wages are normally paid **weekly** for manual work, piece work or the lower grades of clerical work. A **salary** is paid **monthly** to any other kind of employee.

You pay a **fee** for **professional services**, i.e. work consisting of a specific job and not a fixed work period: *medical fees*, an *architect's fee*, *legal fees*, *audit fees*, and so on.

9

Perfect your idioms

The greatest compliment anyone can pay you about your English is to say that you speak good idiomatic English, and that you can handle the idiomatic phrases used in everyday speech and informal writing.

Many of these are verbal idioms; combinations of ordinary verbs and one or two prepositions. They can be found in all Teutonic languages, but English is specially rich in such expressions, which are often the most natural way to speak or write in a given situation.

Suppose someone is double-parked next to your car. You can't drive off and sit there, drumming your fingers, sounding your horn every ten seconds, and fuming generally. When the driver of the other car finally appears, you will probaly tell him off (unless he is a very big fellow). To *tell somebody off* is by far the best expression for that daring act of yours. The 'straight' words *scold, reproach, rebuke, admonish, reprimand, berate* or maybe even *censure* and *reprobate* sound like my grandfather or just funny.

This presentation of only modern and important idioms should make this vast subject manageable and digestible.

1. Be

To be at it means **working** on something:

He got up at six and was already at it by seven o'clock.

You can also use this combination to express exasperation at somebody's habitual action. If someone insists on telling newcomers about his exploits on vacation and other boring subjects, you may groan:

'Oh, no! He's at it again.'

To be in is a short way of saying **to be at home** [Am.: to be home], at/in the **office** or wherever somebody happens to be:_

She will be at home after six: *She will be in after six.*

He's never in the office before ten: *He's never in before ten.*

Logically enough, the opposite is to be *out*. **To be in** can also mean to be **in fashion**:

Who knows? Longer skirts may be in again next year.

You can also use this *in* as an adjective:

The Stardust Night Club seems to be the in-place this year.

To be in on something means being a **party to a secret** or confidential arrangement:

We can talk openly in front of him. He's in on it.

To be inside is a very unfortunate situation: to be **in prison.** The preposition **off** has many possibilities when combined with **to be**:

The concert is off = **cancelled** [Am.: canceled].

The meat is off = **no longer fit** to eat.

This dish is off = **deleted** from the restaurant menu.

'They're off!' = traditional exclamation at the **races** when the horses have left the starting post.

We're off now = **leaving** now.

She's off her food = has **no appetite** (usually (mainly applied to animals) because of indisposition).

When they push you on to the stage, they may whisper:

You're on now!

to indicate that it is **your turn** to sing 'O sole mio'. **To be through** is mainly American, with growing acceptance in the other

quite off her food...

English-speaking countries. It means **having finished**, either a task or the day's work:

I am through now. Let's go home.

It can also mean a more permanent end, either of a personal relationship:

Vera and I are through,

or of a job. The American announcement:

You're through!

is the equivalent of the British English:

We regret to inform you that we are obliged to dispense with your services at the end of the month.

As soon as you manage to climb out of bed, you are **up**. If you are **up to it**, it means that you are **capable** of doing something:

It looks tricky. I don't think I'll be up to it.

If you are not sure what somebody is doing or intends to do, you may wonder what he is **up to**:

They erected some odd-looking machinery. I wonder what they are up to.

To be with it is modern slang. It means being **up to date**, keeping up with modern trends:

She is doing hang-gliding at weekends. She is certainly with it.

2. Call

Call for means **require, need** etc. in an impersonal sense:

The crisis calls for emergency measures.

You can also form this adjective when complaining about somebody's unjustified action:

Your criticism is quite uncalled-for.

Call forth is **provoke, cause**:

The tax increase called forth a wave of protests.

If your TV set still doesn't work after you have hit it three times, why not **call in** a technician, i.e. **ask for** professional **help**? When it is getting too dark for tennis, you could propose:

Let's call it a day!

as a colloquial way of suggesting an **end** to today's play. **Call off** is the same as **cancel**:

The test was called off at the last minute.

Call on has two possibilities. It can mean a **brief visit**:

When passing through Montreal, we called on her parents.

It can also be used in the sense of **request** someone's **help** or services:

When we need an interpreter, we'll call on you.

3. Come

Come about means happen, result from:

The misunderstanding came about through an incorrect translation.

Come across is **find** or meet by accident:

I came across this rare coin in the Portobello Road.
We came across this expression in a news magazine.

If your rich aunt thinks you are wonderful, you may **come into** a lot of money. **Inherit**. **Come in useful** or **come in handy** mean **prove to be useful**:

The spare distributor cap certainly came in handy during our breakdown in the middle of the night.

When you **come into your own**, you find your right place, **gain recognition**:

He never used his Portuguese, but when the Brazilian football team came to town, he came into his own.

When you pull the handle too hard, it may **come off**. That's easy. Less obvious are two almost opposite meanings:

Although everyone was doubtful, the experiment came off

means that the experiment was a **success**. On the other hand,

The play at the local theatre [Am.: theater] *came off after three days*

reports that the play was **withdrawn** from the stage because it was a failure. You could therefore combine the two by saying that the daring new play did not come off and therefore came off after a few days. '**Come off it!**' is an appeal to **realism**, something similar to '**Don't be silly**' or '**Do you think I am stupid?**':

'£6000 for this old car? Come off it!'

Come round can mean three things. Slowly become **converted** to someone else's point of view:

They disagreed strongly at first, but came round in the end.

Also **recover** after an illness or short period of unconsciousness:

She fainted, but came round almost immediately.

An **invitation** to your home could sound like this:

Come round at five for tea.

Come to is similar to **come round** in the physical sense:

I emptied a bucket of water over his head and he came to immediately.

Come to can also be the same as **amount to**:

The total came to £85.

Come on its own can often be the same as **become**:

Her dreams came true.
He knocked at the hinges and the door came loose.
The dress rehearsal was a disaster, but it all came right on opening night.

When you **come up with** an idea, you **devise** it, present it:

The new assistant came up with an ingenious scheme.

4. Do

The verb *to do* is much more widely used than the same word in other languages. A few groups will help.

• As substitute for another verb

To do can be used in several constructions as a kind of multi-purpose verb. The listener or reader sometimes has to guess what might be meant:

He did Marion's hair = **combed** or **washed** or **gave a permanent wave to**.
Have you done your teeth? = **brushed**.
The painter is doing the upstairs study = **painting**.
She'll do your room later = **tidy up; clean**.
He does the books in the firm = is **in charge of the accounts**.
She is doing a book on graphology = **writing**.

Let's do the sights tomorrow = **go sightseeing**.

They did London in two days = managed to **see** all the worthwhile **sights**.

He is doing a new play = **producing** or **writing** or **acting** in it.

My new car can do 120 miles an hour = **go** at a **top speed** of.

When a policeman stops you because you were driving much too fast, look surprised and say: *'But I was only doing thirty!'* (= 30 miles an hour).

Do can also refer to **distance** in place of speed when talking about driving:

When on vacation we usually don't do more than 400 km a day.

● **To avoid repeating another verb**

I know him better than you do.

Be careful, however, not to put in *do* where it does not belong, i.e. where it does not refer back to a preceding verb. Take this sentence:

We asked for the issue of a written guarantee, and they agreed to do so.

The *do* here has no connection with *asked*. End the sentence after *agreed*. It is also incorrect to use *do* when the preceding verb is *to have* or *to be*. This can easily happen where you have a past participle:

If you have ever experienced a typhoon, as I have done, you will know that tablets against seasickness are not very effective.

No need for *done* here.

• To emphasize

The word *do* gives emphasis to a statement, wish or request:

> *I am sure he did write before visiting them.*
>
> *I do wish she would hurry up!*

'*Sit down!*' is fairly rude. '*Do sit down*', with stress on the first word and not shouted as a command, is just as polite as '*Please sit down*'.

• In questions

Needing no special discussion is the use of **to do** in questions containing a **principal verb**:

> *Does she come here often?*

Equally elementary is the rule that **to do** is not required with verbs that can also be used as auxiliaries:

> *Have they?   Can we?*
>
> *Is he?   May she?*

On the other hand, you may have heard or read '**Do you have** a cigarette?', linking **to do** with **to have**. Why? Although British English used to prefer '**Have you** (got) a cigarette?' the American '*Do you have?*' is now acceptable everywhere. Besides, the **have** is here not an auxiliary but a principal verb meaning **to possess**.

• Prepositional idiomatic and other combinations

Do up can mean several things, similar to the occasionally vague possibilities of **to do** discussed in the first paragraph.

> *It's cold outside. Do up your coat* = **button up**.
>
> *Can you do up these presents for me?* = **pack**.
>
> *I have to do up my shoelaces* = **tie**.
>
> *They have had their house done up* = **redecorated**.
>
> *Please do up my zip* [Am.: zipper] = **close**.

Can do with is the same as **need**, but in positive contexts only:

> *I could do with a new dress.*

'Please do up my zip.'

Nothing doing is a useful short colloquial phrase:

We asked them three times but nothing doing.

This means the same as the rather longer and awkward:

We asked them three times but they refused to agree to our request.

Nothing doing therefore indicates **refusal** or some other failure. When something **will do** it means that it will be **enough**:

Three blankets will do for tonight.

If you can't afford something, I suppose you will have to **do without it**, i.e. **exist without** a certain thing. You can even leave out the word **it**:

There is no camembert this week, so we have to do without.

When you think that something will have the **desired effect**, you can say that it will **do the trick**:

If they don't answer our letters, let's write direct to their parent company. That should do the trick.

Do you know the difference between **doing well** and **doing good**? **Doing well** means **prospering**, making good progress. **Doing good** means doing something of **benefit to others**; something that will get you to Heaven. If your gift to charity enables you to reduce your income tax, someone may comment unkindly:

He is doing well by doing good. . . .

5. Drop

In several languages you have the two-verb combination *to let something fall*. In English you need only one verb when you say:

She dropped the ball.

When you **drop a person**, you **terminate** a relationship:

He was dropped from the football team.

When you **drop a project**, you **abandon** it:

The plan was dropped for financial reasons.

Drop a line is write a **short letter**:

Why not drop me a line on arrival?

Drop in is a casual **visit**, nothing formal:

Drop in on Saturday, if you can.

Drop off is the same as **fall asleep**:

We dropped off during the adagio part of the sonata.

You can also **drop off a passenger** by **stopping** your car and letting him or her get out:

No need to drive all the way to my house. Drop me off at the next corner.

When you **abandon** a group activity, you **drop out**:

When she was told that you can pronounce the letters o-u-g-h- in seven different ways, she dropped out of the English class.

There is also the noun **drop-out** (or dropout) for a person with this lack of stamina: *high-school drop-out, university drop-out,* etc.

6. Fall

If your joke **falls flat**, nobody laughs, i.e. it is a **failure**. (Probably not your fault. The audience is a bit stupid.) If it is a real disaster, someone could comment that you fell *flat on your face*. **Fall for** is positive when referring to a person; negative when connected with an action:

Jack fell for Jill = he fell in **love** with her.

They fell for his explanation = they **naïvely believed** what he said.

When sales **fall off**, they **decline**:

Our sales always fall off in February/March.

Cats are supposed to **fall on** their **feet** no matter how they fall or are thrown. This zoological wisdom can also be applied to people:

Don't worry about him. He'll always fall on his feet.

This shows confidence that he will always get **out of trouble** or achieve final success. **Fall out** with a person means **quarrel**, end a friendship:

He fell out with them over an argument at the card table.

If a project has **fallen through**, you know that it was **not continued**, that nothing further was done about it:

The musical festival fell through for lack of support.

(The *for* here means *because of*.)

7. Get

When asked to describe a typical day's activities, someone could tell you that he usually gets up at seven thirty, gets out of bed, gets washed and dressed, gets his breakfast, gets out of the house, gets on a bus, gets to the office by nine, gets the mail, and gets started to get a day's work done. And so on, until he finally gets home, gets to bed, and gets to sleep.

With a little luck some people may reach ripe old age and use not much else besides the obviously over-worked verb **to get**. Some care is therefore required if you want to preserve your reputation as a writer of some freshness and originality.

Here are a few idiomatic combinations with **to get** that could nevertheless help you in conversation or informal writing.

When you **get around**, you **travel widely**:

Our service engineer visited nine countries in ten days.
He certainly gets around.

If your **relations** with other people are **good**, you can boast that you **get along well** with them or **get on well** with them:

He gets along well with his in-laws.

In-laws is the shortened, colloquial form for **parents-in-law**. **Get at** means **imply, hint, mean**, indicating a hidden or obscure (to the reader or listener) meaning:

This letter makes no sense to me. I wonder what he is getting at.

Get away with has a connection with **get away** (escape), but means that somebody did something illegal or daring **without being punished** or running into trouble:

He pleaded that he was unaware of the new regulations, and got away with it.

They asked for a wage increase of 65% and got away with it!

Someone who **annoys** or irritates you **gets** your **back up**:

His arrogant manner gets my back up every time he calls.

Another combination with **back** is **get one's own back** (with stress on the word *own* for **retaliate**, get one's **revenge**:

> *Their noisy radio has been a nuisance for years.*
> *We are now getting our own back: our son was given a trumpet for*
> *Christmas.*

Get by means **manage with limited resources**:

> *You will find it difficult to get by on five dollars a day.*

You can, of course, **get down** from a ladder; but when **something gets** you **down**, it **depresses** you:

> *Their constant pessimism gets me down.*

Adding two words, you **get down to it**, which means you **start work, apply yourself**:

> *If the report was promised for Friday, I have to get down to it immediately.*

Get the hang of something means **acquire a skill, understand**. It is near-slang, but fully respectable:

> *She is a very bright girl. We explained how the new machine works and she got the hang of it in five minutes.*

Get off the ground has an obvious connection with aviation or maybe ornithology, but can also be used in quite neutral contexts when you mean **succeed**, get started. It is, however, mainly used in negative statements:

> *The project was sound, but it never got off the ground.*

As you know, **get on** means **make progress**, but it can also mean **grow old, get old**; with or without the addition of the words **in years**.

> *I saw him again last week after a two-year absence. He seems to be getting on (in years).*

When somebody has promised to do a job for you, but sits there talking to a colleague, you could **stimulate** activities by shouting *'Get on with it!'* When you **complete** a **job**, finish a task, you **get through** it:

> *Holy cow! I will never get through these invoices today!*

Get up is nothing new to you. It's your fate every morning. It can, however, have two additional meanings:

She was got up as an Indian squaw = **dressed**, often at a fancy dress party.

He got up some form of reception committee = **organized**.

Combinations of **to get** and the noun **wind?** I can offer two possibilities. **Get wind of something** derives from smelling the scent of a person or animal, as a dog does. It therefore means **discover**, usually of an unpublicized intention or secret:

They have all gone. They must have got wind of the fact that we need help with the washing up.

Get the wind up means **become afraid**, get scared:

When he heard the howling wind, he got the wind up.

Most common verbs have several noun forms, but **to get** has few useful ones. A **get-together** is a **party** or **meeting**, usually of modest scope:

They are planning an informal get-together on Saturday night.

Getaway means **escape**, always phrased like this:

They made their getaway in a red sports car.

Here is an extra item for emergency use by female readers. When you are being pestered by a drunk or otherwise obnoxious male, what can you say to get rid of him? *'Please leave me alone'* could be too weak, *'Drop dead'* would be too drastic. **'Get lost'** is just right. Not too timid, not too rude, but conveying firmness and finality. It should be effective.

8. Give

Give away can mean **reveal** unintentionally:

He is a poor poker player. His facial expressions give him away.

They gave away their approximate turnover figures by mentioning monthly production in tons.

Give in implies some kind of surrender, but mainly in the sense of letting somebody do what he wants:

Their children are impossible because their parents always give in to them.

Give out in the normal sense of **distribute** can ultimately lead to a situation where stocks give out, i.e. become exhausted:

Fuel supplies gave out after two days.

Give up is the same as **discontinue**, but when you realize the futility, the hopelessness of something, you can make it clear by adding *as a bad job*:

When I had failed the exam for the sixth time, I gave it up as a bad job.

9. Go

Go all out means **maximum effort**:

She went all out to win the trophy.

Go ahead means not only **make progress**, but can also be used as a request or command when asking somebody to **proceed**:

You are now connected with Tokyo. Go ahead.

Go along with is colloquial for **agree with** a decision, opinion or plan:

The idea sounds workable. I'll go along with it.

Go by has three possibilities:

> *Five years went by before we heard from them* = **pass**.
>
> *You cannot go by appearances* = **judge**.
>
> *We can never go by what they say* = **rely on**.

Go down means **catch, get, succumb to** an **illness**:

> *He went down with hepatitis.*

Something can **go down well** or **go down badly** with an audience: they **like it** or they **don't**:

The joke about horse meat went down badly at the butchers' Convention.

When you are quietly heaping caviar on your crackers at the party, your host may implore you:

> *'Hey! Go easy on* (with) *the caviar!'*

He is asking you to **be careful** with it, **use** it **sparingly. Go for** has three possibilities:

> *Quite suddenly the lion cub went for me* = **attack**.
>
> *And that warning goes for you, too!* = **apply to**.
>
> *I certainly go for these new mini-bikinis* = **approve wholeheartedly** (slang).

In colloquial American you will also find a fourth meaning when you hear:

> *She has everything going for her: looks, charm, and brains.*

This phrase **going for her** means that she has the **advantages**, the personal **assets**, often indicating some envy on the part of the speaker. When you have a **hobby**, practise a **sport** or **other activity**, you **go in for it**:

Last year he broke his leg when skiing. This winter he is going in for chess.

Go off can be three things:

The bomb suddenly went off = **explode**.

The party went off well = **go well, succeed**.

The meat has gone off = **turn bad**.

Go off the deep end has no connection with activities around the swimming pool, because it means **become very angry**.

When he heard about the mistake, he went off the deep end.

When you ask somebody about a person you have not seen for a long time, the reassuring answer may be that he or she is still **going strong**, i.e. **alive and doing well**:

Pete? He is still going strong. I met him in London last month.

If Pete is doing **very well**, he may even be **going great guns**:

He started a restaurant and is going great guns.

Go through can mean two things apart from the obvious *He went through the park*:

The customs officer went through all suitcases = **examine thoroughly**.

When I saw a model of the guillotine, I realized what a salami has to go through = **endure, suffer**.

Go to town is something you can do in the middle of a field without moving anywhere. It means **act in an unrestrained way**:

After the concert the Chamber Music Quartet went to town with 'When the Saints go marching in'.

Go in combination with a few adjectives can mean **become, turn, get**, i.e. indicate a change of condition:

go bad   go sour   go rotten   go mad   go deaf   go blind
go bankrupt   go green (before being seasick)   *go straight* (lead an honest life).

When the gearbox of your car suddenly starts making expensive noises, you can **describe the sound** by telling the mechanic:

It suddenly went 'brrrrrrr'!

(An expensive noise brings you the bad news that the repair will cost a lot of money.) **Go** can also be a noun with many useful possibilities, all colloquial:

Wait! Now it's my go = **turn.**

We can send it in one go = **delivery.**

Have a go! = **try it.**

They are on the go all day = **active.**

It was a success from the word 'go' = **beginning.**

We cannot make a go of it = **success.**

She succeeded at first go = **attempt.**

The last has the plural form **goes**:

She managed to park the car in four goes.

The present participle form **going** means **available** when someone asks you, looking deeply worried:

'Is there any more ice cream going?'

10. Have

In English and other languages you can **take** a bath, **smoke** a cigarette, **eat** a meal, etc., but in conversation and informal writing you may find that someone:

Has a bath.

Has a cigarette.

Has a meal.

An invitation or encouragement is simply expressed by **have** in the imperative:

Have a bath before you go to bed!

Have a cigarette!

Have dinner when you get there!

Anglo-American department: when offering a chair to someone, you say *have a seat* in North America; *take a seat* on the other side of the Atlantic. **Have it in for someone** means **bear a grudge against, dislike** a person, often indicating an unreasonable attitude:

> *I once forgot to invite him to our annual party, and he has had it in for me ever since.*

'Let's **have it out**!' may be the depressing remark by your dentist after examining the back tooth that gave you hell last night. It can, however, also mean '**let us talk openly**' about the trouble, the unhappy atmosphere, the bad feeling between us. Typical example:

> *They haven't spoken to us for months. I have no idea what they have against us. I think we should have it out with them.*

You can't have it both ways is a philosophical remark which means the same as the homely phrase **you can't have your cake and eat it**: you cannot enjoy two advantages that can never go together. Typical situation:

> *You spend money like water and then complain that your bank account is always low. You can't have it both ways.*

In other words, the advantage of big spending cannot go together with big savings. Unless you have a few oil wells, of course. The combination **have** and **on** can mean three different things. The first meaning, the easiest, is **wear**:

> *She had a very attractive dress on last night.*

It can also mean **trick, fool** or even **deceive** someone:

Don't believe a word he says. He is having us on.

Third meaning? Have an **engagement**:

We have nothing on next Sunday. We'll be glad to come.

An odd phrase is **rumour** [Am.: rumor] **has it**. It means that there is a rumour going around:

Nothing is known for certain, but rumour has it that they may close down next month.

11. Knock

There are many idiomatic possibilities, most of them a little slangy. **Knock about** means **travel widely**, often implying different and not very regular activities:

After leaving university, he knocked about the world for three years.

More slangy, it can also mean **available**, lying around in a vague kind of way:

Is there any green ink knocking about?

Knocked about can be the description of something that has seen heavy **wear** and tear:

This armchair looks rather knocked about.

You can be **knocked down** by a car, i.e. **run over**, but at an **auction** acceptance of the highest bid is usually phrased like this:

The glassware was knocked down for eight pounds.

Knock off is always in the slang department, but could occasionally be useful:

We usually knock off at six. = We **stop** work.

He knocked off six sausages and an enormous heap of potatoes. This expresses **amazement** at the amount of food or at the speed with which it was consumed.

I saw him knock off two calculators. = **Steal**.

'Knock it off!' means *'Stop it!'* in situations where something annoys you.

While **knock off** can mean eat quickly, drink quickly is **knock back**:

They knocked back four brandies in five minutes.

12. Lay

I don't think I can lay my hands on $1000 this weekend

tells you that the money is **not** readily **available**. This laying one's hand on something therefore denotes a possibility without special effort. **To lay off** employees means **dismiss** them, sometimes only temporarily:

Four hundred manual workers had to be laid off at Factory B.

'Lay off!' can also be a slangy request to **'Stop it!'** If somebody takes a sip of your beer when your back is turned, you may tell him to *'lay off!'* This is very similar to the 'knock it off!' mentioned above. **Lay on** is a slightly slangy way of saying **supply**:

If you bring the sandwiches, we'll lay on the drinks.

To be **laid up** indicates temporary **inactivity** of people or inanimate objects:

She was laid up for six weeks. = **Ill** in bed.

The ship was laid up for two years. = In port; **out of service**.

Lay out is **spend**. That's why the noun is **outlay**:

The repairs will mean an outlay of £580.

The inverted noun **layout** is arrangement, **design**, etc.:

We have to change the layout of our winter advertisement.

13. *Let*

If somebody does not keep a promise or **disappoints** you in some other way, he or she **lets** you **down**. You could also reinforce your request in this way:

I am counting on you as my partner at tennis on Tuesday.
Don't let me down.

When you **assume a responsibility** that turns out to be a nuisance or unexpected trouble, you **let yourself in** for something. Not easy to translate, but a useful expression to describe your rash act:

When I promised to pay for his friends, I let myself in for something.
He brought along 14 of them!

Pressure in a boiler is reduced by letting steam escape. **Letting off steam** can also be quite non-technical when you want to explain somebody's action:

Take no notice of his bad language; he's just letting off steam.

Always used in negative statements, **let on** means tell, **giving away information:**

I asked him twice about her age, but he wouldn't let on.

14. *Make*

Make, without preposition, can mean **reach:**

Their escape made the front page of the evening paper.

It is also a colloquial version of **to be able to come, to keep an appointment:**

Next Friday? I'm afraid I can't make it.

When you run all the way to the station and manage to jump into the compartment just as the train is moving off, you may shout triumphantly:

'We've made it!'

Make it can be a little stronger by implying not merely reaching a goal but being a **success**:

He has been promoted to marketing manager. Not an easy job, but I think he'll make it.

Less optimistically, you could comment:

Gerry as marketing manager? He'll never make it.

Can you manage to **make ends meet**? This question tries to find out whether you can **live on your income**, have enough money to cover your expenses:

If she takes that job, they will be able to make ends meet comfortably.

Make for can be the same as **move towards**:

During the last few minutes of the film many people started making for the exit.

It can also mean **tend to create**:

The new incentive scheme makes for higher productivity.

When you **succeed**, you **make good**:

He emigrated to Canada and made good after a rough start.

You can also **make good damage** when you **compensate** somebody, either with money or through a repair:

They will have to make good the damage caused by the leaky pipe upstairs.

To make money is to **earn** it, as you know. *How much are you making?* expresses an informal interest in your income. This point is freely discussed in America; top secret in all other countries. **Make of** means **think of** in this kind of sentence:

This letter sounds rather unfriendly. I don't know what to make of it.

What do you make of the new teacher?

When you **run away**, you **make off**, sometimes combined with the word *with* to indicate a theft:

He grabbed the necklace and made off with it in the crowd.

There are four possibilities with **make out**. It can mean **issue** or **produce**:

We made out an application for an import licence.

It can also mean **understand**:

Last week they seemed very happy; this week they look depressed. I can't make them out.

If you can't make a person out, it need not only indicate your lack of understanding, as in the last sentence, but can also mean lack of **visual clarity**:

It may have been Tony, but I can't be sure. It was so dark that I couldn't make him out.

How did you make out? means *How did you get on?*, *What was the result?*. In American English this question can go a little further by referring to success in relations with the other sex. In fact, a **make-out artist** is slang for an expert in the art of seducing women. Questions with **make out** have therefore to be used more carefully when dealing with Americans, as they can easily sound highly indiscreet. **Make over** means **transfer** and can be used in formal contexts:

Most of his fortune was made over to his children before his death.

When you **make up a story** you **invent** one:

This seems hard to believe. I think she made it up.

Adding the pronoun *it* produces the meaning of **settle a quarrel, effect a reconciliation**:

They did not talk to each other for three years, but at last they have made it up.

Adding the preposition *for* gives you the meaning of **catch up** in this kind of construction:

He was last during the second lap, but made up for it by a special burst during the final 100 metres [Am.: meters].

Make yourself at home is what the good host says to his guests when he wants them to **relax** and **feel** as **comfortable** as in their own home:

Why not remove your jacket? Take off your shoes (but not socks). Make yourself at home.

15. Play

This is an interesting verb, because most of its idiomatic expressions have no literal equivalent in other languages.

Since Bill and Betty separated in July, he has been playing around

reports that Bill has had a number of girl friends or other **not** very **serious** personal relationships. If you are not serious about an activity, you are just **playing at** it:

He won't send you a horoscope. He is just playing at astrology.

Play ball means **co-operate** and could even refer to a business arrangement:

I don't like the cartel idea, but I suppose we should play ball and sign.

Play by ear has less to do with the ear than with the brain, because it means playing a piece of music **from memory**. The same phrase can also be used when you want to say that something is done **spontaneously**, without prior planning:

We don't know whether a price reduction of 2 per cent will be enough. We'll have to play it by ear at the meeting.

Play down means **minimize** the importance of an event:

The government played down the accident at the nuclear power station.

Logically enough, **play up** is the opposite, **exaggerate**:

The newspapers played up the accident.

Play up can also be something quite different: misbehave, **make difficulties**; applied to people as well as objects:

When the children played up last night, the parents just smiled tolerantly.

This front tooth has been playing up for the past three days.

If you want to prevent your opponents from seeing that you hold the ace of spades during a card game, hold up your cards, close to your chest. **Playing it close to the chest** is a descriptive expression for being **careful** not to disclose anything of value to others:

They have stopped all visits to their assembly plant.

They are now playing it close to the chest.

Probably because a new model is the big secret.

16. Pull

Pull in and **pull out** can refer to the movement of a road vehicle or train.

The train is pulling into the station

reports that it is slowly entering it.

The train is just pulling out

brings the bad news that you have just missed it. **Pull off** is colloquial for **succeed**:

> *It looks difficult, but I think they'll pull it off.*

Another meaning of **pull out** is withdraw from a commitment, **cancel** an arrangement:

> *He wants to pull out of the poker group.*

People or businesses can **pull through**, i.e. **recover**:

> *It may take two years, but I think the company will pull through.*

Pull up can be the simple **movement** of an object:

> *Pull up a chair and join us.*

When you drive at 70 km past one of those signs that says '40', a policeman may **pull** you **up** for speeding, i.e. **stop** you. It may involve a ticket (fine) or at least a **warning**, as in:

> *The teacher pulled me up about my homework.*

For no obvious anthropological reason **pull a leg** is **tease**, not being serious:

> *Take no notice. They are only pulling your leg.*

When your socks slip down to your ankles, you have to pull them up. When offered as advice or admonition, it means that you should make an **effort to improve**:

> *Bottom of the class again? You'll have to pull your socks up.*

The person so warned may then start **pulling his weight**, i.e. making a full contribution, **work hard:**

> *If these robots don't pull their weight, we may have to use real people instead.*

17. *Push*

Having just pulled, what could be more logical than continuing with **push?** Its idiomatic meanings are for some reason mainly slang. **To be pushed** indicates a **shortage** of something, usually of time:

Sorry, I can't come tonight. I'm terribly pushed.

By adding the preposition *for* you explain what you are short of:

They seem to be pushed for money.

When someone **promotes** the **sale** of a product, he may be said to push it:

His lecture on skin care was interesting, but he was probably pushing his company's new moisture cream.

Similarly, **push** as a noun is an energetic, sustained **effort**:

Sales are very slow. We need a big push during the trade fair.

An aggressive person tends to **push** other people **around**, i.e. tell them what do do, **order** them **about**:

Say something! Don't let them push you around.

*I have to **push off** now* is a highly informal announcement of your **departure**. Equally informal is **getting the push** for being **dismissed** from a job. A **pushover** is a very **easy task**:

The physics exam was a pushover.

A person can also be a **pushover** if he or she is an **easy victim**:

If he refuses, just burst into tears. He'll be a pushover after that.

Are you fit? If not, why not get up five minutes earlier tomorrow morning? Lie flat on the floor, face down, and push yourself up by your arms. Like this happy gentleman:

He is doing **push-ups**. (I prefer the hyphen here. 'Pushups' looks a little strange. Like some special meat dish from the Balkans.)

18. Put

Put across is a useful expression for **explain, communicate, convince** in a usually successful way:

He put his ideas across very forcefully.

She put this tricky subject across in an easily digestible manner.

We all know **put down** in the sense of **write** down, but you can also **put down** other things. When you buy a house, you probably put down an initial **deposit**:

We had to put down 10% when we signed the contract.

You can say that you **paid** 10 per cent **down**. Hence the noun **down payment** for a deposit. Oddly enough, you can also **put up** a sum of money, but this is more in the nature of a **financial guarantee**:

They showed their faith by putting up a bond for $5000.

The difference between putting down and putting up is therefore not very great. Revolutions, rebellions and other upheavals are sometimes effectively dealt with by being **put down**, i.e. **suppressed**:

The revolution was put down without loss of life.

When you have a theory about something and **attribute** it to a certain cause, you **put it down to** something else:

I put their losses down to poor stock control.

You can **put a person down for** something. In that case you write down a name in the nature of a **commitment**:

We'll contribute. Put us down for £200.

Your feet can also be used in idiomatic English. You can **put** your **foot down** (only one) and be **firm, assert** your **authority**:

This pudding tastes of soap. Put your foot down. Send it back!

Put in for something means to **apply**:

She put in for an extra week's leave in July.

Making a tactless remark or some other kind of **blunder**, or **faux pas** is called **putting** your **foot in it**. Someone may comment:

Every time Jim opens his mouth he puts his foot in it.

Anatomically difficult (except for babies); metaphorically easy. **Put off** has more meanings than the elementary one of **postpone**. Something that **distracts** your attention can **put** you **off**:

I can't study while the TV is on. The noise puts me off.

Also distracting but more with the idea of **losing interest**, appetite, sympathy, etc. is **put off** in this type of comment:

It's a famous restaurant but please don't go into their kitchen. It will put you off.

Off-putting is the corresponding slangy adjective:

A look into their kitchen can be off-putting.

Put on means **pretend**, ranging from mild hypocrisy to dishonesty:

He didn't sprain his ankle. I think he is putting it on.

More physical, **put on** can also mean **gain weight**:

Terrible! I put on two kilos over Christmas.

Are you **put out**? I hope not. It means to be **annoyed**. Preposition: **by**.

She seemed rather put out by his innocent remark.

Put up need not only mean **raise** (when you talk about prices), but can also be **accommodate**:

When we missed the last train, they put us up for the night.

Built for such emergencies is a piece of furniture that can be quickly converted from a sofa into a bed. This is a **put-you-up**. (Mainly British English.) When you **tolerate** something, you **put up with** it:

I am not going to put up with this shoddy workmanship.

A person can be **put up to** something. In that case **somebody else** provided the **encouragement**:

> *He would never have the nerve to do such a thing. I am sure his brother put him up to it.*

Don't you want to **move**? Then it is best to **stay put**:

> *I don't want to go out in this weather. I am staying put.*

19. Run

In other languages you have the physical meaning *run to the bus stop*, perhaps the idiomatic expression *run a risk*, and maybe one or two more. In English you can do very much more with this verb.

• The verb without preposition

When you **run a business** or other enterprise, you **manage** it. You may own it or you may be employed:

> *He ran the company for 35 years.*

You can also **run a car**: you **own** it and **use** it regularly. **Running a temperature** is having a **fever**:

> *She has to stay in bed. She is running a temperature.*

When you need a bath, you have to **fill the bath tub** with water. You call this useful act **running a bath**. When the word **running**

follows a time definition, it means **in succession**. Examples:

For ten years running = **every year** during a period of ten years.

Three days running = on three **consecutive** days.

The phrase **in a row** means exactly the same:

Five days running = five days in a row.

(The **row** is here pronounced to rhyme with 'slow'.) When you take someone along in your car, **give** him **a lift** to a certain destination, you **run** him there:

Jump in. I'll run you to the station.

A **hereditary trait**, an aptitude or other characteristic inherited from your parents, may be something that **runs in the family**:

His father is an accomplished violinist. His mother used to be an opera singer. He plays the bongos. Music runs in that family!

• Combined with a preposition

When someone **runs down** a pedestrian, he hits the poor fellow with the vehicle he is driving or riding in. **Run over** is more or less the same. People can also be **run down** by words. It then means **talk badly** about someone, speak in a **derogatory** way. If Dave says to Jack that Tom is hopeless at his job, he is running him down. Are you feeling tired and irritable? You may be **run down**, physically **exhausted**. It can happen to you. It can also happen to a car battery. When you jump into your car on the way to work, singing happily (as you always do in the morning), turn the ignition key and nothing happens, your battery is probably run down. It is likely that your singing will then stop rather suddenly. **Run-down** is a noun and possibly quite useful in business. It means **summary**, usually a verbal report:

Could you please give me a run-down on what happened at the board meeting.

To run for it sounds a little odd. Why the *for it*? It simply means **to run away**:

He grabbed his coat and ran for it.

Run in is near-slang for **arrest**:

He was run in last night for drunken driving.

When you **meet** a person quite unexpectedly, you **run into** him or her:

I happened to run into her on Fifth Avenue.

Run over can also be harmless when it is used to mean **look at** something written, give it a quick check:

Could you please run over this statement.

When you **run through** a sum of **money**, you **spend** it:

He ran through a small fortune during his stay in Las Vegas.

Run through need not cost you a penny, if it means read, sing or act from start to finish, often when **rehearsing** for a performance:

Let's run through this chorus without the orchestra.
We'd better run through the second act again.

Run through can also mean **check, verify**:

Please run through this report before I send it off.

Exhaustion is also implied when something has **run out**, i.e. when the **supply** has **dried up**:

Disaster! We've run out of ice cubes.

When you **run up a bill**, you **create a debt**, usually at a hotel or restaurant:

During our week's stay we ran up a bill of £1100.

The noun **run** is also highly versatile. **In the long run** means **sooner or later, eventually**:

The machine is still working quite well, but it will have to be replaced in the long run.

If something is **ordinary, average, nothing special**, it can be called **run of the mill**:

I expected something sensational after all that publicity, but the new model seems rather run of the mill.

If somebody is very much **better** at something than some other people, he or she **runs rings around** them. A little slangy, but quite suitable for occasional use:

> *She beat all competitors in straight sets. She is running rings around all of them in this tournament.*

20. See

There are several useful meanings without preposition. Let's see:

> 'The capital of Peru?' – 'Let me see. . .' = **Think**.
> 'Five plus six is eleven.' – 'I see.' = **Understand**.
> 'Please see that the door is locked.' = **Make sure**.
> 'Let's wait and see.' = **See (what happens)**.

See can often mean **accompany**:

> *She will see you to the door.*
>
> *The porter will see you out* (of the house).
>
> *He saw her home.*

The last sentence can mean two things, depending on how you interpret the word *her*:

> *Her* = personal pronoun: he *accompanied* her to her home.
> *Her* = possessive adjective: he *had a look* at the place where she lived.

See about can mean **attend to** or obtain information:

> *We'll have to see about visa formalities.*

See off can also mean **accompany**, but suggests absence for a certain period, the more elaborate farewell where you stand waving:

> *We should all see them off at the airport.*

When you stay up until midnight on December 31st, you **see** the New Year **in**. At the same time you **see** the old year **out**. **See to** can be similar to see about for **attend**, do:

> *Don't order the tickets. I'll see to it.*

Apart from **seeing through** a window, you can also see through something in three other ways:

> *Having started the course, she should see it through.* = **Complete** it.
>
> *Two crates of beer should see us through the evening.* = **Be sufficient for**.
>
> *When we read the small print in the contract, we saw through their offer.* = **Detected the trickery** in.

21. Take

Take after means **resemble** in character, not in appearance:

> *He has a terrible temper. I think he takes after his grandfather (who also started throwing plates when upset).*

Take for means **think** in a few constructions. An indigant *What do you take me for?* means *What kind of a (silly) person do you think I am?*

> *When I heard his voice, I took him for a Dutchman.*
>
> *You are her sister? I took you for her mother!*

(The last remark will give you a very low popularity rating.) When you **take in** something, you **absorb knowledge**, acquire information:

> *Our new teacher talks much too fast. It is very difficult to take in everything he tells you.*

When a **person** is **taken in**, it means something quite different: **to be deceived**:

> *We were all taken in by his story about how he lost his wallet on the train.*

Take + it offers several possibilities:

> *I take it that they told you about it*

means

> *I assume that they told you about it.*

When you are able to **take it**, you can **tolerate** something, are **unaffected** by it. This can show **physical** stamina:

It's a very steep climb but she can take it.

It can also refer to **emotional** tolerance, i.e. a thick skin:

They are always very unfriendly to newcomers in that office, but he can take it.

If he accepts this kind of treatment in a **passive** way, he is **taking it lying down**!

Say something! Don': take those insults lying down!

Take it from me is not necessarily a generous offer, but can also mean no more than **believe me**:

They may look poor, but take it from me: they have more money than all of us put together.

You can take off (remove) your jacket, but you can also **take off (depart)** in an aircraft:

The next plane to Frankfurt takes off at 10.15.

It is also possible to **take off a person**. It means **imitate** a **mannerism or voice**:

She can take off Grannie perfectly.

Take on has two meanings. If something takes on, it **becomes popular**, widely accepted:

Our latest fur-lined boots never took on in Hawaii.

When you **take on a person** or a **difficult task**, you **accept the challenge**, i.e. you do not run away:

Although heavily outnumbered, they took on the entire gang.

He must be mad to take on this thankless job.

Take out can mean **obtain** when used in connection with a **licence** [Am.: license], insurance cover or other document. It is then quite formal, not at all colloquial:

They took out a patent on their new lawn mower.

He took out a life insurance policy when he was 30.

When something **exhausts** you, it **takes it out of you**:

I don't mind exercise, but walking all the way to the tenth floor took it out of me.

When exhausted, why not **take it easy**? Yes, **relax**:

Sightseeing? No, I prefer taking it easy today.

This relaxation can also be in the sense of **calming down**, not getting excited:

Don't be upset about it. Take it easy.

When people **take to** you, they **like** you:

The children took to their stepfather immediately.

Take up an activity means **start** it, usually a hobby or sport:

She took up horse riding last year.

As a noun, **to take** has three possibilities. **Takings** is the **money collected**, the gross income. It can be what the owner of a shop [Am.: store] takes home at the end of a day; it can be the amount obtained from a charitable or other collection. **Intake** is what is taken in i.e. **received**:

Today's intake of orders was high.

It can also apply to people. A hospital may refer to an intake of new patients; a training camp to the intake of new recruits. Are you quick on the **uptake**? This near-slang expression refers to the

ability to understand. You can be quick on the uptake; you can be slow on the uptake:

> *Jim is not exactly brilliant, but his younger brother is very quick on the uptake.*

22. Tear

Here you have an interesting colloquial idiomatic meaning: **move fast**:

> *They tore along the motorway at 200 kph.*
>
> *She tore down the lane, pursued by three dogs.*
>
> *He tore up the hill in a cloud of dust.*

You may note two things. Firstly, that you can tear both on foot and in a vehicle; and secondly, that tear is always followed by an indication of **direction**. In the above examples *along, down*, and *up*. You can therefore not implore that madman driving your car 'Don't tear' when you want him to drive more slowly. What you can say ranges from the polite 'Not so fast, please!' to the rude 'Slow down, idiot!'.

23. Turn

When young Claude is listening to some very loud rock music, his long-suffering father may shout *'Turn the damn thing down!'* as a more forceful version of 'Would you be kind enough to reduce the volume of your record player'. Apart from turning down something noisy, you can also **turn down** a **request**, i.e. say 'no'.

> *Our application has been turned down.*

This is by no means colloquial, but a perfectly respectable alternative to the verb *refuse*. **Turn in** can mean **deliver** or **produce** in this kind of report:

> *He turned in a first-class analysis of sales prospects in China.*
>
> *Our team turned in some excellent times during the pre-Olympic trials.*

A **transformation**, usually of a fairly drastic nature, can be described by **turn into**:

The hairy caterpillar turned into a beautiful butterfly.

You can turn on the light, of course, but if a dog **turns on** you, it means he **attacks** you:

I was only pulling his tail in a friendly manner, when he suddenly turned on me.

To **be turned on** can be connected with narcotics to indicate the temporary **stimulus** induced, but you can also be turned on by much more harmless things. In a slangy way:

His clarinet turns me on. = I **love** the way he plays the clarinet.

I am sorry to report that **turn out** has seven different possibilities.

They were turned out of the hotel. = **Evicted** from.
The new manager turned out to be a success. = **Proved to be**.
The customs officer made them turn out their pockets. = **Empty**.
They are turning out 20,000 units a day. = **Producing**.
It turned out that he had no qualifications. = **Became known**.
300 people turned out for the wedding. = **Attended** the wedding.
She is always immaculately turned out = **Dressed** (passive) or **groomed**.

There is also a noun **turnout** for **attendance**:

800 spectators was a good turnout.

You can **turn to** *him for advice* assures you that you can **apply** to him, seek his help. **Turn up** means **arrive**, usually with the implication that someone was late:

They managed to turn up at eleven.

A similar meaning of arriving, but more in the nature of **being found** is in this depressing message:

Your parcel turned up in Perth, Australia, instead of Perth in Scotland.

When somebody has reached a certain age, you could phrase it like this:

Grandma turned eighty last week.

Upturn is an **improvement** in the economy or your personal fortunes. Yes, **downturn** is the opposite. A **turning** is a **road** at an angle to the one you are on. It need not be a secondary, smaller road:

Take the second turning on the right.

A **turnoff** (or **turn-off** in case the joined word looks like something in Russian) is where you leave the road you are on. You may watch out for your turnoff when on the motorway. It can also be a small **side road**:

The industrial area starts at the next turnoff.

As we have just discussed *turn up* for arrive above, it may be useful to add that there is also the slightly more slangy idiom **show up**. It often implies some mild disapproval on the part of the speaker:

They were meant to join us at four, but finally showed up at six.

Airlines may disapprove when a passenger with a confirmed seat fails to arrive. There is a noun for this elusive passenger: **no-show**.

10
Perfect your conversation

This chapter deals with a few conversational expressions you should find useful.

1. Greetings, friends!

Everyday greetings are not quite as international as you may think. Did you know that 'Good day' is not exactly the same as 'Guten Tag', 'Bonjour', 'Buenos días', 'Goedendag', 'Buon giorno', 'God dag', and all the others? Some of the most common English forms of greeting are a little different from those in other languages.

Good day

Be careful: this is **not** an **arrival** greeting, as in other languages. *Good day* is used when **leaving**, but even then not very often. It

(← English →)   (→ Foreign ←)

sounds very formal. When terminating a meeting, the chairman may gather his papers and say *Good day, ladies and gentlemen* before leaving the room.

An abrupt *Good day* can also indicate that the person departing is angry.

Good morning

Logically enough, this is used during the morning hours, but only **on arrival**, i.e. when meeting someone for the first time during the day.

Good afternoon

This serves you during the afternoon, mainly as an **arrival** greeting. If somebody says to you *Good afternoon* very slowly, it can indicate irony about your being late. When used on departing it sounds very formal or (if said abruptly) angry.

Good evening

A little later you have this greeting, but used exclusively **on arrival**.

Good night

This is a **departure** greeting only, used when you will not be seeing somebody again during the same evening or night. You could therefore bid someone *Good night* as early as 8 p.m.

More informal **arrival** greetings are:

Hello (also sometimes written Hallo and Hullo)

This is a general-purpose greeting for people you know. You would not, for example, say it on arrival in a strange office or shop [Am.: store].

Hi (mainly American and Scandinavian)

Much more informal than *Hello*, this is often used when meeting a group of people. At a cocktail party, for instance, you may join three familiar-looking bores near the bar and vaguely greet them *Hi*.

As *Good day* is rather formal as **departure** greeting, here are a few better possibilities when leaving:

Goodbye [Am.: also **Goodby**]

You may have read somewhere that this is only used when you do not expect to see somebody again for a long time, e.g. when emigrating to Australia or leaving for a two-year expedition to the drearier parts of Central Africa. Not at all. Good-bye is also all right when you have to face the same person again the next day.
    Variants are **Bye-bye** and (mainly on the telephone) **Good-bye for now**.

See you

This seems to be the most popular casual greeting of the moment, suitable for use face to face as well as on the telephone.

Take care

This friendly farewell greeting is mainly American. It is less common than the others, but possibly useful for the sake of variety.

Have a nice day!

Although this American farewell wish is usually well meant, it sounds a little odd to visitors from other English-speaking countries.

2. How do you do? How d'you do?

Etiquette and good manners are international. Or at least fairly international since I have no idea how some natives on the Upper Amazon hold their knives and forks. Some aspects of etiquette are a little different in English-speaking countries because of what people there may say or do in certain social situations.

As you may know, the English ritual of introducing people to one another is a little unusual. Let us assume that someone with the very short name of 'A' tries to break the ice between two equally laconic persons called 'B' and 'C':

> A: *'May I introduce Mr B? This is Miss C.'*
> B to C: *'How d'you do?'*
> C to B: *'How d'you do?'*

The two questions *'How d'you do?'* do not indicate the slightest interest in health matters. They are therefore mumbled in a flat monotone, without the usual intonation used when asking a question.

It's a silly performance, I admit, but before you start giggling, may I remind you that a straight translation of what you say in some other languages does not make much sense, either:

- In German: 'Pleasant!'
- In French and Spanish: 'Enchanted!'
- In Dutch: 'How do you make it?'
- In Italian: 'Pleasure.'
- In the Scandinavian languages: 'Good day.'

Any better?

As you may at some time have to play the part of **A, B** or **C**, here are a few comments.

You are A

Here are a few ideas for your introductory repertoire:

> *'Mrs C, may I introduce you to Mrs B?'*
> *'Miss C, I'd like you to meet Mr B.'*

'Mrs C, have you met Mr B?'
'Miss C, this is Mr B.'
'Mrs C, I'd like to introduce you to Mr B.'
'By the way, Miss C, this is Mr B.'
'Oh, this is Mr B, this is Miss C.'

You have some variety here, depending on the degree of informality.

Be sure to observe the following order of priorities: always first introduce a man to a woman. Exception: if the man is very much older, you present the woman first. When you have your grandfather on one side and young Annie, aged 16, on the other, for example.

When introducing people of the same sex to one another, introduce the younger to the older one, if the age difference is considerable.

You are B or C

B and C are more restricted, as we have seen in the very first introduction. In North America they may say 'Pleased to meet you' or 'Glad to know you', but this sounds a little uneducated on the other side of the Atlantic.

Young people, unimpressed by this kind of ritual, may say 'Hi', mentioned in the preceding chapter.

First names are used fairly freely at informal gatherings, even though the people may not be exactly teenagers. In other countries Mr. B may be introduced as 'Professor Doktor Schmidt' and maintain his titles and dignity for the rest of the evening. In English-speaking countries, however, he may be presented:

'Have you met Jack Schmidt?'

and walk around as plain 'Jack' from then on.

The ritual of shaking hands is not as common in English-speaking countries as elsewhere. When you are being introduced informally, especially when meeting a group of people, you need not go from one person to the other to pump hands vigorously. Not shaking hands is never considered bad manners.

On the other hand, you will be pleased to hear that there is far more kissing going on between women and between members of the opposite sex when meeting or saying good-bye. Don't get over-optimistic: it does not mean 'I love you', but is merely a friendly version of 'Hello, nice to see you' or 'Good-bye' among friends.

3. Can I help you?

Someone looks a little lost when entering an office or standing at a street corner. An offer of help in other languages will probably contain the word 'désirer', 'wünschen', 'desiderare', 'önska', 'desear', 'wensen', and others. A straight translation into English could be 'What do you want?'. This sounds very rude.

Your best solution is:

'Can I help you?'

This is a wonderful phrase, suitable for a wide range of situations. It establishes you as a helpful, friendly citizen, not just an inquisitive person. Telephone operators attending to breakdowns or helping callers with difficult connections are often trained to come on the line with 'Can I help you?'.

If purred gently, this question should soothe the most agitated nerves of someone who has been struggling for twenty minutes to call a number.

Other possibilities when approaching somebody in need of help at the office are:

'Are you being attended to?'

'Is there anything I can do for you?'

'Is anyone looking after you?'

Assuming that you have to take the visitor to a waiting room or somewhere else, you may be tempted to say 'Come along, please'. Don't. That's what you would say to a child of five or your poodle. Better ideas:

'Would you come this way, please.'

'May I show you the way.'

'This way, please.'

'Would you like to come this way, please.'

'Would you care to come this way, please.'

If you want to suggest that the visitor should sit down, don't say 'Sit down', not even 'Sit down, please'. They sound like commands. Try the more gentle

'Would you like to take a seat?'

If some waiting cannot be avoided, your next diplomatic move could be:

'I'm afraid you will have to wait a few minutes.'

'Do you mind waiting a few minutes?'

'Mr. Smith won't be a minute.'

This last 'minute' need not be taken too literally. It could be anything up to ten minutes. When busy Mr. Smith is finally ready, you may again escort the visitor, leading the way with any of the phrases given above. When arriving at the right door, your final piece of helpful information could be:

'Here we are.'

4. Don't mention it

'*Don't mention it*' is still being taught as a standard response to an expression of thanks. There are several others:

> '*That's all right.*'
> '*That's quite all right.*'
> '*Not at all.*'
> '*It's a pleasure.*'
> '*You're welcome.*'

'*You're welcome*' is American, but being used increasingly in the other English-speaking countries. '*That's OK*' and '*Forget it*' are more slangy.

When someone thanks you after a party or meal, you could also say:

> '*Im glad you enjoyed it.*'
> '*I'm glad you liked it.*'

5. Hello, hello!

Whether you like it or not, the telephone plays an important part in business and private life. Let's make sure we know the words and phrases connected with the art of telephoning.

The main parts of the telephone are the **receiver** (the part you lift off the **cradle**) and either the numbered **keys** (to *press*) or the **dial** (to *turn;* or just to *dial a number*).

Your connection is called a **line**. If you cannot hear much, you complain about a **bad line** or a **poor line**. You ask '**Please give me a line**', if the switchboard has to plug you in before you can dial yourself. If the people you are calling are talking to somebody else, you say that the **number is engaged** in British English, that the **line is busy** in American English.

Other languages probably have three or four different ways of saying **to telephone**. In English you have nine:

*I'll **telephone** tomorrow.*

*You **phoned** last week.*

*He **rang** twice.*

*She **called** three times.*

*We ought to **call** them **up** immediately.*

*You should **give** him **a ring**.*

*They tried to **give** us **a call** this morning.*

*Why not **give** me **a buzz** tonight?* (slang)

*I'll **give** you **a shout** as soon as I'm finished.* (slang)

In British English you say **ring, give a ring**, etc.; in American English you **call, give a call**, etc.

As discussed on page 150, the **figure 0** is pronounced '**oh**' on the telephone. All other figures are pronounced in the normal way. A **double digit** is treated like this:

55 = '*double five*' [Am.: '*five five*'].

As in other languages, you can answer the telephone in several ways, either by giving your number

'Two oh three five two seven oh'

or by saying:

'Hello.'

'Evans here.'

'Johnson speaking.'

'Marks and Spencer.'

If you are a man, do not put '**Mr**' in front of your name when answering. It sounds a little uneducated. At least in British English.

When you have to ask somebody to wait, you can say:

'Hold the line, please.'

'Just a minute, please.'

An operator announces his or her presence with:

'Number, please.'

'Can I help you?'

You can make your wishes known with any of the following phrases:

'Could you get me. . . , please.'

'I'd like to call. . . , please.'

'I'd like to speak to. . . , please.'

If you want to make sure that you are only connected when the person you wish to speak to is available, you ask for a **personal call** in British English, for a **person-to-person call** in American English.

Have you finished the conversation? All right, **hang up**, please, i.e. put the receiver down.

6. *What's the time?*

When you want to know the time, you can say:

'What's the time?'

'What time is it?'

'What do you make the time?'

'What time d'you make it?'

The last two questions assume that the person you are asking is wearing a watch. Using the same idiom with the verb **to make**, the reply could be:

'I make it ten to seven.'

This implies 'at least by my watch'.

There is another question you can use when your time is limited and when you are worrying about some other commitment. If, for example, you can spend only ten minutes with a friend because you have to catch a train, you may ask after five minutes:

'How is the time?'
'How is the time going?'
'How are we for time?'

The time can be written and read aloud in several ways. Assuming that it is twenty-five minutes past nine in the morning, you have:

Written	Pronounced
9.25 or 9:25 or 9^{25}	nine twenty-five
0925	oh nine twenty-five
9.25 a.m. or 9:25 a.m.	nine twenty-five 'ay-em'

In the 12-hour system you use **a.m.** (ante meridiem) for the hours before noon, and **p.m.** (post meridiem) for the hours after noon. It is always 'ay-em' and 'pee-em', i.e. the Latin versions are never pronounced in full.

Twelve a.m. is **mid-day** or **noon**. (**Noon** is preferred in North America.) Twelve p.m. is **midnight**. You never combine noon with a time announcement, i.e. you do not say 'it is five minutes to noon'. You can however, mention midnight. At 23.50 on New Year's Eve you may shout into the kitchen:

'Quick! Get the champagne out of the fridge. It's ten minutes to midnight.'

In the 24-hour system the word **hours**, abbreviated **hrs.**, is sometimes added, specially by the armed services:

The next H-bomb will go off at 18.00 hrs.

The full hour is here pronounced like a year: 'eighteen hundred hours'.

As you know, eight-thirty can also be called half past eight. What else is worth knowing in the spoken department? If it is **before** the full hour, it is **to** in British English (ten to three), but **of** in American English (ten of three). If it is **after** the full hour, it is **past**; in American English also **after**:

| 6.15 | quarter past six |
| | quarter after six |

The word **o'clock** is used with the **full hour** only:

It is now five o'clock

but

It is now ten to five (no 'o'clock').

In the UK you may sometimes hear 'half-eight'. This is half past eight; not, as speakers of German, Dutch or the Scandinavian languages may think, half past seven.

When you are not quite sure about the exact time, you can use the following expressions:

*He is usually here at **about** nine thirty.*

*It is supposed to start **around** six.*

*They should arrive **round about** ten.*

If, on the other hand, you are sure about the time, you can show your reliability with the following phrases:

*I'll be there at eight o'clock **sharp**.*

*They always arrive **on the dot**.*

*The plane was **dead on time**.*

American slang has **on the button** and **on the nose** to denote extreme accuracy:

Here is your train. 3.25. On the button!

Let's see if we know everything about **clocks** and **watches**.

The time-measuring device that needs no springs or battery is the **sun dial**. Yes, it is called **dial**; not 'sun clock', as you may be tempted to translate from some other languages. What you carry on your person is a **watch**; **wrist watch** or **pocket watch**. Everything else is a **clock**. Every clock or watch (unless of the digital kind) has **hands** (**hour hand, minute hand, second hand**). They move **clockwise**, i.e. to the right in a circular sweep. The opposite movement is called **counter-clockwise** or **anti-clock-**

wise. These expressions are used in technical instructions:

Increase the pressure by turning the knob clockwise.

In several other languages you would say 'turn the knob to the right'. This is not quite accurate, as 'to the right' could also be movement in a straight line, not rotary.

The **small hours** are those **very late** (or very early) **hours** after midnight:

He says he gets his best ideas when lying awake during the small hours.

Somebody who works from nine to five and is always out of the building by 17.01 is probably a **clock watcher**:

He has become a bit of a clock watcher since he got married.

He used to work long hours. Now he rushes off to Emily at five as if the office block was on fire.

7. How much?

This is probably the most important question when you come to a new country. Here are a few English words and phrases connected with this vital subject.

Expensive means that something costs a lot of money. The price may be fair; it may be too high.

Dear also means a high price, but with the implication that it is too high. *This watch was expensive* merely reports that you paid a considerable amount of money. *This watch was dear* is a complaint.

Pricey is close to **dear**. It shows that the speaker thinks he is paying too much.

Costly is similar to **expensive**. No reflection on whether you are getting value for money, but merely a comment on the fact that your bank balance went down. **Costly** is mostly applied to the high price of **services**, not of goods: costly medical treatment, a costly repair job, a costly law suit.

Reasonably serious comment on a high price can be expressed by:

*That figure is quite **outrageous**.*

*$350 seems **exorbitant**.*

*Their prices are **sky-high**.*

More relaxed remarks would be:

*This boat cost me a **packet**.*

*Her mink coat cost a **bomb**.*

*£700 is **daylight robbery**.*

*Their new house cost the **earth**.*

Having to be a little careful with our money, we had better study words and phrases connected with a low price.

Inexpensive means that you did not pay much. No reflection on quality. What you bought was certainly no luxury item, but it was not shoddy, either.

Cheap often implies inferior quality. If you buy an inexpensive present for a friend, he or she may be delighted with it. It may easily be good value for money. If you buy a cheap present, you may be in trouble. The word **cheap** is therefore usually avoided in advertising.

Here is how it can be done:

Low-cost accommodation!   **Sensational** offer!   **Unbeatable** value!
An **economy** weekend!   **Budget** car rental!   **Bargain** sale!

A small complication is added by the fact that if you use **cheap** as predicative adjective, it does not condemn quality to the same extent as when used attributively. As mentioned earlier, an attributive adjective stands next to a noun, usually in front of it.

He bought a cheap car.

This reports that he bought something that is unlikely to last a lifetime.

A predicative adjective is linked to its noun by a verb, usually by **to be**:

This car is cheap!

Here someone reports a bargain, something that is worth more than it costs. In extreme cases you can call something **dirt cheap**. The combination of cheapness and low quality can be made quite clear by using **cheap and nasty**:

They tried to sell us some cheap and nasty bracelets.

Relaxed, or slangy comment on a low price is:

*The painting was sold **for a song**.*

*Five dollars is **peanuts**.*

*That's a **give-away** price.*

*Eighty cents? **Chickenfeed**!*

You are now ready to do business in any English-speaking country, making disgusted or appreciative remarks about goods and services of any price level.

8. Cheers!

Are your spirits revived by a gin and tonic or do you gain that new strength from a glass of cold milk? Whichever your preference, you may now and again join people from English-speaking

countries for a drink. It would then be better to know some of the phrases they actually use rather than try translations of what you might say in your own language.

If it's you who is going to pay or supply the drinks in your own home, don't ask 'What do you want?'. As we already discussed in section 3 of this chapter, this sounds rather rude. Try any of these instead:

> *'What would you like* (to drink)?'
>
> *'What can I get you?'*
>
> *'What are you going to have?'*
>
> *'Do you feel like a drink?'*
>
> *'How about a drink?'*
>
> *'Would you care for a drink?'*
>
> *'What's yours?'*
>
> *'What's it to be?'*

An answer to these generous proposals can be phrased in one of several ways:

> *'I wouldn't mind a . . . , please.'*
>
> *'Can I have a . . . , please?'*
>
> *'I'd love a . . . .'*
>
> *'A . . . would be great.'*
>
> *'I'd like a . . . , please.'*
>
> *'Could you get me a . . . , please.'*
>
> *'I think I'll have a . . . .'*

You **buy** other people a drink; you **stand** them a drink; in Australia and New Zealand you **shout** them a drink. **'Have one on me'** is the signal that it is your invitation.

Before you drink the stuff, you generally just say *'Cheers!'* nowadays. There used to be several other possibilities ('Your health!', 'Bottoms up!', 'Chin-chin!', 'Cheerio!', 'Down the hatch!', etc.) but these sound rather old-fashioned nowadays. The Scandinavian *'Skaal!'* is not unknown. (Rhymes with 'pole'.)

Short drinks are those strong alcoholic ones of which you only get a small glass. **Long drinks** are refreshing drinks, either non-alcoholic or alcoholic but strongly diluted. **Soft drinks** are always non-alcoholic. If you want them to contain those bubbles, ask for a **fizzy** drink. An undiluted strong drink is called **neat** in British English, **straight** in North America: a neat/straight whisky, for example. **On the rocks** is a neat/straight drink **with ice cubes**.

When you order 'a beer' in the UK and the Irish Republic, you will generally be served what is known there as **bitter**, the preferred brew in those countries: not so bubbly and probably too warm for your liking. If you want to receive something that resembles what you are used to at home, ask for a **lager** (pronounced the German way).

Beer in bottles? **Bottled beer**, of course. If from a barrel or tank somewhere under the bar, it is **draught beer** [Am.: draft beer]. Pronunciation: rhymes with 'raft'.

Cheers!

9. Perfect your manners

You may find these useful as part of your repertoire:

Please? Please! Please.

This is a true story, but let us start it like a fairy tale:

Once upon a time there was a waiter at a hotel in Austria. His name was Josef. I suppose his friends called him Sepperl. He knew only one word of English, the useful and polite '**please**'.

Someone had told him that it was the English equivalent of the German '**bitte**'.

Although this represented a very modest vocabulary, unlikely to create much scope for making mistakes, our friend Josef managed to use 'please' wrongly every time he served his guests from English-speaking countries at mealtimes. Let's turn on our tape recorder and listen to this short conversation between Josef and the Tourist.

Tourist: Josef!

Josef: Please? (in response to a call you say 'yes, sir').

Tourist says something which Josef does not understand.

Josef: Please? (when you want something repeated, you can use any of the phrases on the opposite page).

Tourist orders his meal, Josef brings it, and sets it down in front of him.

Josef: Please! (when handing somebody something, you either say nothing or perhaps 'here you are'. Waiters sometimes say 'thank you', presumably in recognition of the fact that you were kind enough to move your fat arm out of the way).

Tourist: Thank you, Josef.

Josef: Please. (responding to an expression of thanks, you say 'you're welcome', 'that's all right').

There you are: one very simple word, used wrongly four times. Looking worried, some readers may ask 'but when **do** I use "please"?' Only when you **ask for** something:

'Three kilos of potatoes, please.'
'Please get me Mr Smith.'
'Would you like another one?' – 'Yes, please.'

● **Eh?**

This question is a rather rude method of asking a person to repeat what he or she has said. When you have not heard properly, try any of these:

'Pardon?'

'I beg your pardon?'

'Pardon me?'

'Sorry, but I didn't quite hear what you said.'

'Sorry, but I missed that.'

Less polite are *'What?'*, *'What did you say?'*, and *'Come again'*. (Further down the line we have grunts, but these are not for you.)

• Hello!

Speakers of some Teutonic languages sometimes use this in English to attract a person's attention. That's wrong.

The best general-purpose expression is *'Excuse me'*, said with sufficient volume. In a restaurant the reluctant waiter could be summoned *'Waiter!'*; and when shopping, you could try *'Miss!'* to interrupt the conversation between the salesgirls at the far end of the store. Not recommended are *'Hey!'*, *'Hey, mister!'*, *'Yoohoo!'*, *'Oy!'*, *'Psst!'* or whistling, except when the above more polite versions have failed completely.

• 'Bon appetit'/'Mahlzeit'/'Eet smakelijk'/'Velbekom'

When sitting down to eat in some countries, you will hear these expressions of mutual hope that the meal will be enjoyable and that there will be no ill effects afterwards.

Although table manners in English-speaking countries are no worse than in yours, people there **say** absolutely **nothing** before a meal. So please do not try 'Good appetite' or similar expressions of incorrect as well as unnecessary politeness.

- ### 'Hup-choo!', 'Atishoo!' and similar noises

When somebody sneezes, you may be used to saying something polite. In fact, saying nothing will seem impolite. In countries using British English, however, you are not displaying any lack of manners by quietly ignoring this explosive sound and keeping silent. When children or close friends sneeze, some people say *'Bless you'*.

In the United States you say 'Gesundheit', using one of the many German words you find in American English.

11

Perfect your vocabulary

Although every page in this book is meant to expand your vocabulary, not every word or expression fits under the main headings of *Grammar, Correspondence, Verbal Idioms, Conversation*, and so on. *Vocabulary* is a general-purpose home for many meanings that may be new to you. Usually in quite ordinary words, not in those rarities of five syllables you may hardly ever use.

1. Single words

Answer

In English you not only answer questions but also several other things:

There is someone at the door. Please answer it. = **Open**.

Please answer the phone and tell them I'm busy. = **Pick up the receiver**.

Quietly ignoring this rule is not the answer. = **Ideal solution**.

This watch does not answer the description in the advertisement. = **Conform to**.

Does your circle of acquaintances include someone who pretends that he knows everything, that he has heard it all before? He is obviously a **know-all**. This unfortunate characteristic can be described in this way:

Do you know Cedric? – Oh, yes. He knows all the answers.

Around

You probably know this word as a harmless little preposition:

There is a wooden fence around the house.

More colloquially, it has a few additional meanings. **To be around**, applied to persons, means **here** or **alive**:

Where's Mother? – She's somewhere around (the house). = **Present**.

My grandfather died 15 years ago, but grandmother is still around. = **Alive**.

Applied to things, it means **in existence**:

'Sploosh' is the finest soap powder around!

To get around has two possibilities. **It gets around** refers to the **spreading** of **news** or information:

The restaurant is now always empty after it was fined for indescribable conditions in its kitchen. This sort of thing gets around.

It can also mean **travel widely**:

He visited ten countries in two weeks. He certainly gets around.

Feminists will be furious to hear that:

He has been around. = He has **travelled** [Am.: **traveled**] **widely**.

She has been around can mean that she has had many (too many) **male friends**.

Around is also an informal way of saying **approximately** in connection with figures:

I believe we paid around sixty dollars.

Bore

When something is not very interesting or you have nothing to do, you may sit there and conjugate:

ich langweile mich

tu t'ennuies

han keder sig

ella se aburra

wij vervelen ons

essi si annoiano.

What's so remarkable about this depressing chorus of international boredom? Just this: English is the only language that does not use the reflexive form, but **I am bored**: verb 'to be' plus adjective. Another charming example where English fails to conform to what you would normally expect.

In English you also have the noun **bore**. This can mean two things:

Kate is a dreadful bore!

This opinion tells you that when Kate is present, people are in danger of falling asleep. A boring person is simply a bore. Most other languages have no short noun derived from the verb.

Those formalities are always such a bore!

This complaint does not mean that you tend to go to sleep. In fact, you are probably wide awake while struggling to complete those forms in quintuplicate. Here the word **bore** means **nuisance, inconvenience, bother**.

There is also the technical verb **to bore**. It looks very much like the Teutonic 'bohren', 'booren', 'borra', but has the more restricted meaning of **enlarging an existing hole**. You re-bore the cylinders of an engine, you bore out a tube. When you produce a fresh hole, you **drill** it. The noun **bore** can mean **inside diameter** or **hole**:

The casting has a 160 mm bore.

The clean bore of the rifle.

But

You probably learned at school that the conjunction **but** introduces a contrasting or in some way unexpected statement, as in all other languages:

He is very fat, but a light-footed dancer.

Quite correct. The word **but** is, however, far more versatile in English. **But** can mean **only**:

She is but a child.

He had but one son.

They have but one aim in life.

I suppose we can but try.

As you may suspect, these constructions are to be found in formal writing rather than everyday conversation. **Nothing but** means **nothing except, only**:

They heard nothing but praise.

All but has the sense of **almost completely**:

Better street lighting has all but eliminated burglaries.

But for means **without**:

It would never have happened but for their interference.

This sounds very formal. In normal speech you would probably say:

If it had not been for their interference.

Anything but means **not at all**:

We are anything but satisfied with you.

The exclamation *'Anything but that!'* means *'Oh, no!'* in this kind of exasperated cry:

'Another tango? Anything but that!'

If you have to make a correction in the 16th line of a typed sheet of 17 lines, you do so in the **last line but one**. The **but** has here the meaning of 'except'. Another example:

Go down this road and take the next turning but one on the right.

This means that you should walk past the first turning, but take the second one.

Fair

This simple-looking adjective has six different meanings:

Fair hair = **blond** (or at least not dark).

Fair maiden (old-fashioned) = **beautiful**.

Fair weather = **good**.

A fair chance = **reasonably good**.

The quality is fair = **not too good**.

A fair decision = **just, equitable, correct**.

Although people in English-speaking countries by no means have a monopoly in the sense of fairness (as in *fair play*), some other languages have adopted the word **fair** when expressing this noble attitude.

Fix

The verb **to fix** is basically **to fasten, secure**. Beyond the basics we have the meaning **settle, determine, decide**:

We haven't fixed the selling price yet.

I fixed the broken switch! reports that you **repaired** it. American English also has **prepare** when you talk about food or drink:

Jack is fixing his special milk shake.

Can I fix you a drink?

Fix up can be a little vague. The question *Are you fixed up?* can mean anything between *Have you found a hotel room?* and *Did you find a partner for the dance on Saturday?* The noun **fix** is a **dilemma** of varying importance:

I was in a terrible fix: I had forgotten my credit cards!

Fun

The noun **fun** is not just **amusement**, something that makes you laugh, but in a wider sense **entertainment**. Even a person can be fun:

Bill is fun

reports that William (Bill is the short form) is an entertaining, lively fellow; not necessarily a comedian who makes you roll on the floor with laughter. In American English he could even be called a **fun person**. A **fun place** (also American) is usually a restaurant where in addition to a decent meal you can be sure of an unusual, lively evening.

The adjective **funny** has two meanings, exactly like its German counterpart 'komisch'. It can mean **humorous** or **strange**. So when you hear the comment that someone is a funny fellow or girl, you do not always know what is meant. To find out, you can ask:

Do you mean funny/haha or funny/peculiar?

Fun and games is usually not funny to the speaker who is likely to describe activities of which he does not approve:

The staff in the Accounts Department was working normally, but the General Office was having fun and games.

No games were played. They were simply **fooling about**.

Anthropological information: at your elbow the ulnar nerve is near the surface. When you knock it, you may get an almost electric, numbing effect. I am sure this has happened to you many times. The bone of the upper arm is called **humerus** in Latin. A long time ago some humorous doctor or medical student translated this as **funnybone**. This word has stayed in the language ever since. So when you next knock that sensitive spot, you can say

Ouch! That was my funnybone.

Hand

The English word **hand** offers far more meanings and expressions than in other languages.

Give me a hand means the same as **Help me**. **Hand** can also be two kinds of persons. One is an employee or unpaid **assistant**, usually required for work that does not call for too much brain power:

We need an extra three hands for the unloading job.

It can also be a person with a lot of **experience** or length of residence:

He is an old China hand. (He spent many years there.)

An **easy victory** is one with **hands down**:

They won the tournament hands down.

A **used** car can also be called a **second-hand** car. Marketing people are never quite sure which is the better psychological term in advertising.

When you have been dealt 13 cards in a game, you look at your **hand**, i.e. the **cards**, not your fingers. *A strong hand* therefore means a hand with *many points*. **In hand** means **available**, in reserve:

We used up three dozen, but still have one dozen in hand.

I can't tell you **offhand** is an admission that you cannot give information **without preparation**, a look at reference books, calculations or other sources. But *That waiter was rather* **offhand** reports that he was **curt** and **rude**. **Giving** somebody **credit** for something can be put like this:

You have to hand it to her: she's got courage!

Handy is the same as **useful**. A handy travel guide, for example.

In some languages you use the word 'side' when you contrast two statements. English prefers the word **hand**:

On the one hand it's an ideal home, but on the other hand it will cost the earth to maintain.

As the **fist** has a close connection with the hand, it is quite useful to know that **tight-fisted** is a descriptive adjective for someone who **hates to spend money**, who keeps a tight grip on that bank note or coin:

He's a dear old soul, but a bit tight-fisted.

A **hand-out** is something **given away**, usually money in response to a request:

The new association is expecting a hand-out from the government.

Mind

This versatile verb can mean much more than having an objection to something:

Don't mind him. He is only trying to impress us. = **Don't take any notice of.**

Mind the step at the bottom! = **Be careful of.**

Mind you, at least it's cheap. = **Yes, but at least it's cheap.**

He is minding the store today. = **Looking after, attending to.**

The last **mind** is also what a babysitter does: *he or she is minding the baby.*

When somebody is standing on your foot in a crowded compartment, your reaction can be anything between rudeness and a polite request to stand on someone else's foot for a change. An in-between possibility is the following:

Do you mind?

This question, with even stress on all three words, is a firm, not overly polite expression of your sentiments.

Odd

The word **odd** is rather odd, because it can have five different meanings. The easiest is **strange, unusual, peculiar**:

They never wash. They are a very odd couple.

When preceded by a number and joined by a hyphen, it means **approximate**:

The dance hall holds 500-odd people.

Did you know that **odd** can also mean the same as **occasional**?

Our visitors are mainly local residents, but we do get the odd tourist.

Numbers divisible by two are **even** numbers: 2-4-6-8-10, and so on. What do you call the others in between: 1-3-5-7-9, etc.? These are the **odd** numbers.

Something can be called **odd** if it does **not conform** to other objects or people:

We sorted this pile of shoes into pairs, but are left with one odd brown shoe and two odd black ones.

These three are not like the others which are in pairs. They are therefore the odd ones. **Odd man out** is the colloquial way of describing someone who prefers to be different:

They all ordered soup, except for Percy who asked for shrimp cocktail.

In this group Percy is the odd man out.

Outfit

The most common meaning is **equipment**:

Before leaving for the underwater exploration he had to buy a special diving outfit.

You can also mean what people **wear**:

She arrived in a green outfit with stripes.

More colloquially, it can also mean a **military unit**:

They served together in an intelligence outfit during the war.

More slangy, you can also use it when referring in a light-hearted way to a **company** or other **organization**:

She works for some electronics outfit.

He belongs to a temperance outfit.

Picture

This is not only the immobile kind of image you may have in a photo album or on the wall of your living room. It can also mean a moving picture, a cinema film. Although the word **film** is indeed used in English-speaking countries, you will sometimes also find **picture**. This usually refers to a full-length film, not Tom and Jerry:

They are showing a good picture at the Odeon.

The term **moving picture** has produced the American word **movie**:

Let's see a movie tonight!

Place

Combined with a possessive pronoun, the word **place** can mean **home**:

Come round to my place at six.

The party will be at their place on Saturday.

When you enumerate a few facts or factors, you usually say **firstly, secondly, thirdly**. As these can sound very formal, you can also say:

I don't like this plan. In the first place, it's too complicated; in the second place, it may not be quite legal; and in the third place, we can't afford it.

If you are not too happy in certain company, possibly embarrassed by certain shortcomings, you may feel **out of place**:

When they started discussing their next expedition to Mount Everest, I felt rather out of place. (I get dizzy when I look down from a third-floor balcony.)

A **decimal place** is the position of a figure after the decimal point (the English version of the decimal comma):

3.141592653 is pi exact to nine decimal places.

I cannot **place him** can mean two different things: *I am unable to find a* **vacancy** *for him* (employment or educational) or *I have seen him before, but I can't* **remember** *where.*

To take place has one meaning only: **to happen**, as in:

The celebration took place on the 18th of the month.

This means that it **happened, occurred, was held, was staged**. Do not use **take place** as an attempt to translate 'prendre place', 'plaats nemen', 'tage plads', 'tomar asiento', and similar foreign versions of a physical action. You then mean the English **take a seat** or **sit down**:

They took a seat in the last compartment.

Point

English has many expressions with the noun **point**. Most of them are frequently used and seem to have no literal equivalent in other languages.

The *point*, normally a round object, can be made oval in English when you **stretch a point**. It means **make a concession**, go beyond the limit, as in this unlikely decision by an insurance company:

His life insurance policy expired on the 15th. He died on the 16th. Let's stretch a point and pay out the £100,000.

When there is **no point** in doing something, it is **useless**:

There is no point in trying again.

You could also say that it is **pointless** to try again. When you **make your point**, you **convince** others, usually with verbal arguments, sometimes with a silent demonstration:

She fanned herself throughout the lecture. I think she was trying to make her point that the room was much too hot.

When you **make a point** of doing something, you do something **specially**:

Whenever we visit Copenhagen in the summer, we make a point of going to the Tivoli Gardens.

If something is **increased** from ten to twelve per cent, it goes up by two per cent, of course. You can also say it went up by two **points**.

Point can be the important, the **essential** thing. Instead of asking: *Do you understand what I am trying to say?* you could ask:

Do you get the point?

An **irrelevant** remark can be called **beside the point**:

He was nowhere near the accident. His comments are quite beside the point.

If you are **evasive** or vague, someone may complain

Come to the point!

On the other hand,

You have a point there

concedes that your argument makes sense, has merit; that you are **right**. Are languages your **strong point**? If so, a knowledge of languages is your **special strength**.

I hope I have made my point about *point*. If not, the exercise will have been pointless.

Poor

This adjective is not only the **opposite** of **rich**, but also of **good**. In the latter sense it is often neglected by my foreign friends. Here are a few combinations for practice:

The service in this hotel is rather poor.

He gave a poor performance last night.

Last month's sales were poor.

They had a poor opinion of his administration.

She seems to be in poor health.

June	July	August
3.4583	4.5204	1
8.6947	2.8588	5
10.5285	11.6386	3
9.4666	12.4241	2
32.1481	31.4419	11
=======	========	==

Last month's sales were poor.

Combining the two meanings, you could say that the painter is poor because he is a poor painter.

Remember

You may remember Old Bill, your rich uncle's birthday, and the capital of Paraguay, i.e. persons, events, and facts; but did you know that in English you can also **remember one person to another?**

Remember me to your mother means the same as:

Give my regards to your mother.

It even sounds more elegant. Try it next time.

Reservations

When you order tickets or book accommodation, you make reservations. That's nothing new. **Reservations** (in the plural) has an additional meaning. If, for example, someone puts forward a plan and you do not quite agree, have certain **doubts** about it, you have reservations about the idea:

It sounded like the ideal solution when they suggested it, but now I have reservations about it.

Sell

The salesman sells a product. In English, however, you can also say that **the product sells** when you mean that it is **being sold**. It may look a little strange to you but it is perfectly correct:

The new camera sells for £235 duty-free.

When something is a big **success** and is being sold very quickly, you say that: *It sells like hot cakes.*

Sell can also assume the functions of a noun in the terms **soft sell** and **hard sell**, the **subtle, indirect** approach to selling a product and the **direct** appeal to the consumer. If you produce deodorants, for example, you could advertise a series of cartoons showing how somebody becomes a big success at parties, with members of the opposite sex, in his job. At the end you would mention something about 'De-Smello' deodorant. This subtle theme is a soft sell. The hard sell would be just a direct slogan:

Do you stink? Use 'De-Smello'.

She

Gender can be a tricky business in many languages. Is it **der, die** or perhaps even **das**? Should I use **el** in place of **la**? Is **het** better here than **de**? Would I be wrong when preferring **en** to **et**? Maybe I should have written **la** instead of **il**. . . .

English is wonderfully easy in this respect. **She** is simply a woman, ranging from your Aunt Gertrude to your female hamster. No guesswork, no complications. Exceptions? Very few, so let's deal with them straight away. **She** can be applied to a mechanical object (usually large), if you have some personal relationship or interest:

I bought this car six years ago. She is still running like a dream.

The yacht was at anchor. She had extremely graceful lines.

The female article is for some reason confined to things that move (cars, ships, planes, trains, etc.), while other objects close to your heart may still merely be *it*:

This is our summer house. It was designed by my son.

The end of a personal feeling can also mean the end of a *she*-denomination. Seamen call the ship they sail in **she**. A book on supertankers makes the interesting point that these huge vessels have become impersonal through their very size. Result: seamen call them **it**.

Countries can be called **she** if there is some personal feeling. A book on my shelf promises in the introduction:

*This pictorial record of Canada shows you how **she** really is.*

On the other hand, a more detached news report may state:

*Upper Boobooland became independent in June. **It** applied for foreign aid in July. (The Rolls-Royce for the new President is still held up by the London dock strike.)*

The moon is called **she** in English. The sun is a **he**.

Shoot

Bang! Bang! Yes, that's shooting; you hear a **shot**. There are, however, two noiseless meanings:

The film will be shot in Africa.

This harmless shooting is **filming**. You can also shoot a still picture. A **snapshot** is an impromptu, usually unposed picture.

We had shots against cholera.

These shots are noiseless but can hurt. They are **injections** with a hypodermic needle. There is no verb form for this kind of shooting, i.e. you cannot say 'they shot us against tetanus'.

Mainly American is a **shot** in the sense of a **short drink**, usually drunk in one gulp: a shot of vodka. Also American is the adjective **shot** for **exhausted** or **worn-out**, applied to people after a tiring day as well as to old cars after 80,000 miles.

A **big shot** (slang) is someone who has reached a **high position** in his career:

We started together twenty years ago as office boys. He is now a big shot in Detroit.

Sleep

This simple verb not only means what you are doing when you have your eyes closed, are breathing steadily in and out, and perhaps snoring in that charming way of yours. It can also mean **accommodate**, indicating the **number of beds** available:

Our yacht sleeps only 12.

Their country house sleeps six.

Way

When explaining how to do something, when demonstrating a manual task, you use the words 'comme ça', 'so', 'así', 'così', 'zo', 'så här', 'sådan', etc. The best English equivalent is **this way**:

Look. Do it this way: move lever A to the left, set the spindle speed, and press button B.

Like this means exactly the same as **this way**. The word **way** is used many times in everyday conversation. When offering to **accompany** somebody, you could say

Come this way, please.

An **extra effort** can be phrased

They went out of their way to be helpful.

To be in a bad way can apply to the **health** of a **person** or **organization**:

I saw him last night. He seems to be in a bad way.

According to this article the United Sausage Co. is in a bad way.

In many countries a car coming from a street on your right may drive into you, and it will still be **your** fault. This law means that traffic from your right has the **right of way**. If there is **no alternative**, if something has to be done, you can say that **there are no two ways about it**:

Joe has to finish the report tonight. There are no two ways about it.

By way of can mean **via**, or **through**:

They came by way of the Panama Canal.

Way = **far** (colloquial) when you hear that:

This is being sold at way below cost.

Informal American usage has **way back** to mean a **long time ago**:

It happened way back (in 1874).

No way is a slightly slangy and emphatic **no**, or **definitely not**:

We couldn't persuade them. No way.

2. Colour [Am.: color] scheme

When someone hits you in the eye, you may develop a **blue eye** in German, Dutch and the Scandinavian languages. In Spanish you will have a **purple eye**, but in English the same unkind treatment will result in a **black eye**. (In French you will even have an eye with black butter.)

A dirty joke is called *green* in Spanish, but *blue* in English. Colours are not so international when it comes to figurative usage, so here are a few 'colour-full' English expressions not found in most other languages.

A **white lie** is a **small**, usually forgivable **lie**. It is often told for the sake of tact. When you are invited to what may be a very boring party, you may say:

I am terribly sorry, but I can't manage Friday night. My rehearsals, you know.

(There are no rehearsals.) **Lie** is a very strong term to describe your piece of diplomacy. **White lie** is less damning. A **white elephant** is not only an albino, but can also be something that is **expensive, useless, difficult to get rid of**:

The Olympic Stadium is a white elephant.

It was built for the Games many years ago. It is much too big for normal local sports events and is therefore hardly ever used.

A **red herring** is a **false clue**, something designed to deceive or divert attention. Half-way through a detective novel you may suspect that the murder was committed by the debt-ridden

white elephant   white elephant

nephew of the old tycoon. No, that was merely a red herring introduced by the author to increase your surprise at the real solution at the end. A **red carpet** may be rolled out before the arrival of important people. Specially **good treatment** (with or without a carpet) can be described in this way:

We got red-carpet treatment at our hotel on the island.

They rolled out the red carpet for us last year.

In the UK you have the expression **redbrick university**. This means one of the **newer** universities, not the ancient ones with their old stone buildings. **Red tape** is **bureaucracy**, time-wasting procedure:

The importation of this component will involve a lot of red tape.

When a business is **making a profit**, it is **in the black**. When it **loses money**, it is **in the red**:

After two disastrous years Amalgamated Lollipops are again in the black.

Grey [Am.: **gray**] has two possibilities. **Grey matter** means **brains**:

A nice fellow but perhaps lacking a little in grey matter.

Your lawyer may refer to a **grey area** when he means something **not clearly defined**, neither black nor white:

It is not expressly forbidden in the contract, but I remember that objections were occasionally raised. We seem to be in a grey area here.

Yellow means **cowardly** in a slangy way:

Come on. Jump in. Or are you yellow?

Something **unexpected** comes **out of the blue**:

His promotion came quite out of the blue.

The reason for this happy development may be that he has always been the **blue-eyed boy**, i.e. somebody **specially popular with superiors**:

The new Marketing Manager seems to be the blue-eyed boy of the Board.

'Blue-eyed girl' does not exist, but it will come, no doubt.

Pink is for some reason connected with the act of tickling. **To be tickled pink** means **to be very pleased**:

She was tickled pink with the award of the trophy.

If you are good at **making things grow**, if your garden or balcony boxes look pretty, people may say that you have **green fingers** (British English) or that you have **a green thumb** (American English).

3. Please control 'control'

In many languages you have the noun **control**. You also have the verb **control**. One obviously has a close connection with the other. But not in English where something subject to control need not be controlled. Sounds like nonsense? Let me explain. The English noun **control** means the same as in your language, but **to control** usually does not. Here are a few examples to show what goes on in departments where control is exercised:

Customs control

When you go through customs at the airport, they may **check** your luggage [Am.: baggage], not control it. If they want to find out what you are hiding in your underwear, they may even **search** you.

Health control

If on arrival from an overseas country you look a bit green in the face, they may **examine** you medically.

Quality control

In production you have quality control to maintain a high standard of the goods manufactured. One noun **control**, but four verbs: you **check** or **inspect** each workpiece; you make sure that it has the dimensions or finish specified. Inspecting is usually more thorough than checking. If you do not know the dimensions, you **measure** it. You can also **test** it. If you want to know the hardness of a piece of steel, for example, you test its hardness. **Test** can also mean making sure that something functions properly. The brakes in your car, for example.

Control of accounting records

Your work does not involve controlling the books but **audit**ing them. A Controller is not an auditor, but the **Chief Accountant**.

Staff control

This probably means the supervision of people and the verb **to supervise**.

Performance control

The Flight Engineer in a jumbo jet sits in front of an instrument panel. One of his jobs is:

> To **monitor** *engine performance on take-off.*

To monitor means **keep an eye on, watch**:

> *The Bycheep supermarket chain monitors its competitors' prices.*
>
> *A special department monitors foreign broadcasts.*

Verify is another verb which in certain situations could be 'control' in other languages. If someone makes a report or

Monitoring engine performance.

statement to you, it may be necessary to find out whether it is true. You then verify the matter.

A Danish magazine recently advised housewives that before buying a dishwasher they should 'kontrollere' certain desirable technical features. Here the best equivalent would be to **make sure** that the appliance meets certain standards.

There you are: the noun **control** may be all right most of the time, but the corresponding verb could be **check, search, examine, inspect, measure, test, audit, supervise, monitor, verify**, and **make sure**. Slightly nervous, you may ask, '**Is** there an English verb **to control**?'. Yes. It has two meanings, best explained by examples:

Vertical movement is controlled by a handwheel.

All subsidiaries are controlled from Brussels.

This **control** is a very **direct** influence, not merely supervision as the corresponding verb in your language may suggest. The handwheel directly actuates the movement; Brussels is directly involved in the running of the subsidiaries. The second meaning is **restrict, limit, guide**, or otherwise put a brake on something. It is often used in an adjectival sense. **Controlled immigration** means putting a limit on the number of people entering a country. A **controlled flow** of liquid in a manufacturing process does not mean that the flow is being constantly measured, but that it is strictly limited.

The verb **to check** can also mean exactly the same as **control** in the sense of keeping something back:

They are trying to check inflation through a price freeze.

He wanted to protest, but checked himself at the last minute.

Do you know the collective name for the steering wheel, pedals, hand brake, and knobs in your car? **Controls**.

4. Please check 'check'

The verb **to check** has far more meanings than you may have suspected. Demonstration:

The epidemic was checked by stopping the municipal water supply.

This **check** means that this action **stopped, slowed down, curbed, restrained, arrested** the spreading of the illness. When something is **kept in check**, it is **kept within limits, controlled. To check** for **examine** can mean anything between a very quick glance of a few seconds to a day's hard work:

She checked the day of the week on her watch.

She checked 386 invoices.

When you **check** your **belongings** (baggage, coats, hats) in North America, you mean that you hand them over for safekeeping. Your receipt is called a check. In American English you can also use **check** for **agree**:

The waybill checks with the delivery note.

When playing chess, you say *Check* to your opponent after a move that threatens his king. The chessboard has black and white squares, but when you have a similar pattern on fabrics, wallpaper, and other material, you call it **checks**:

She wore a checked shirt.

At a hotel you **check in** by **registering** at the reception desk; you **check out** when you pay on **leaving**. (Mainly American.) You also **check in** at the airport, hoping that they haven't overbooked again. **Check out** can also mean **investigate**, verify, examine in a systematic way if you want to be sure of the best or cheapest:

> *Check out all excursion fares before making any booking.*

After a restaurant meal you receive a **check** in North America, a bill in the other English-speaking countries. You may pay by **cheque** (British and American spelling) or **check** (American spelling only). If you are planning a trip, a conference or some other project, you may want to make a summary of the things to do beforehand. Why not make a **check list**?

5. *Please decrease 'decrease'*

What is the opposite of **increase**? **Decrease**? Well, usually not. Although in theory you may be right, you very often use a different verb or noun. Here are a few examples, with the perfectly acceptable **increase** on the left and better alternatives to **decrease** on the right:

price *increase*	price *reduction*
increase in expenses	*cut* in expenses
increasing sales	*falling* sales
increase in popularity	*decline* in popularity
increase in demand	*falling-off* in demand
increase in profits	*drop* in profits
increased expenditure	*curtailed* expenditure
increasing danger	*receding* danger
increasing prospects	*dwindling* prospects
increasing influence	*waning* influence
increasing scope	*diminishing* scope
a *slight increase* in reserves	a *dip* in reserves
a *steady increase* in rates	a *slide* in rates

What then about the neglected word *decrease*? You could apply it to a statistical trend (*a decrease in juvenile crime*) or to a slow, deliberate action (*the pilot decreased power when crossing the coast*), but even here you could talk about a *decline* in crime and report that the pilot *reduced* power, or *throttled back*.

I never use *decrease* and feel fine.

6. Watch your figures

Figures are supposed to be international, leaving little scope for making mistakes when translating from one language into another. Don't be so sure. Here are a few points where English differs from other languages.

Decimal comma/decimal point

In English you have a decimal point. Other languages use a decimal comma.

Foreign	English
12,3%	12.3%
DM 18,50	DM 18.50
3,1415	3.1415
11,4 km	11.4 km

Although the International Standardization Organization has advocated the universal use of the decimal comma, I am sure that people in English-speaking countries will happily stick to the decimal point for many years to come.

Thousands division point/thousands division comma

You write 250.000. English has 250,000. This dividing comma is not needed when you deal with:

street numbers, e.g. 1275 Green Lane
year figures, e.g. 1945
telephone numbers, e.g. 677 820
page numbers, e.g. Page 1052

If a figure has four digits, you may use the comma, but you do not have to:

£4,658 or £4658
2,300 bearings or 2300 bearings

Writing figures/writing words

When mentioning figures in **normal correspondence**, it is best to write them in **words**, as in the following kind of sentence:

We had only ten minutes to spare.

They expect about three hundred applicants.

It cost us nearly four thousand dollars.

On the other hand, if the figure has **statistical** significance or has to be **accurate**, you should write:

Yesterday the trip took 28 minutes, today only 19.

They received 312 applications.

It amounted to $4075.

Ordinal numbers (lst, 2nd, 3rd, etc.) are also best treated in the same way:

It will be our third visit to Japan.

Please delete the 17th line from the bottom.

Plural of figures

Add a small *s;* formerly also apostrophe + *s:*

It happened in the early 1970s (1970's).

Shortened millions

If you are used to handling millions with your famous nonchalance, you may be interested to hear that you can abbreviate them in written form:

$10,000,000 = $10 million = $10m.

Hand-written figures

Be very careful when writing two figures by hand in letters to English-speaking countries: the **one** and the **seven**. The British and American **one** has a plain downstroke: I . In other countries it often has a short tail. Like this : 1 . The English **seven** is **not crossed**: 7 . In other languages it usually looks like this: $\not{7}$.

The following mistakes can arise unless we pay attention to these differences. If you write 11 **Shore Road** for **11 Shore Road**, the postman in Britain [Am.: mailman] at destination – not accustomed to your tail-equipped 11 – may easily think that this means **77 Shore Road**. On the other hand, if I write Gartenstrasse 77 as my version of $\not{77}$, anyone used to crossed sevens may deliver the letter to No. 11.

7. More figure work

A few English expressions are connected with numbers. Here are some not found in other languages.

Don't expect Jack to contribute. He always looks after No. 1 first.

When you hear this, you can conclude that careful Jack is an **egoist**. As the figure '1' looks like the first personal pronoun 'I', looking after No. 1 means looking after oneself in a selfish way.

One in front of a name indicates **doubt, ridicule** or **contempt:**

These 'eternal youth' pills were invented by one Professor Vologradoff

expresses doubt about the 'Professor' or the 'Vologradoff'. (His real name is probably Smith.)

By the way, putting the indefinite article **a** before a name shows some **uncertainty** when announcing a visitor.

Mr Benson is here to see you

indicates that the receptionist assumes that Mr Benson is known to the person to be visited.

A Mr Benson is here to see you

shows some doubt that Mr Benson is known.

You know those gambling machines where you pull a lever to start three drums, which always stop in the wrong position. These machines are aptly called **one-armed bandits**: they have one arm (the lever) and must be bandits because they take your money.

One for the road is the **final drink** before departure, often the result of some persuasion:

No thanks, I've had enough.

– Come on. One for the road.

Two-faced is a descriptive adjective: a person with two faces, i.e. insincere, **deceitful**. Some men with dark hair look a little **unshaven** by late afternoon and may need another shave. This unfortunate condition is called **five o'clock shadow**:

Your shirt is all right, but you will have to do something about that five o'clock shadow.

'Take five!' can be heard in show business or at rehearsals in North America to announce five minutes' **rest**.

He didn't write it down. Ten to one he'll forget about it.

Here the speaker offers betting odds of 10:1, i.e. he is quite **certain** that something will be forgotten. If something is very **common**, readily available, you have these comments using numbers and money:

Unofficial money changers are ten a penny at the airport.

These exotic flowers are a dime a dozen in Brazil.

Millions, billions, trillions, etc. are very high numbers. If you want to impress people when mentioning an **enormous** quantity without being too specific, you also have the slangy American **zillions**:

How many bottles do you sell on a hot summer's day?
– Oh, zillions!

As we are on the subject of figures, you may have come across some with an **-ish** at the end. Why *fortyish*, for example? When you are not quite sure about the **shape** or **colour** [Am.: color] of an object or the **age** of a person, you can use the colloquial suffix **-ish** to denote **approximate, more or less**:

She wore a greenish coat.
It came in a squarish package.
He is dark-haired, of medium height; fortyish.

If you measure 1.76 m in your stockinged feet, they may call you **tallish**, not tall. Indications of time can also be equipped with *-ish*, if you cannot be too exact. When asking a friend for coffee after dinner, you may say *Come about eightish*. The vague *about* is for some reason always added to the equally imprecise *eightish*.

8. Good and bad

When used in certain combinations, these very elementary words can in most cases not be translated literally.
   In good time means **sufficiently early**. If you arrive at the airport in good time, you will be there before you start getting a little nervous. **Good for** means **valid** or **serviceable** for:

This voucher is good for two balcony seats.
This suit will be good for another season.

For good means **for ever, permanently**:

The house has been empty for two years. It seems they have left for good.

Good eating is not an attempt to translate 'Bon appetit'. It refers to a kind of food that makes a **good meal**:

Grilled monkey paws are good eating.

(You do have odd tastes.)
Good combined with measurements indicates **not less than**:

It takes a good hour to walk to their home.

It's a good two miles from here to the station.

If you are impressed with somebody's achievements, good fortune or attitude, you say **Good for you!**, with stress on the last word. This becomes **Good on you!**, with stress on the first word, in Australia and New Zealand:

Glad to hear about your promotion. Good for you! (Northern Hemisphere.)

You were right to refuse the offer. Good on you! (Australasia.)

No good is worse than *not good*, because it means **useless**:

Give it up. It's no good trying any further.

This washing powder is no good.

Bad also offers a few interesting meanings. A debt is a sum of money somebody owes you. If it is paid, you're lucky. If not, you have a **bad debt** on your hands. **Bad blood** cannot be changed through a blood transfusion. It means **bad relations**:

The wives get on very well, but there is bad blood between the men.

Bad temper can mean two things:

*He **has** a bad temper*

indicates that he is easily upset, becomes furious quickly. This is a permanent defect, a fault of character.

*He **is in** a bad temper*

refers to a temporary bad mood, something that can happen to all of us. Someone who has a bad temper may throw something at you. Someone in a bad temper may do nothing more drastic than sit there sulking in a corner.

Just too bad is American slang. Don't try to translate it literally.

It expresses the sentiment *I can't do anything about it*, *They will have to get used to it*, and similar reactions indicating **indifference**:

If he doesn't like this room, that's just too bad.

If they are not happy with a reduction of 10 per cent, that's just too bad.

We can combine **good** and **bad** in the nouns **goodies** and **baddies**. They are easy to identify in Wild West films, for example. John Wayne will lead the goodies, i.e. the forces of law and order, while that unshaven and dirty-looking lot represent the baddies.

Baddies

The adverb **badly** can also mean exactly the same as **very much**:

The news of the accident affected him badly.

They were badly beaten in the finals.

I am badly in need of a change.

9. Hot and cold

Hot and **cold** are very ordinary words, used literally (*a hot day*) or figuratively (*she gave him the cold shoulder*) in all languages. As usual, English can be a little different when it comes to figurative usage. Here is a collection of words and phrases not found in several languages.

Hot when applied to food does not only mean **heated**, but can also mean **spicy**:

Her speciality is an extremely hot curry.

In some languages you use the adjective 'sharp' for strong-tasting things. Not in English, so be careful. **Hot air** could be something that comes out of your hair drier. It can, however, also mean **verbal** (not written) **nonsense**:

Most speeches at the meeting were a lot of hot air.

Getting into **hot water** means getting into **trouble**:

This unlimited guarantee could get us into hot water.

In most languages you can talk about a 'warm meal', 'warm milk', 'warm rolls'. Not in English, where the word **warm** when applied to food means *lukewarm, inadequately heated,* and other uninviting descriptions.

You have a **hot** meal, **hot** drink, **hot** rolls.

There are are two kinds of hot vehicles in the automobile field. A **hot car** (mainly American) is a **stolen** car. A **hot rod** is a specially adapted car, stripped of all but essentials to give maximum performance for **racing**. **Hot seat** (originally meaning **electric chair**) is any situation in which someone may face **awkward questions**:

When the auditors find that doubtful stock valuation, the controller is likely to be in the hot seat.

When you feel **hot under the collar**, you can feel one of three emotions: **angry, resentful** or **embarrassed**:

After waiting for two hours, I was getting pretty hot under the collar.

A **hothead** is a person who **acts hastily**.

Not too hot or **Not so hot** is a rather lukewarm comment. It means **not very good, nothing wonderful, fair**:

The concert was not too hot.

Do you know the expression **so-so**? It means very much the same and shows a very low degree of approval. Just like the Italian 'così, così':

How was the food? – So-so.

Let's cool off a little and look at the word **cold**.

Cold feet cannot always be cured by thicker socks or by

propping them on the nearest radiator. They can also mean **fear, apprehension, lack of courage**, and similar mental attitudes;

When he looked down from the diving board, he suddenly got cold feet. (He refused to dive; got scared.)

Cold when applied to drinks is all right in the UK where the production of ice cubes is not a national industry. In the United States and tropical countries be sure to make matters clear by saying **iced** drinks. **To be out cold** means to be **unconscious**:

After bumping his head on the ceiling he was out cold for twenty minutes.

To be out in the cold is different. It means being **left out**, being without the benefits or advantages others may enjoy:

They all received a balloon, but little Hubert was (left) *out in the cold.*

Cold sweat is that chilly feeling that results from a **shock**:

When he realized that the door was locked from the outside, he broke out into a cold sweat.

When you sniffle and cough, you probably have a **cold**, medically also known as the **common cold**. If it's not very cold, it is probably

cool. This word also offers a few possibilities: **Controlled emotions** can be called **cool**.

She seemed very cool about it. = **Unexcited**.

Keep cool! = **Keep calm**.

Cool in front of a sum of **money** indicates that the speaker or writer is impressed with the amount:

Their new house cost a cool two million guilders!

In English you can **cool your heels** without putting your feet into a bucket of cold water. This expression means **wait**:

We had to cool our heels for two hours before being able to see the minister.

The expression **a cool customer** means a **daring** person, someone who takes risks:

The bank robber seemed a very cool customer: he counted the money before running out of the bank.

Cool can also be American teenagers' slang for something or somebody **wonderful**. A *cool dude* is the highest of praise for a young man; a *cool cat* expresses the same kind of admiration for a member of either sex.

10. Do you like 'like'?

There are a few things you should know about the simple word **like**.

Do like I say! (?)

In British English you say:

*Do **as** I say!*
*He spoke **as if** he meant it.*
*Please leave the bathroom **as** you wish to find it.*

In American English you will hear:

*Do **like** I say!*
*He spoke **like** he meant it.*
*Please leave the bathroom **like** you wish to find it.*

The use of **like** as a conjunction, as in the above sentences, sounds uneducated to someone brought up on British English. It is, however, acceptable in American English, so take your choice according to circumstances.

Perfectly correct on both sides of the Atlantic is the use of **like** as preposition or prepositional adverb when it introduces a **comparison** and is not followed by a subordinate clause:

She writes like her father.

What is it like?

If you listen carefully, you will find that people in English-speaking countries prefer the combination **what. . .like** to **how** in these sentences:

What's the weather like today?

What was the film like last night?

I wonder what the party will be like tomorrow.

Did you see him? What is he like?

The last question asks *What do you think of him* **as a person?**, **How** is *he?* expresses interest in his **health**.

What does she look like?

This question makes it quite clear that you are interested in her more permanent **features**: size, shape, complexion, colour [Am.: color] of hair, facial characteristics, and so on.

How does she look? shows an interest in her **present appearance**, i.e. whether she looks healthy or not. In other languages you have only one way of putting these two questions. **Look like** is also a good phrase for your daily weather forecast:

It looks like rain

Do you feel like a piece of cheese?

In other languages this question sounds funny. Not in English because all it means is *Would you like a piece of cheese?*. A few examples:

I feel like a cold drink.

He felt like a game of squash.

She didn't feel like going out.

This **feel like something** is therefore close to **avoir envie/Lust haben/tener gana/zin om hebben**, and other phrases you may sometimes have found a little difficult to translate into English.

An English brochure I once found in a foreign hotel described the accommodation and amenities in glowing terms but ended with this doubtful assurance:

You will feel like being at home!

The translator meant to say 'You will feel at home here' but he really told his readers:

When you are here, you will wish you were at home.

11. Murder class

Death, killing, and murder are not exactly light-hearted subjects. Except in English, where you can use these macabre words in many colloquial or slangy ways that can be quite positive or even cheerful. In several languages you can also say *I am dead tired* and *I am dead sure*, but English has far more combinations in which **dead** is merely the same as **very**:

dead certain	*dead right*
dead easy	*dead serious*
dead funny	*dead straight*
dead level	*dead wrong*
dead lucky	

Dead beat means very tired indeed. **Dead** can simply mean **inoperative**:

The transmitter went dead last night.

When two contestants finish **alongside** one another in a race, it's a **dead heat**:

I think they crossed the line together. Looks like a dead heat to me.

Strong **opposition** is indicated when you read:

*The government is **dead set** against a tax cut.*

When a project is no longer under consideration, **no longer alive**, you could comment:

The oil exploration project is dead,

or even:

The oil exploration project is a dead duck.

Extreme **disapproval** can be expressed like this:

That yellow pullover? I wouldn't be seen dead in it!

Dead to the world is no more than being in **deep sleep**, usually as a result of an exhausting activity:

They went straight to bed and were dead to the world for ten hours.

Even *dying* can be quite harmless when you gasp to your friends on a hot summer's day:

I'm dying for an ice-cold beer!

to indicate your **desperate** thirst.

All Teutonic languages have *die out* for becoming **extinct**, but in

English (and Dutch) you can use *die down* for **decline** or diminish in other ways:

The forest fire has died down.

The wave of strikes has died down.

When you are tired after dragging yourself through three museums, you may complain to your companions:

My feet are killing me!

Murder can mean nothing more drastic than physical **inconvenience** in these complaints:

Seville in August is murder! = **Terribly hot**.

Christmas shopping is murder! = **Very tiring**.

Saint Tropez in July is murder! = **Overcrowded**.

12. *Nocturnal news*

In most languages the word **night** refers to the hours of complete darkness. In English it can also mean **evening**:

Let's meet tomorrow night

can be any time after work.

I think we should have a night out

need not suggest anything more adventurous than a visit to the cinema at 8 p.m.

We danced all night!

in other languages probably boasts about the fact that breakfast was served after the last waltz. In English it may only refer to an event that went on until very late. When coming home from the usual night out, you will tell friends that you had a good evening, not a good night. A good **night** means a good rest, a good night's **sleep**.

Do you know what **moonlighting** means? Nothing to do with illumination, but work, because it refers to a paid activity besides your usual job, i.e. having **two jobs**:

After normal office hours he moonlights for three hours in a disco.

13. Thing and nothing

Thing and **nothing** have been old friends of yours for a long time. They may be more versatile in meaning than you may have suspected. Let's find out.

He always has a cold shower first thing in the morning.

She likes a cup of cocoa last thing at night.

No need to explain what **first thing** and **last thing** mean in this context, but could you translate these sentences without resorting to 'as soon as he gets up' and 'before she goes to sleep'?

Things is a very general and vague term. It can mean **conditions, morals, living standards, business, clothes**, anything. A few translations:

Things are looking up. = **The outlook is getting better.**

Pack your things. = **Pack your belongings.**

How are things? = **How are you?**
How is business?
How is the job? etc. etc.

Things aren't what they used to be. . . is a clear sign of middle age, a lament that life was easier in the good old days. **Thing** can also be the conventional, correct act or action:

It's hardly the thing to do

is the same as:

It's hardly the done thing.

Belching after a meal, for example. At least outside China.

Thing can also mean **complex, phobia**, and other aversions that bother people:

He has a thing about heights

means that he hates to look down from a balcony, roof, mountain or other elevated places.

The word **something** can be the highest praise in American English when someone exclaims *That's really something!*. This means *That's remarkable!, I am impressed!*, and other expressions of **admiration**. Two hundred years ago the sight of a tropical sunset may have provoked a poem of 24 lines. Now someone may mutter *Ain't that something!*, and leave it at that.

Nothing has the colloquial form **not a thing**, which is used extensively:

I didn't feel a thing during the operation.

The trip did not cost us a thing.

They didn't have a thing to do all day.

Not a thing can manage to sound more emphatic than **nothing**:

He attended the meeting, but said nothing.

He attended the meeting, but didn't say a thing.

The first sentence merely reports his silence. The second one expresses some surprise that he did not open his mouth. Maybe he followed the philosophy I once heard somewhere:

Better keep your mouth shut and let people think that you're a fool than open it – and remove all doubt. . . .

If **nothing** is colloquially **not a thing**, can nobody be **not a body**? Sorry, no; but you do have a colloquial alternative: **not a soul**.

We wandered all over the estate, but there was not a soul in sight.

The plural form **nothings** exists, but only in the report that

He whispered sweet nothings into her ear.

This means that he made soft, amorous, probably inane noises into the long-suffering girl's ear.

Nothing doing is a useful short way of saying that you did not get a positive response:

I asked him for a day off, but nothing doing.

We asked for a discount, but nothing doing.

Nothing followed by a preposition has three interesting possibilities. **Nothing for it** (not American usage) means that there is no way out, no alternative:

We simply have to cut overheads. There's nothing for it.

If you add the suggested solution, you add the words **but to**:

We're in deep trouble. There's nothing for it but to cut overheads.

Nothing in it, applied to a rumour [Am.: rumor] means that it is not true:

I heard a rumour that they are planning a big reorganization, but there is probably nothing in it.

Nothing to it is slang. It means **It's easy!**

Swimming across the Channel? Nothing to it!

14. *Weather report*

The weather is a frequent topic of conversation. Not surprising that several idiomatic expressions are connected with it.

I feel under the weather. = I **don't feel well**.

You'll be as right as rain. = You'll feel **all right** again.

He hasn't the foggiest (idea). = He **knows nothing** about it.

She took a rain check. = She preferred to **come another time**.

We did a snow job on the boss. = We managed to convince him with our **glib** (or high-pressure) presentation.

You are under a cloud. = You are **unpopular**.

The last sentence is often the result of an omission or mistake. If you forgot to send off that important fax message on Friday night, you will be under a cloud (with the boss).

It's raining cats and dogs! to describe very heavy rain is not used nowadays. More modern is the unimaginative *It's pouring!*, said in a suitably awe-struck tone or, if you insist on something descriptive, *It's coming down in buckets!*

15. Geography

Relax! Geography comes into this chapter, but only within the general aim of perfecting your English.

• GB = UK?

Most people in the British Isles speak English. Of a sort. That, however, does not make all inhabitants Englishmen. There are plenty of Scotsmen, Welshmen, and Irishmen who will not be impressed when you write or speak about 'exports to England' or 'English customers' if you may also be dealing with Scotland, Wales, and Northern Ireland.

You need a good all-round term that will not upset anyone. **England** is not suitable for the reason just explained. **Great Britain** and **Britain** are constitutionally imprecise, as they exclude Northern Ireland. **British Isles** is a reasonable geographical definition, but by far the best is **United Kingdom**.

Although unity may at times be doubtful, this term is unlikely to infuriate anyone in Edinburgh, Cardiff or Belfast. **UK** is the commonly accepted abbreviation. It serves as noun as well as adjective. So from now on please refer to *exports to the UK* or *our UK buying agents*.

If you do find a UK product marked *Made in England* it means that it is indeed manufactured in the geographical area known by that name.

Your handling of the word **Ireland** also needs special care. If you mean the part belonging to the UK, it is **Northern Ireland**. If you refer to the independent republic in the South, it is **The Republic of Ireland** or **The Irish Republic**. The terms **Ulster** (for Northern Ireland) and **Eire** (for the Irish Republic) are not recommended, as somebody or other over there may object on certain emotional grounds.

• NL = Holland?

Shouldn't it be *Netherlands*? The **Netherlands** is indeed correct when you refer to political, legal, economic, and other sober matters: the government of the Netherlands, the property laws of the Netherlands, etc. Although **Holland** is only a part of the country geographically, in English this word has a certain **warmth**, an **emotional** content, which Netherlands lacks. That's why you will find references to:

My friends in Holland,

The windmills of Holland,

Our vacation in Holland,

as well as a big sign at Amsterdam airport that says WELCOME TO HOLLAND.

• USA = America?

Again emotion is involved because **America** sounds far warmer than **United States**. Patriotic songs are always about America. However this usage encourages neglect of the rest of the continent of America, of which the USA is only a part.

• USSR = Russia?

More emotion! The word **Russia** may evoke visions of a troika in the snow; a samovar, and maybe an onion-domed church or two. **USSR** has a much more sober ring about it, although more strictly accurate.

Take care in all these cases. The patriotic feelings of whole nations are at stake.

16. Medicine

Here is some interesting information connected with being ill, doctors, and that sort of thing. As it is merely meant to expand your vocabulary, it can still be a pretty cheerful subject.

• Sick/ill

The difference between the two is interesting. **Sick** is usually less serious than **ill**, if used predicatively: if your colleague has a bad cold, you will report that he or *she is sick*; not ill. Sick can also have a close connection with a stomach disorder when you may have to **vomit**. *I feel sick* or *I am going to be sick* clearly indicates the impending disaster. *He is sick*, with strong emphasis on the word *sick*, means that he is mentally ill, i.e. slightly **mad**. **Sickly** is not an adverb, but an adjective, meaning of **unhealthy** or chronically sick appearance: a *sickly complexion*, for example. If *sick* is used attributively, i.e. in front of a noun, it does denote something serious. The statement *He is a sick man* should certainly give cause for concern.

Ill is not used attributively. You do not say 'he is an ill man'. That's why all compounds have *sick* in it: *sick leave, sick bay, sick pay, sick list*, etc. **I am sick of it** or in extreme cases *I am sick and tired of it* has nothing to do with health. It means that something or somebody is a nuisance, that you are **irritated**:

We are sick of their complaints.

Sick and tired of their complaints

● Doctor/physician/general practitioner/specialist/surgeon

A medical doctor shows his acquired degrees by initials after his name. The most common are MD, MB, BS, and MS. In the UK you also have MRCS, LRCP, FRCS, MRCP, and FRCP.

A medical man can be a *general practitioner* (usually called GP) or a *specialist*. The term *physician* means specialist in the UK. In North America it can be both specialist and general practitioner. A *surgeon* is a specialist who performs *operations*. In the UK, surgeons are addressed as *Mister* and not *Doctor*. There is an interesting story behind this odd convention.

During the reign of Henry VIII the physicians were given a Royal charter when they formed their College. Operations were in those days mainly performed by barbers in a rather barbaric fashion. The physicians showed their disapproval by barring from membership of the College anyone who used a knife. The early surgeons could therefore not call themselves doctors. In the 19th century the qualified surgeons founded their own College, and in order to show their contempt for those bigoted doctor physicians, who had so insultingly snubbed them, they insisted on being called *Mister*.

17. Zoology

I know you are an excellent driver – careful, skilled, and considerate to others – but when in heavy traffic in a foreign town you may possibly do something silly that could annoy the locals. Depending on where you are, some other motorist may lean out of the window and shout '*Chameau!*' (camel), '*Rindvieh!*', '*Rund!*' (cattle), '*Foca!*' (seal), '*Åsna!*' (donkey), '*Okse!*' (ox) or '¡*Animal!*'.

In English-speaking countries you will hear none of these zoological insults. Not because the people there are more forgiving or polite, but because all these animal terms mean nothing insulting to them. In English a camel has some vague connotation of thirst, cattle may make you think of docility, a seal could describe agility under water, a donkey has an image of stubbornness, and an ox could have something to do with strength. On the other hand, English does have expressions involving animals that you do not find in other languages. Here are some that you may meet in writing or conversation. One for each animal.

When you are **in the dog house**, you are **in disgrace**, temporarily unpopular:

He forgot his wife's birthday and was in the dog house for a whole month.

The cat appears in the adjective **catty**. It means **spiteful** and is applied to verbal comment only, not action. Here comes a catty remark:

When I showed her my new diamond ring, she said, 'Yes, these new imitation diamonds are really fantastic'.

Don't be upset. Men can also be catty. **Horseplay** is friendly but **rough play**, as you can see in any boys school at break time. In American English you also have the verb form **horsing around**. There is no implication of being dirty when someone **makes a pig of himself**. It means **eating** or **drinking too much**:

We all had one piece of chocolate cake. Angela had five! She made a pig of herself, as usual.

The sheep is not very aptly used in the adjective **sheepish**. It means **embarrassed**:

When I asked him why he had done such a silly thing, he just looked sheepish.

The **chicken** emerges in an unexpected way as adjective. In American slang it means **scared, afraid**:

Why don't you jump into the pool? Are you chicken?

Donkey work is essential but **not** very **interesting** work:

He travels; we stay behind and do all the donkey work at the office.

Bulls and **bears** appear in stock market reports. When prices tend to **rise**, it is called a **bull market**; when they fall, you have a **bear market**. Adjectives? Conditions are **bullish** or **bearish**. The cow gives us milk as well as the adjective **cowed**, meaning **subdued, docile**:

When the boisterous visitors saw the bill, they suddenly became rather cowed.

Monkey business is something suspicious, probably **dishonest**:

This revaluation of their assets looks a bit strange. I think there's some monkey business going on.

Fishy is an adjective meaning **doubtful, suspicious-looking**:

Don't sign the contract. There is something fishy here.

A highly **enjoyable time** is called a **whale of a time** in American English:

We had a whale of a time in Rio.

High grass can be a good hiding place for a snake. Someone who is called a **snake in the grass** is **deceitful**, somebody you cannot trust:

She went straight to the boss and told him. What a snake in the grass!

In some towns you find open-air markets where you can buy anything from rusty bicycle parts to double beds. Reminding you of what you may acquire in the mattresses, this is called a **flea market**. A small, third-class cinema? A **flea pit**. **Flies** find it difficult to settle peacefully on somebody who is always moving about, maybe someone who is **active** and full of **initiative**. Admiration of such a person is expressed by *There are no flies on him!*, with the stress on the last word. The **louse** is quoted extensively in American English where you find the slang term **lousy** (the s is pronounced as in 'rose') for **very bad**:

The service in this restaurant is lousy!

Rats live in a very competitive environment, rushing around to get food and stay alive. The **rat race** describes modern, **high-pressure life**, usually in business:

I am going to live on a tiny island in the South Pacific.
I'm getting out of the rat race.

12

International mistake museum

May I invite you for a stroll through our Museum with its collection of exhibits gathered in many countries? The reasons for the mistakes – with comments where necessary – extend across language borders. Errors found in German-speaking countries often also apply to Holland and Scandinavia. Others seen or heard in France may be the same as those recorded in Spain and Italy.

1. Tricky words

Backside

In German you have the word 'Rückseite', the Scandinavian languages offer 'baksida' or 'bagside', and in Dutch you find 'achterkant'. Relying on the Teutonic heritage in English, some people translate this as **backside**. Please don't! The **backside** is that part of your body on which you sit, at least in countries where British English is spoken. Mistakes can obviously cause embarrassment or giggles, so here are three less risky alternatives:

> The **back** of the house is being repainted.
>
> The guarantee is printed on the **reverse** of the sheet.
>
> The pump is attached to the **rear** of the machine.

In American English you do have **back side** (two words) with no anatomical connotation. During the moon landings the TV commentator used to mention that the command ship was orbiting the back side of the moon. Quite all right in North America; very funny elsewhere.

Barracks

In several languages this word means a poor kind of small building, a hut, a shack. In English it is used in the plural only and means a place where soldiers or other military personnel are housed. Barracks can therefore be quite luxurious.

Caricature

In all languages a caricature is a **grotesque presentation**, a distortion, an over-emphasis of certain features, usually of a person. This can be in the form of a written description, a performance on a stage or a drawing. A funny drawing, however, is not a caricature in English, but a **cartoon**. Caricature has a slightly negative, often malicious ring, whereas cartoon is usually more good-natured:

It was easy to draw a cartoon of De Gaulle.

The hand-drawn films first produced by Walt Disney and later by others were originally called **animated cartoons**, now just **cartoons**.

Chef

In France and some other countries this is the **Big Boss**. In English he is also the boss, but only in the kitchen: he is the **chief cook**. Pronunciation: 'sheff'.

Clever

An advertisement in an American news magazine, sponsored by a German investment firm, invites readers to join 'thousands of clever businessmen in many countries'. This sounds odd because the word **clever** can also have a negative sense, especially when applied to business people. It can then imply **cunning**, some degree of dishonesty. Those probably terribly rich businessmen described in the above advertisement should better be called **smart**. Here are a few other combinations in which some people may be tempted to use the frequently doubtful **clever**:

Astute management   A **wise** precaution   **Sensible** reserves.

Conductor

An English **conductor** can have two widely differing activities. He may conduct an **orchestra** or a choir, i.e. he directs the players or singers. He may also be a **bus conductor**. Although the verb **to conduct** looks like a relative of 'conduire', 'conducire', etc., it has here nothing to do with driving the bus. That's the **driver**'s job. The bus conductor is the other person on a public transport bus who **sells tickets** to the passengers. In London, for example.

Crayon

This French word exists in English, but not in the sense of pencil. It is that waxy type of writing implement (usually not enclosed in wood) used for colouring [Am.: coloring].

Critic

This word looks like 'Kritik', 'crítica', 'kritiek', and other cousins. Don't rely on it. The foreign words are abstract terms, but the English **critic** is a **person**. He or she is often a journalist or other professional writer who gives an appraisal of books, films, stage plays, concerts, sports events, and other presentations. The resulting report is not called 'criticism', but **review**, or **notice**:

Her latest novel received excellent reviews in the press.

The play had poor notices everywhere.

You could, in fact, say that a film critic *reviews* new films. The abstract term **criticism** is not quite the same as in other languages where it can be good or bad. The English **criticism** usually finds something wrong somewhere:

The proposed town plan met with widespread criticism.

Only **literary criticism** is more open-minded and can refer to a positive appraisal of a piece of writing.

Engineer

In all countries an engineer is someone qualified after studying some branch of engineering. The British engineer can indeed be the same kind of expert, but sometimes he is merely a mechanic. *'An engineer will call at your house at eleven o'clock'* promises nothing more than that someone with a hammer and a few other tools will visit you at half past eleven, look at your defective washing machine, scratch his head, and recommend that you should buy a new one.

In North America the engineer is at the controls of your **train engine**, i.e. the locomotive.

If you want to make it clear that you mean somebody qualified and not just the fellow with a toolbag, say *graduate engineer*, *mechanical engineer* or whatever other branch of engineering he may be qualified in.

Exposition

No, this is not a public display of products, works of art, etc. It is the noun of the verb to **expound** which means **explain in detail**:

He expounded his economic theories.

He gave an exposition of his theories.

If you put something on show, you stage an **exhibition**.

You have seen EXPO in connection with World Fairs? That is a concession to internationalism and languages that have exposition (French), exposición (Spanish), etc. Besides, the abbreviation 'EXHI' would not work. It sounds like a hiccup.

Fabric

There is no connection with 'fabrique', 'Fabrik', 'fábrica', etc. The place where something is being produced is a **factory**, in America also called **plant**. The English **fabric** is something **put together**. It may be **cloth**:

They brought out a new synthetic fabric.

It may be a **building structure**:

There is a weakness in the fabric of the roof.

It may be **figurative**:

His story was a fabric of lies from start to finish.

You could also call that a *complete fabrication*.

Fire

When you are desperate for a cigarette, but have forgotten your lighter or matches, you will have to ask somebody for help. Asking for 'fire' in English would be quite wrong, even if you are used to *feu/Feuer/fuego/fuoco/vuur*, etc. In English you ask for a **light**, not fire:

Can I have a light, please?

Gay/queer

These two adjectives used to be harmless and unambiguous: a **gay** person was **fun-loving** and **lively**, just about the opposite of someone who sits at home with a long face. **Queer** was more or less the same as **odd, strange, unusual** or **peculiar**.

Considerable care is now required with these two words, because they also serve as adjective as well as noun for **homosexual**. The difference between the two? **Gay** sounds much more tolerant and has therefore largely ousted **queer**. That's why there are self-styled gay bars, expressions like gay population, etc.

Play it safe by not using **gay** or **queer** in their original sense when referring to people. Use the synonyms mentioned above.

Genial

In many languages this adjective has a connection with the noun **genius**, somebody who is brilliant. In English it just means **jovial, cheerful, easygoing**, etc. i.e. attributes that have nothing to do with brains.

Inflammable

This has always been a misleading word because of the negative-looking prefix **in-**. You know **incomplete, inconsistent, involuntary**, and other words, in which the **in-** means 'not'. Associating the 'flammable' -part with **flame**, anyone can think that **inflammable** means that something will not burn. No. It's more or less the opposite: something inflammable is dangerous because it will burst into flames very easily.

Trucks carrying highly combustible fluids in the USA often bear the warning FLAMMABLE. Not really correct, as this word does not exist, but at least you and I know that it would be silly to light a cigarette while that fluid splashes on the ground.

Invaluable

Another word with a misleading prefix. There are the opposites **sufficient/insufficient, visible/invisible, definite/indefinite**, and so on, but **invaluable** does not mean 'not valuable'. It means **very valuable indeed**:

Their help was invaluable during these difficult months.

Labour [Am.: labor]

An Austrian company tells its customers about 'subsidiaries and fellow-labourers' in an English-language brochure. No; a **labourer** is not any kind of worker, but someone doing **unskilled**, often rough work. This may be on a building site, in road construction, general duties in the factory or wherever muscles are specially important. Depending on the exact meaning intended, the above 'fellow-labourers' can be **fellow-workers, colleagues** or **collaborators**. **Hard labour** is the physical **hard work** sometimes added to a prison sentence. **Labour troubles** are **strikes** and other difficulties with workers, not troubles with the work.

Labour is also the **pains before childbirth**. A woman is **in labour** immediately before the child is born.

Liquor

This word (pronounced 'licker') may make you think of that sweet after-dinner drink, the French 'liqueur'. There is a family connection, but not much more. **Liquor** is any kind of drink containing alcohol and has therefore a very much wider application. It (the word, not the substance) is more common in North America. The comment *He can hold his liquor* means that he can drink a lot without showing it.

That sweet after-dinner drink is called **liqueur** to make thinks easy for you. Its pronunciation is, however, 'lick-yure' in the English way, sometimes also as in French ('li-cur') in North America.

Music hall

This is not a building where concerts are presented. It is the general term for the old-fashioned kind of British stage show, where you may have singers, a conjurer, a comedian, and other varied fare. The American equivalent is **vaudeville**. Both terms are mainly used as adjectives:

A music hall artist.

On the vaudeville stage.

The modern equivalent of this mixed entertainment is called **variety**, the word you use in a few other languages:

A variety show at the Palladium.

Someone at the back of the class may ask 'But where do I go to hear Beethoven's Symphony No. 6 in F Major?' Then you are looking for a **concert hall**.

Original

Two meanings of the English **original** coincide with those in other languages. The first one is **genuine**, when you talk about an original painting by Goya, for example. The second one is **imaginative**, novel when you comment on someone's *original project*. The third meaning, however, is quite different: **first**, as in this sentence:

The original plan was to start construction in May.

Adverbially, **originally** means in the **beginning, initially**:

They lived most of their lives in New York.
Originally they came from Montana.

Pause

The English **pause** (noun and verb) refers to a **very short interruption** of speech or movement:

The comma marks a natural pause in a sentence.

She walked to the corner, paused to look at the notice, and came back.

In other languages 'pause' means unoccupied time or recreational period. When you are in a theatre [Am.: theater] there is some time between the acts to enable you to sneak out for a smoke or a dry sherry. This is called the **interval** in British

English; the **intermission** in American English. Any other interruption to give you a rest is a **break**. This can be minutes, it can be months:

There is a ten-minute break after the third lesson.

Reclamation

In several languages this word means complaint, request for replacement of something defective, claim for reimbursement, etc. The English **reclamation** has a much narrower meaning: creating cultivable land; land on which you can grow things. You can reclaim land from the jungle, from the desert or – most spectacularly – from the sea. The Dutch are very clever at putting up dykes and converting sea into arable land.

Reclamation in the sense of **getting something back** can also apply to the **recovery** of material: the reclamation of certain metals from industrial waste, for example. So if your video still doesn't work after your local dealer charged you a fortune for repairing it, **make a complaint**. Not a reclamation.

Secretariat

In many languages a similar word refers to the place where secretarial work and some administration is going on. That would be a **General Office** or maybe **Registry** in English. The English secretariat is always in a non-profit-making organization: the secretariat of the United Nations, of a trade union, of a professional association, etc.

Self-conscious

Taking this adjective to pieces, we get *being conscious of your own self*, but only in the sense of being **aware** of your **defects** and other shortcomings. These may be inability to dance the tango, a hole in the seat of your pants, brown shoes with a blue suit, and other minor weaknesses. These may make you **embarrassed** or **shy**. That's what **self-conscious** means.

The German 'selbstbewusst' and the Dutch 'zelfbewust' look like its cousin, but mean **full of confidence, self-confident,** almost the opposite. Danish goes even further: 'selvbevidst' means **arrogant**.

Sensible

In many languages this word has something to do with sense or feeling. It describes a person who has to be treated very carefully because he or she may be easily hurt or annoyed by what you may say or do. This is obviously a negative kind of characteristic. Not in English, where **sensible** has to do with common sense, with good sense. A sensible person is somebody described elsewhere as 'sensé', 'vernünftig', 'sensato', 'förnuftig', 'verstandig', etc. All these are positive features. A few examples for practice:

This seems a sensible move. = **Wise**.

She is very sensible for her age. = **Knows what is right**.

It's the only sensible thing to do. = **Correct**.

The English adjective for your 'sensible' in the sense of **touchy, thin-skinned, easily hurt** is SENSITIVE:

He is very sensitive about his big ears.

Sensitive can also mean easily affected in a more physical way. If you have a sensitive skin, you may easily get sunburnt or you may get irritations from that new cream. The film in your camera is sensitive to light.

Sensible

Sensitive

Serviceable

When someone tells you that a machine is serviceable, you may possibly think that it can be serviced, i.e. that it can be repaired. No. **Serviceable** means that it is **suitable for service**, ready for use:

After six weeks in the workshop the engine is again serviceable.

Smoking

If you are a man and are invited to a formal dinner or other event, you may be asked to wear a **dinner jacket**; also **tuxedo** in American English. (Don't be misled by the word **jacket**; it refers to the complete suit known in some other languages as 'smoking'.)

Here is something strange: an English word that does not exist in English. **Smoking** is the present participle or gerund of the verb **to smoke**, and nothing else. The expression **black tie** describes the need for a dinner jacket, and a dinner party where it is required can be called a **black tie dinner**. A **white tie** event calls for the other kind of formal men's wear with those tail-like extremities on the jacket, also called **tails**. So whatever you pull out of mothballs for the occasion, it is never a 'smoking'. At least not in English.

Social

No complication if you are thinking of **social security, social welfare**, and similar concepts found in your own language as well as in English. The English **social** can also be applied to **communal life** and **relations**. When you invite lots of people five times a week, you have an active **social life**, extensive **social activities**. A **social evening** is an evening with friends. Someone who likes this sort of thing is called **sociable**. If you prefer staying at home with a good book, people may call you **unsociable** or **anti-social**.

Spare

What do you call the fifth wheel in your car? Probably something combined with the word 'reserve' or similar. In English, however, you call it a **spare** wheel. When going on that long trip by car, why not take a few **spare parts** along?

Undertaker

This word may remind you of the French *entrepreneur* or the German *Unternehmer*, the **independent businessman**. The English undertaker has a very restricted function: he arranges **funerals**.

Uneasy

This is not the opposite of *easy* in the sense of *not easy*, i.e. difficult. It means **worried, perturbed, not relaxed**:

He is two hours overdue. They are getting uneasy.

Her temperature is still high. She spent an uneasy night.

We never trusted him fully, and our relationship was always a little uneasy.

Ventilator

What's so remarkable about this international leaflet? The fact that it is called **fan** in English, not ventilator.

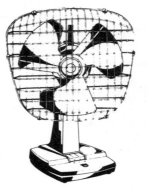

VENTILADOR GARBI
GARBI FAN
VENTILATEUR GARBI
GARBI VENTILATOR
VENTILATORE GARBI
VENTILATOR GARBI

Warehouse

Speakers of the Teutonic languages often think that this must obviously be the English cousin of their **Warenhaus, varuhus, varehus** or **warenhuis**, the big retail store where you can buy a wide variety of goods. No, a **warehouse** is a more modest establishment. It is a place where you **store** goods, not sell them. It is sometimes just a big single-storey hut.

A big retail store is called a **department store**.

2. Typical mistakes made by foreigners in correspondence

This collection of mistakes from several countries is grouped according to whether the key word is a noun, verb, adjective/ adverb, preposition or from the mixed department of our Museum.

• Nouns

The after-calculation showed that we made a loss of 6 per cent

German and Dutch have useful accounting terms that are sometimes translated literally as 'pre-calculation' and 'after-calculation'. The correct English expressions are quite different. If you have to quote a price **before** you know the final cost of an article or service, you make an **estimate**.

Afterwards, when you have all cost factors available, you can do the **costing**:

'Pre-calculation' = **estimate**
'After-calculation' = **costing**.

Although the verb **to cost** is irregular in its more common intransitive form (it **costs** £5 today; it **cost** £4 last week; it **has cost** us a fortune), it remains regular when used in the sense explained above:

No wonder we have been losing money on the radiator. It has not been **costed** *since 1972.*

Can we have five exemplars a month?

The English **exemplar** is more restricted in meaning than the similar-looking 'exemplaire', 'Exemplar', 'exemplaar', 'eksemplar', 'ejemplar', etc., which means one unit. That can be anything. The English **exemplar** also means unit, but implies that there are not many in existence:

You may find an exemplar of this bible in the British Museum.

When you refer to something printed, you use the word **copy**:

Please send me ten more copies.

We bought our copy at the station.

Let's discuss it under four eyes tomorrow

The expression 'under four eyes' is very descriptive: if no more than four eyes are present, it must be a meeting of only two people, i.e. a private one. The only trouble with this phrase is that it does not exist in English. Better say or write:

Let's discuss it privately.

In combination with nouns you have:

A private talk or meeting.

A talk in private.

A confidential talk.

If a more personal matter is being discussed, you can also call it a **heart-to-heart** talk. Another part of the anatomy but the same idea as that of the four eyes.

Leader of the Research and Development department

You may be the leader of a sports team or military unit, but in the more peaceful environment of your company it is better to use the word **head** whenever **manager** does not apply:

Head of the Library.

Head of the Statistics Department.

We handle machineries for the paper-making industry

A leaflet in English, produced in Japan, mentions 'machineries' and 'equipments'. Both are collective nouns that have only the singular form:

We handle machinery/we supply equipment.

If you want to stress your versatility, you can say

*We handle **various types** of machinery/equipment.*
*We handle **many kinds** of machinery/equipment.*
*We have a **wide range** of machinery/equipment.*

Equipment in the plural can also be expressed as **accessories**:

A number of extra accessories can be supplied.

This costs DM 32 per piece

In many languages you say 'per piece' in this kind of price information. In English it is **each** or the abbreviation **ea.**:

*The chromium-plated wheels are £4.50 **each**.*
*200 bearings Type KT 456 . . . . . $17.30 **ea**. . . . . . . $3460.*

We wish you a good receipt

In French you may wish someone 'une bonne réception', in German 'einen guten Empfang', but you cannot translate these wishes into English. If you look at it closely, it is not even very logical. If I send you something, I should really wish myself a 'good receipt', not you. I'll be the loser if the parcel does not reach you. You will probably get a replacement, anyway.

If you do want to express your optimism and cover both sender and recipient, simply say:

We hope that the goods will reach you safely.

They formed a separate society for their export sales

No. The commercial organization meant here is a **company, firm** or maybe **corporation**. When the word **society** refers to an organization, it is always an **association** of people with a common interest:

> *The Royal Society for the Prevention of Cruelty to Animals.*
>
> *The American Society of Amsterdam.*

She had great success with this show

The combination 'to have success' is quite all right in other languages, but in English it sounds wrong. Better versions:

> *She was highly **successful** with this show.*
>
> *Her show **was** a great **success**.*

• Verbs

We wish to annul our membership at the end of the year

No. The general word when you simply mean 'no more, thanks' to a current or intended arrangement is **cancel**. You cancel an appointment, a lease, an order. This can be verbal or in writing, but involves no special judicial procedure. Far more formal and usually requiring the intervention of a court is an **annulment**. This means that something is **officially declared invalid**, and always applies to the more weighty obligations tied up in contracts.

They assisted at the meeting

If you did indeed help by carrying in the chairs, dusting the table, and sweeping the floor, you admittedly gave some assistance.

On the other hand, there is 'assister à une réunion' and related versions in Spanish and Italian, which mean that you were there. The above sentence should then be any of these three:

> *They **attended** the meeting.*
>
> *They **took part in** the meeting.*
>
> *They **were present at** the meeting.*

We dispose of the latest aircraft

An East European airline makes this doubtful boast in a leaflet. Readers in English-speaking countries will react by saying 'We hope not!'. Why? Because **to dispose of** means **throw away, get rid of**:

She disposed of the worn-out carpet.

(Dictionaries will tell you that there is indeed another meaning: **have authority over**, but this is now so rarely used that **to throw away** is today the principal meaning associated with this verb.)

You have **disposable** towels, made of paper. You throw them away after use. Your **waste disposal** unit under the kitchen sink grinds up the scraps to get rid of them. So if you do not throw away your aircraft, but simply **own** them, just put:

We operate the latest aircraft.

We appreciate your amusing way of learning us English

The Belgian writer must have been thinking of the Flemish/Dutch 'leren' which means both **teach** and **learn**. No. The **teacher teaches**, but the **student** (I hope) **learns**. The same mistake is sometimes made in less educated circles in German-speaking countries where 'lernen' has a slight similarity to 'lehren'.

They made a lot of publicity on television

This Spanish misuse of the verb **to make** in this kind of construction could also happen to someone speaking most of the other European languages, where you 'faire publicité', 'Reklame machen', 'gøre reklame', and so on. Therefore almost a 'trans-European' mistake. In English you need another verb. A few ideas:

*They **undertook** a lot of promotion* (better than 'publicity').

*They **did** a lot of promotion.*

*They **ran** a lot of advertising.*

They passed three weeks in Finland

A typical mistake made by speakers of the Romance languages. The English **to pass** is usually a **physical** movement:

The car passed us at very high speed.

If you refer to **time**, you need the verb **to spend**:

*They **spent** three weeks in Finland.*

We profit from the occasion to send you our latest brochure

Good French, but poor English. Solution:

*We **take this opportunity** of sending you our latest brochure.*

In this phrase the word **opportunity** must be followed by **of** + the gerund, not by 'to' + the infinitive, i.e. 'to send you' is wrong.

We hope to read you soon

Speakers of French will recognize this as their 'en espérant de vous lire'. Speakers of only English will be puzzled, as they are used to reading something printed, but never a person. Improvement:

We hope to hear from you soon.

The plan can be realized in six months

You can indeed 'réaliser un plan' in French, but a literal translation is not the right solution here. While in English you can realize an ambition, the English verb to realize is mainly a mental process: *they realized that they had lost the match.*

What you can do with your plan is **carry** it **out, implement** it, **complete** it, **execute** it.

We want to subscribe for your magazine

To is the correct preposition to go with **subscribe/subscription**:

*We wish to subscribe **to** your publication.*

When using the word **subscription**, you usually phrase it like this:

*We wish to **take out** a subscription **to** the trade journal.*

• Adjectives/adverbs

The project is no longer actual

The English word **actual** means **real** and not much else:

Although the estimate sounded reasonable, the actual cost was very high.

You should compare projected sales with actual sales.

The similar-looking foreign words 'actuel', 'aktuell', 'aktueel', etc. do not mean the same. They refer to things that are **current, up to date, of the moment**. The best English word for something that has a bearing on current events is **topical**.

A topical play   A topical article   A topical TV series.

If, as in the heading, you want to talk about a project or idea, you can say:

*The project is no longer **under discussion**.*

*The project is no longer **under consideration**.*

*The project is no longer **alive**.*

We have almost no old stock left/we have nearly no spare parts in stock

The combinations **almost no** and **nearly no** exist in most languages. Translated into English, they sound odd. What you do use instead is **hardly any**:

We have hardly any spare parts left.

You can also use the phrase **next to**:

Although we ship to many countries, we have next to no breakages.

He is one of my ancient pupils

old students

ancient students

Speakers of French, Spanish or Italian sometimes wrongly use **ancient** when translating their 'ancien', 'antiguo' or 'antico'. The English **ancient** refers to people and things that go back in **history**: the Ancient Romans, ancient books, ancient monuments, ancient history, ancient treaties, etc. **Ancient** is also occasionally used when you want to exaggerate:

We saw an ancient Greta Garbo film.

As the pupil mentioned in the above sentence is unlikely to be 300 years old and the remark presumably not meant to be funny, you simply use **old** instead, as it can also mean **former**:

*He is one of my **old** pupils.*

We may come eventually

Eventuellement, eventuell, eventualmente, eventueel, eventuelt mean:

perhaps   maybe   under certain conditions   possibly   could be

They all express **uncertainty**. The English **eventually** means:

definitely, but later   in the end   sooner or later   it will happen, but not right now

All these express **certainty**, but indicate some vagueness about the timing. You could therefore say that the English **eventually** is almost the opposite of the seemingly identical word in other languages.

When President De Gaulle was at his most negative about Britain's joining the European Economic Community (now *EC*, before *EEC*; and formerly *Common Market*), he told a journalist from a London newspaper that 'Britain will join eventually'. To UK readers this sounded very positive; a remarkable change of mind. Far from it. De Gaulle's 'eventuellement' merely meant *maybe, perhaps, under certain conditions*. Not much of a change.

Friendly regards

Regards are indeed friendly in all Teutonic languages, but in English you send:

Kind regards,

Best regards,

or just

Regards.

It represents an important price increase

Although the French 'important' and the Spanish/Italian 'importante' are usually the English **important**, I would in this kind of combination recommend other adjectives:

A ***considerable*** *price increase.*

A ***major*** *rise.*

A ***marked*** *advance.*

Thank you heartily

The heart is acceptable in 'herzlich', 'hartelijk', and 'hjärtlig', but the English **hearty** is mainly limited to: a *hearty meal* (**filling** meal), a *hearty welcome* (**warm** welcome) and *hearty laughter* (**uninhibited** laughter). Gratitude, although quite possibly coming straight from the heart, should be phrased:

Thank you very much indeed.

Thanks a lot (colloquial).

'Hearty greetings' could become *Best wishes*.

We await your soon reply

You cannot use **soon** as attributive adjective, i.e. placed in front of a noun. The word you then need instead is **early**:

Your early reply.

Their earliest departure.

Our early decision.

Early can have three different meanings:

The store opens early = at an **early hour**.

They like to come early = **before** the required **time**.

The early inauguration = **soon**.

You probably associate the word **soon** with time. Quite right, but you can also use it when expressing a **preference**:

*I would **sooner** fly than take the boat,*

means *I **prefer** to be scared stiff for one hour to being seasick for twenty.*

*I would **just as soon** forget about the incident*

means *I prefer to forget it.*

It will be ready within short

'Within short' does not exist in English, even though Dutch has the misleading 'binnenkort' and Swedish the tempting 'inom kort'. Remedy:

*It will **soon** be ready.*

*It will be ready **shortly**.*

● **Prepositions**

She sat on our table

A friend of mine, who speaks excellent English, recently surprised me with this remark. The preposition **on** here can only mean **on top of**. If she is a little eccentric she may indeed sit on top of the table while you are munching your Wiener Schnitzel, but more normal would be **at**, i.e. on a chair by the side of the table:

*She sat **at** our table.*

We saw it in television/heard it in the radio

Many languages use the preposition **in**. English has **on**:

It was on TV last night

They mentioned it on the radio.

It was sent on your own risk

Danish preposition trouble, which could also happen to speakers of German and Dutch. You need **at**:

*It was sent **at** your own risk.*

The shipment is destined to Veracruz

Something is **sent to, consigned to, shipped to, mailed to, dispatched to**, and so on; but when the verb is **to destine**, it is always **for**:

*The shipment is destined **for** Veracruz.*

For is also used with the verbs **to leave, to sail**, and **to depart**:

Our friends left/sailed/departed for Thailand.

You can sail **to** a place, but then you are thinking more of movement than of the act of departing.

We are fully dependent of one supplier/independent from them

Be careful with two prepositions: you are dependent **on**, independent **of**.

To my opinion this sounds wrong

A small correction, please: use **in** in place of **to**:

In my opinion this sounds wrong.

Maybe the speaker got things mixed up with the phrase **to my mind**, which means exactly the same:

In my opinion she is right = **to** my mind she is right.

Please address the envelope to my attention

You bring something **to** the attention or notice of somebody, but you send it **for** his or her attention.

I hate to confuse you, but you do bring something to my attention by addressing it for my attention. . . .

Are you coming with?

With is what you can say on its own in any of the Teutonic languages, but in English you need a personal pronoun as well:

*Are you coming with **us**?*

Another possibility is:

*Are you coming **along**?*

The price was increased with 15 per cent

A mistake often seen and heard in Holland and Scandinavia. There you do use 'met' and 'med', but in English it must be **by**. Exercise:

Increased **by** 10 per cent.

Reduced **by** half.

Raised **by** three feet.

With other words, they are bankrupt

Located in Austria, but also possible in countries where they speak Dutch or any of the Scandinavian languages. The preposition should be **in**:

***In** other words, they are bankrupt.*

• Non-existent abbreviations

Foreigners sometimes make mistakes by using abbreviations that don't exist in English. German speakers, for example, have 'u.s.w.' for 'and so on' and assume that this should be 'a.s.o.' in a letter to an English-speaking country. It means nothing over there, so be careful with such home-made products. Here are a few:

abt.   This abbreviation for **about** does not officially exist in English-speaking countries. Excepting **Rd** for **Road**, people seem to take the view: **if an abbreviation does not save more than two letters, don't bother.**

a.o.   This non-existent shortcut is often used by corres-pondents who remember the German 'u.a.' for 'unter anderm' and the Dutch 'o.a.' for 'onder andere', their phrase for **among others**.

Mistaken logic: 'a.o' must mean among others. It means nothing whatever to people in English-speaking countries.

a.s.o.   Possible confusion can be avoided by using the correct **etc.** in place of the unknown a.s.o.

f.e./f.i.   Unless the people you write to have read this book, they will not know what these letters mean. They are not the accepted way of shortening **for example** and **for instance**, which have only one correct abbreviation: **e.g.** (exempli gratia):

> *Many machine tools are now made locally, e.g. lathes, millers, grinders, drills, and so on.*

MD   Placed after a person's name, this means *medicinae doctor*, i.e. *Doctor of Medicine*. As it is not the accepted abbreviation for Managing Director, please be careful.

Nr.   This is not short for *number*, as in some languages, but for *near*; Westham nr. Eastbourne, for example. *Number* is abbreviated **No.**: No. 10. Plural: **Nos.** 10 and 11.

VD   In German-speaking countries VD is sometimes used for 'Vizedirektor'. There is unfortunately only one interpretation known to people in English-speaking countries: venereal disease. Anyone so afflicted should keep quiet about it. Except to his doctor, of course.

• Mixed department

Her hairs are blonde

Depends what you mean. If you are thinking about the **whole head**, you say:

> *Her hair is blonde* (singular).

If you are referring to **individual strands** of hair, you can use the plural:

He has hairs on the back of his hands

means the normal bit of growth. *He has hair on the back of his hands* expresses surprise at more than the usual density.

The parts we need immediately are as follow

It is always **as follows**, with the verb in the third person singular, even if you are introducing more than one item.

How is this called in English?

A frequently heard mistake, because you can indeed use the equivalent of 'how' in several languages. In English you need **what**:

***What** is this called in English?*

How is correct when the sentence contains other verbs:

How do you say it in French?

How would you translate this?

How do you express this correctly?

He is no more employed by us

Speakers of the Teutonic languages sometimes use 'no more' here, a straight translation of what they are used to. The best English in this construction is **no longer** or **not . . . any longer**:

*She is **no longer** with us.*

*He is **not** living here **any longer**.*

It will be ready one of these days

This has little to do with the French 'un de ces jours', the Dutch 'een dezer dagen', the Spanish 'uno de estos días' or the Danish 'en af dagene'. All these promise that something will happen **very soon**. The English *one of these days*, however, is very **vague** and means no more than some time in the future, if you are lucky, if all goes well, if we can manage.

If Uncle Bob promises to mend that broken fence in the garden 'one of these days', you can be sure that it will still be hanging loose when you come again next year. Better versions of the foreign phrases:

Within a day or two.

Within a day or so.

Within a few days.

We remain, dear Sirs, Yours faithfully

The complimentary close in French is 'Agréez, Messieurs, nos salutations distinguées', bringing in that last-minute 'Messieurs', but the English version should simply be the one-liner:

Yours faithfully,

or

Very truly yours

or any of the other possibilities given on page 104.

We have not seen him since long

'Since long' does not exist in English, even if French may have 'depuis longtemps' and German 'seit langem'. Correction:

We have not seen him for a long time.

A related mistake is the combination 'since days', 'since months', 'since years', and other indications of time. In English you use the **continuous form** of the **present perfect tense** and the preposition **for** before the time unit:

They have been producing calculators for years.

She has been waiting for months.

Word index

Major subjects, as given in the Contents on pages vii–xv, as well as key words treated in some detail, are in bold letters. Chapter headings, such as *Perfect your grammar*, can be found under **Grammar**.

Several main chapters contain hundreds of words, as, for example, those dealing with irregular plurals, British/American spelling differences, collective nouns, and others. Words in these chapters are not individually listed, as the reader is more likely to look them up under the main subject headings.

Abbreviations 43, 94, 317
-able/-ible 82
aborigine 147
absolutes 31
abstract nouns 125
accidentally 78
accommodation 78
according to our records 111
acquaintance 78
actual 311
actually 113
address 78
adequate 183
adherence 158
adhesion 158
admirable 147
admission 159
admittance 159
Adverbs 11
ad(vertisement) 94
advise 117

affect 159
aggressive 78
agree/on/to/with 73
all but 249
almond 149
alms 149
alternate 119
alternative 119
although 39
America 287
american cloth 86
American English/British English
(see **Universal English**) 131
amiable 159
amicable 159
amp(ère) 94
ample 183
ancient 312
anemone 147
angry about/at/with 73
annul 308

321

answer 245
anticipate 117
anti-clockwise 236
antipodes 147
anybody 25
anyone 25
Apostrophe 47
appreciate + *-ing* 117
aproximately 113
apt 182
around 246
as per 114
assassinate 174
assist 308
assuring of best attention 111
astute 295
At 64
at earliest convenience 106
at early date 106
at random 67
at times 67
attached herewith 111
audit 265
awaiting your reply 110

baby carriage 95
bachelor 78
backside 293
Bad 273
baddie 275
badly 275
balk 149
balm 149
bankruptcy 78
bargain 238
barracks 294
basically 79
Be 185
bear market 291
beautiful 180
because 122
Belgian/Belgium 79
below 183
benefited 79
beside/besides 160
B/F (brought forward) 96
big 178, 179
black 262

black tie 303
blink 160
blue 262
blush 161
board 28
boat 181
bomb 149, 238
bore 247
bow 147
bra(ssière) 94
break 301
brethren 86, 91
Britain/British Isles 286
British English/American English
(see **Universal English**) 131
brussels sprouts 86
budget 238
budgie/budgerigar 94
bull market 291
bus conductor 295
but 248
buzz 233
by 317
by return of post 105

Call 188
calm 149
Cambridge 147
Can I help you? 230
can/may 38
Can this be right? 38
Capitals 84
cardinal numbers 270
caricature 294
cartoon 294
Case against *case* 125
catastrophe 79
catty 290
caulk 149
-ceed/-cede 83
cemetery 79
C/F (carried forward) 96
cheap 238
Check 267
check 265
Cheers! 239
chef 295
chemist 139

chicken 290
chicken feed 239
childish/childlike 161
clerk 147
clever 295
Cliché collection 105
client 162
climb 149
clockwise 236
Cold 275
Collective nouns 27
Colon 46
Colo(u)rs 262
comb 149
Come 188
Comma 57
commenting relative clauses 26, 61
commitment 79
committee 28, 79
company are/is 29
comparable 147
compare to/with 73
Comparisons 30, 36
complimentary endings 104
compound adjectives 51
concerned about/with 74
concert hall 300
conductor 295
congregation 27
constant 162
consult/consult with 143
content/contents 161
continual/continuous 161
Control 264
controller 265
Conversation 225
cool 277
copy 306
cordially yours 104
Correspondence 98
cost/costing 305
costly 238
could 39
counter-clockwise 237
cowed 291
cradle 232
crayon 295
crew 27

critic/criticism 295
customer 162

Dash 54, 150
date (in letters) 101
daylight robbery 238
dead + adjective 280
dear 237
debt 144
decimal comma/point 269
Decrease 268
deem 118
deep 12
defining relative clauses 26, 61
definite/definitive 162
department 163
department store 305
desert 79
dessert 79
destined for 316
developed 79
dial 232
dinner jacket 303
Diplomacy 126
dirt cheap 239
discreet/discrete 79
disinterested 179
dispose of 309
distinct/distinctive 164
distribute 157
Dividing words 53
division 163
Do 190
dog house 290
donkey work 291
Don't mention it 232
dot 149
doubt 149
dough 146
draft/draught 241
Drinking expressions 239
Drop 194
druggist 139
dues 96
duly signed 114
dumb 149

each 167, 307

early 314
earth 238
eatable 164
eccentric 80
economic/economical 164
economy 238
ecstasy 80
edible 164
effect 159
efficient 165
e.g. 165
egoist/egotist 166
Eire 286
either 39
elder 175
electric/electrical 166
embarrass 80
enclosed please find 116
enclosures (in letters) 104
Endings 104, 109
engineer 296
England 286
enough 183
enthusiastic 80
Envelope 99
error 167
Esquire 99
estimate 305
even 254
eventually 312
every 167
everybody/everyone 25
ex- 181
exaggerate 80
exam(ination) 94
examine 265
exceptionable/exceptional 167
Exclamation mark 44
exemplar 306
exhibition 296
exorbitant 238
expensive 237
exposition 296
Eye, let's hit him in the 41

fabric 297
fair 249
Fall 194

family 29
fan 304
farther 168
fast 168
feasible 118
fee 162, 184
fewer 172
fiery 80
Figures 269
fire 80, 297
fishy 291
fix 250
fizzy 241
flammable 298
flea market 291
flea pit 291
flexible 80
flies 291
floor 169
flu 94
flush 161
folk 149
For 67
for years 141
for your information 112
Foreign Office 163
former 181
forty 80
forward 114
fourteen 80
french fried potatoes 86
fuchsia 148
fulfil(l) 80
full stop 43
fun 250
funny bone 251
further 168
Future 4, 169

gage 148
gang 27
gauge 148
gay 298
general office 301
genial 298
Genitive 16
Geography 286
gerund + possessive pronoun 120

Get 196
getaway 198
Ghoti, pronunciation of 152
Give 199
glasses 96
Go 199
golf 149
Good 273
good afternoon 226
good day 225
good evening 226
good morning 226
good night 226
goodby(e) 227
good-looking 180
goodie 275
goose egg 151
government 27
Grammar 1
Great Britain 286
green 264
Greetings 225
gray/grey 263
gross 148
gym(nasium) 94

hair 318
half an hour 144
hand 236, 251
handkerchief 80
handsome 180
hardly any 311
harass 80
Have 202
head 306
heading (in letters) 103
heart-to-heart 306
hearty 313
height 80
hello 243
Hello, hello! 232
henceforth 107
hereafter 107
herein 107
hereof 107
hereto 107
herewith 107
hesitate 107

Hi! 227
hiccough/hiccup 147
high 12
hippo(potamus) 95
historic/historical 169
Holland 286
horse face 181
horseplay 290
horsing around 290
Hot 275
How do you do? 228
How much? 237
human/humane 169
Hyphen 49

-ible/-able 82
Idioms 185
i.e. 165
if 39, 170
ill 287
impersonal *it* 124
imply 170
in/into 36
in/to 74
in due course 106
in the amount of 107
in years 141
incidentally 80
incredible/incredulous 171
independent 80
independently 80
india rubber 86
indict 148
indispensable 80
inexpensive 238
infamous 148
infer 170
Infinitive, split 35
inflammable 298
inspect 265
insulated 171
intake 221
intention + of 117
intermission 301
**International mistake
museum** 293, 305
interval 300
Introductions 228

invaluable 298
Inverted commas 55
involved 112
I.O.U./IOU 97
Irish Republic 286
irregardless 119
irreparable 148
-ise/-ize 83
-ish 273
isolated 171
it's me 19

job 199
journey 181
jury 27
just too bad 275

Keep it simple 121
key 232
kindly 115
Knock 204

Lab(oratory) 95
Labo(u)r 95, 299
lager 241
lamb 149
large 178
last 171
late 181
latest 171
Lay 172, 205
leader 306
legible 177
lengthy 173
less 172
Let 206
Let's hit him in the eye 41
Letter 101
Letter endings 109
liable 182
lie 172
light 297
lightening 80
lightning 80
Like 278
likely 182
limb 149
line 233

liqueur 299
liquor 299
literature 81
little 178
long 173
long drinks 240
looking forward to 110
loose 13, 81
lose 81
loud 13
lousy 291
love 151
low 12
lying 81

mad about/at 74
major 313
majority 29
Make 206
Manners 241
many 174
margarine 148
marked 313
marmalade 81
mattress 81
may/can 38
MD 318
me 19
**Meaningless phrases and
     words** 111
measure 265
Medicine 287
Mediterranean 81
meet/meet with 144
memo(randum) 95
might 39
mike 95
mind 252
minority 29
mistake 167
monitor 265
monkey business 291
More figure work 271
More scope for improvement 113
mortgage 148
movie 255
much 174, 179

murder 174, 282
Murder class 280
muscle 148
music hall 299
myself 19

nature 124
neat 241
Netherlands 286
next to 312
nil 151
no longer 319
no one 25
nobody 25
Nocturnal news 282
North/Northern 87
Northern Ireland 286
not a thing 284
not so . . . as 36
Not what the teacher said 34
Nothing 283
notice 296
nought 150
Nouns, collective 27
null and void 152
number 29

O, pronunciation of 150
oblige 112
occurrence 81
odd 253
odd numbers 254
offer 174
official/officious 175
older 175
On 69
on time/in time 175
One 22, 271
Only 41
op(eration) 95
orchestra 27
ordinal numbers 270
original 300
o-u-g-h 146
Out 71
outfit 254
outrageous 238

pack 182
package 182
packet 182, 238
palm 149
panama hat 86
paraffin 81
parcel 182
pardon 242
parliament 81
participle clauses 34, 60
pass/past 175, 310
Past 1
pastime 81
patient 162
pause 300
peanuts 239
per 114
per piece 307
perambulator 95
perhaps 118
Period 43
perm(anent wave) 95
permissible 81
person-to-person call 234
personal call 234
personnel 28, 81, 149
phrasal compounds 52
physician 288
picture 255
pig 290
pink 264
place 255
Play 209
please 241
plumb, plumber 149
Plurals 87
plurals, apostrophe in 48
P.O.B./POB 100
point 256
poor 257
practicable/practical 176
pram 95
precede 83
preface 149
prefer 39
preferable 149
Prepositions 64
prepositions, at end of sentence 37

pretty 180
prevent 120
price 176
pricey 238
principal/principle 177
prior to 115
private school 139
prize 176
proceed 81
pro(fessional) 95
professions 162
proficient 165
promissory 81
Pronouns 19
  impersonal 22
  intensive 21
  interrogative 35
  possessive 20
  reflexive 20
Pronunciation 81, 146
pronunciation, of 'ch' 150
psalm 149
P.T.O./p.t.o./PTO/pto 97
public school 139
publicly 79
Pull 210
Punctuation 43, 100
Push 211
Put 213

qualm 149
queer 298
query 177
question 177
Question mark 44
questionnaire 81
quick 168
quotation 174
Quotation marks 55

rain 285
rain check 285
rat race 292
rather than 39
ratio 149
re 108
readable 177

realize 310
receiver 232
recipe 149
reclamation 301
red 262
reference (in letters) 101
regards 313
registry 301
relative clauses 60
relevant 113
remember 258
Republic of Ireland 286
reservations 258
responsible 81
rest assured 108
review/reviewer 296
revs. (revolutions) 95
rhino(ceros) 96
row 149
RSVP 97
Run 215
Russia 287

said 115
salmon 149
salutation (in letters) 102
same 108
satellite 81
search 265
secretariat 301
See 218
see you! 227
self-conscious 301
sell 259
Semicolon 46
sensible 295, 302
sensitive 302
Sentence fragments 37
separate 81
series 91
serviceable 303
shall/will 7
She 259
sheepish 290
ship 181
shoot 260
short drinks 240

sick 287
signature (in letters) 104
silent *b* 149
silent *l* 149
Silent parade 76
sky-high 238
sleep 260
slough 147
small 178
smoking 303
smooth 81
snake in the grass 291
snow job 285
sociable/social 303
society 307
soft drinks 241
solicitor 81
somebody 25
someone 25
soothe 81
spare (part) 303
spartan 86
specialist 288
specs (spectacles) 96
Spelling 78, 132
Split infinitive 35
staff 29
standby 88
State Department 163
stationary/stationery 81
stimulant/stimulus 178
storey 169
straight 241
Stress 146, 152
stroke 150
Style 105
subject line (in letters) 103
Subjunctive 8
sub(marine) 96
sub(scription) 96
sub(stitute) 96
subscribe/subscription 82, 311
subtle 149
sufficient 183
sun dial 236
superfluous 149
superintendent 82

supervise 265
surgeon 288

table 145
Take 219
take care! 227
talk 149
tall 179
teach/learn 309
**Teacher, not what the teacher
    said** 34
team 27
Tear 222
Telephone terms 232
telly 96
tendency 82
test 265
thanking in anticipa-
    tion/advance 110
That 26, 33
Thing 283
though 33, 40
thousands divisions 269
through 77
thumb 149
time, in/on 175
Time, what's the? 234
to hand 108
to my mind 316
tomb 149
transpire 119
trip 181
truly 82
try and 40
Turn 222
turpentine 82
tuxedo 303
tyranny 82

UK (United Kingdom) 286
Ulster 286
under 183
under the weather 285
underneath 183
Understatement 128
undertaker 304
uneasy 304

uninterested 179
United Kingdom 286
Universal English 131
  opposite meaning 145
  prepositions 141
  pronunciation 140
  spelling 132
  terminology 135
USA 287
USSR 287

variety 300
vaudeville 300
VD 318
venetian blind 86
ventilator 304
verify 265
very 179
vessel 181
vet(eran) 96
vet(erinary surgeon) 96
victuals 149
visit/visit with 144
Vocabulary 245
voluntary 82
voyage 181

wages 184
walk 149
warehouse 305
wash/wash up 143
wastage/waste 180
waste disposal 309

Watch your figure 269
way 260
Weather report 285
wellington boots 86
West/Western 87
whale of a time 291
What's the time? 234
when 33
whether 170
Which 26
Which of the two/three/four? 158
Which preposition? 73
whiskey/whisky 180
white 262
Who/whom 35
whose 41
will/shall 7
wink 160
wise 295
Word divisions 53
work at/for/in 75
would 39
Wrong usage 115

Yellow 264
yolk 149
yours cordially/faithfully/sincerely/
  truly 109

Z, pronunciation of the letter 149
zero 151
zillions 273
Zoology 289